LOCAL-AREA NETWORKS

and their

ARCHITECTURES

LOCAL-AREA NETWORKS

and their

ARCHITECTURES

(Lokal'nye Informatsionno-Vychislitel'nye Seti)

Eduard A. Yakubaitis

Institute of Electronics and Computer Science
(Latvian Academy of Sciences)

translated by Martin Morell

Allerton Press, Inc./New York

Library of Congress Cataloging in Publication Data

ÎAkubaĭtis, Ēduard Aleksandrovich.
  Local-area networks and their architectures.

  Translation of: Lokal'nye informatŝionno-vychislitel'nye seti.
  Bibliography: p.
  Includes index.
  1. Local area networks (Computer networks) I. Title.
TK5105.7.I2413 1986 004.6'8 86-70929
ISBN 0-89864-018-0

TABLE OF CONTENTS

LOCAL-AREA NETWORKS

and their

ARCHITECTURES

INTRODUCTION

The theory of computer networks [1-13] is providing us with architectures of ever-increasing diversity, with the result that new types of networks are appearing and the methodology of data processing, transmission, and storage is becoming more refined and sophisticated. Local-area networks, which were formerly of secondary importance, have undergone an explosive development in recent years. The part played by such networks in the hierarchy of current data processing facilities is growing rapidly.

The appearance of local-area networks has been promoted by the fact that around 80-90% of all information generated in science, control, and business and industry circulates inside organizations and enterprises. Only 10-20% of the information is generated by external interactions of these organizations. Advances in computer science have made possible the efficient and economical integrated transmission and processing of all types of information that concerns the operation of the various sectors of the national economy.

For instance, over the last 20 years the cost of data processing has decreased by around a factor of ten every 10 years, and this tendency is currently continuing. The cost of electronic data entry and storage is also decreasing rapidly, dropping by up to 25% per year. Ultra-high capacity disks are currently under development, and video-disks are coming into widespread use.

Local-area networks are currently a powerful data-processing tool which provide the following:

- extensive information and computer capabilities, distributed throughout the organization or enterprise;
- a wide spectrum of information resources: mathematical models, data bases, information retrieval and reference services, and so forth;
- efficient shared use of all available resources;
- high degree of reliability of data processing, through redundancy and duplication of resources;
- integrated transmission and processing of data, speech, and graphics;
- capabilities for utilizing computers of all types and sizes;
- simple forms of network expansion, alteration, and reconfiguration.

The use of separate networks for transmission of data, graphics, speech, teletype, etc., is not economically justifiable. Nor is it justifiable to create separate and unrelated computerized control systems for management functions, design and technological operations, and production. All these processes can be carried out economically and efficiently in a single local-area network or a group of interconnected networks, which store, transmit, and process all the information pertaining to the operation of the organization or enterprise.

Because of computerization of production and control, access to computer resources has become something of a dynamic social phenomenon. For instance, whereas at the beginning of the 1980's there was one computer terminal for every 45 workers in the most highly developed countries of the world [14], at the end of this decade, on average, every 10 workers will have their own terminal. It is anticipated [14] that by 1985 around 75% of the workers in the sphere of control will employ the information and computing resources of local-area networks.

All this requires the creation of highly efficient networks capable of executing economically advantageous and dynamic data processing, transmission, and storage. These processes are implemented in a variety of computers, data-preparation devices, and information transmission and storage facilities.

This book offers a straightforward account of the theory of local-area networks. The architecture of such networks is considered, and network hardware and software are analyzed. Particular attention is paid to network standards, defined by their protocols and interfaces. The analysis is illustrated by examples of network designs and operating networks.

The structure and method of the book are such that it can be used for various purposes. Readers who are familiarizing themselves with local-area networks for the first time may prefer to read the contents in their entirety. Specialists who wish to improve their knowledge in a particular area can find the necessary material by referring to the table of contents. In the event an unfamiliar term is encountered, the reader is referred to the glossary. Finally, the book can also be employed as a handbook or reference work. A detailed subject index is furnished for this purpose.

The author wishes to thank Corresponding Member of the Academy of Sciences of the Latvian SSR V. Pirogov, Candidate of Technical Sciences S. Trainin, Candidates of Technical Sciences P. Treis, Ya. Kikuts, and A. Liven for valuable advice upon reading the manuscript.

4

CHAPTER 1

ARCHITECTURE OF LOCAL-AREA NETWORKS

In considering any complex entity, it is first necessary to define the task it is intended to handle and to identify the principle characteristics and parameters which the entity should possess. For this purpose we will employ a general model that defines the characteristics and functions of both the entire network and of its principal components. The description of this model is called the **computer network** (or **data network**) **architecture.**

1.1.
STRUCTURE AND CHARACTERISTICS OF COMPUTER NETWORKS

Let us introduce some definitions. Entities that generate or consume information will be called **subscribers.** These include the following:

— computers and computer installations;
— on-line and external storage devices;
— terminals (displays, plotters, printers, etc.);
— teletypes;
— copying and facsimile equipment;
— television cameras and monitors;
— telephones and dictaphones;
— robots, automatic machine tools and mechanisms;
— test instruments and equipment, radio receivers, television sets, tape recorders, etc.

Each user is connected (Fig. 1.1) to a **station,** this being an arrangement that executes auxiliary functions associated with data transmission. The aggregate of subscriber and station is called a **subscriber system.**

A **physical medium** is required to support interaction between subscribers. Such a medium is provided by space (the "ether") or material (copper, light guide) whose properties ensure propagation of the signal conveying the necessary information. The concept of physical medium also includes the data circuit-terminating equipment that is directly connected to the space or material in question. The physical medium provides the basis for the **communications subnetwork,** intended for transmitting data between subscriber systems.

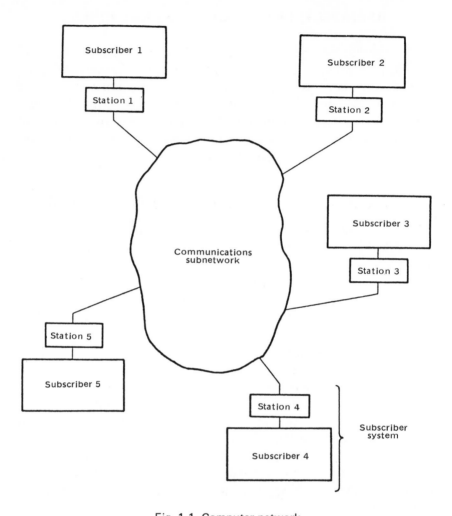

Fig. 1.1. Computer network

The association (Fig. 1.1) comprising subscriber systems and communications subnetworks will be called a **computer** (or **data**) **network.**

The resources of a computer network are intended to serve the personnel of organizations and enterprises. All such personnel will henceforth be called **users.** Either directly (from terminals) or through the use of available programs, they specify the necessary tasks and obtain the information they require.

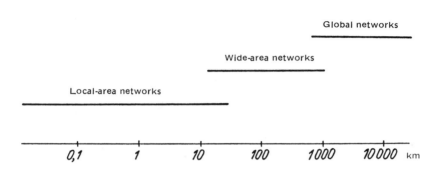

Fig. 1.2. Classification of computer networks on the basis of geographical coverage.

Computer networks are divided into three types depending on their size (Fig. 1.2). A **local-area network** is one in which the distance between users is small. Usually, local-area networks cover a single building or a few adjacent ones. However, a radial-control network, for example, may have an extent that is measured in meters, whereas the network of an industrial combine may span a territory 10—15 km in diameter. **Wide-area networks** link subscribers at considerable distances from one another. Subscribers within a city, county, province or even a small country may be included.

The third type comprises **global networks,** which link users in different countries or on different continents. Global networks are generally satellite-based. The advantage here is that satellites can "see" enormous areas. When a transmitter/receiver is installed on a satellite, large numbers of subscribers can be connected by one or more radio links.

By combining global, wide-area, and local-area networks, it is possible (Fig. 1.3) to create multinetwork hierarchies that provide powerful and economically advantageous facilities for processing huge amounts of data. Local-area networks are basic elements in such associations.

The continuous nature of most processes with which human beings are familiar led to the creation of various devices, installations,

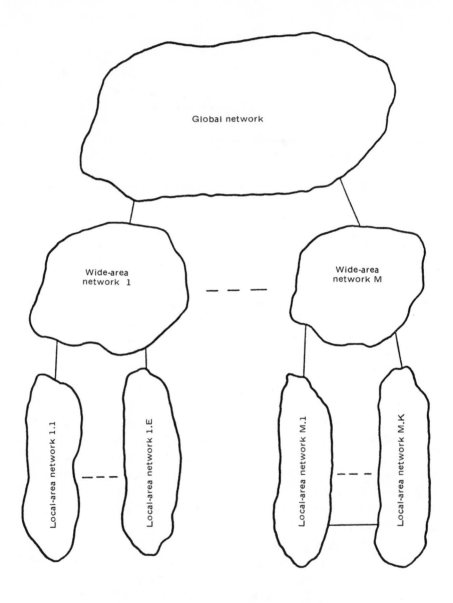

Fig. 1.3. Hierarchy of computer networks.

and networks that provide reception, transmission, and delivery of large amounts of analog information. These include radio, telephony, and television. Correspondingly, analog radio, telephone, and television networks were created.

The appearance of computers brought with it the unaccustomed discrete or digital form of information representation and processing. Initially, attempts were made to train people to use binary codes directly and to employ punchcards and punched tape. But the rapid and extensive development of methods of data representation and the creation of the requisite hardware, as well as the penetration of computer science into literally all areas of human activity, resolved the problem of creating forms of representing computer-readable information that are convenient for human beings.

In contrast to analog methods, **digital methods** make it possible to employ logic algebra and automata and set theory and provide exceptionally high reliability and accuracy of data processing. However, analog methods of information representation are employed in many spheres of human activity. This contradiction was resolved by the creation of an extensive variety of analog-to-digital and digital-to-analog converters. Thus, data processing, transmission, and storage became digital, while its forms of representation, when necessary, could be analog.

The successful development of computers and of data conversion methods compelled a re-examination of the structure of traditional information services. Thus, it became possible to create powerful new multipurpose information and computing networks employing computers, digital telephony, radio, and television.

Direct analog-to-digital speech conversion yields a data stream with a rate of roughly 64 kbit/s.* Methods are currently available, however, which provide compression of **audio information,** i.e., information which can be perceived by the human hearing apparatus. Admittedly, individual voice coloring is lost, and only the content-bearing part remains. To eliminate this shortcoming, attempts are being made to create acoustic models of the human organs. This will make it possible to set the model parameters for an individual speaker at the outset and to transmit them to the model at the receiving end. As a result, reproduction of the original speech with an adequate degree of fidelity becomes possible.

---

*Here and henceforth, in defining data transmission rate or volume of data, the following notation: k = 1024, M = 1024·1024 will be employed.

A new form of audio information, known as the voicegram, is coming into wider and wider use. Voicegrams are monologues uttered by speakers, which are then encoded and transmitted in the form of bit sequences. Voicegrams make it possible to transmit information over channels that operate at arbitrary slow speeds.

Analog-to-digital and digital-to-analog conversion of audio information is done in two ways. In the first way, the telephone instruments are left unaltered, while the necessary data converters are installed at digital telephone stations. In the second way, the converters are installed in the telephone or directly in the handset. For example, Bell has developed a converter [15] which is fitted into a capsule that is inserted in the handset. The capsule contains a filter and an acoustical signal generator.

After telephony, radio is the second method of transmission of audio information. Its general nature is the same. Radio and telephony differ only in terms of the types of channels used for transmission. Therefore, radio is digitized in more or less the same ways as telephony.

Digitization has also begun to invade the field of phonograph recording. Digital technology is being used to develop universal devices and phonograph records that are equally suitable for both computing and domestic applications.

Conversion of home record players to digital method will make it possible to enhance record quality by an order of magnitude. In most cases, data is read off a digital recording by a laser beam. In the reproduction process, the data is converted from digital to analog form. Special integrated circuitry that performs D/A conversion has been developed for this purpose.

Digitization of television involves more complicated problems. These problems stem primarily from the fact that the transmission of **video information,** i.e., information that can be perceived by the human visual apparatus, is at very high rates. For example, direct conversion of a standard television image yields a data stream at rates up to 150 Mbit/s. At the same time, it has already proved possible, through compression, to reduce this stream to a few tens of millions of bits per second.

A second problem is the large amount of image that each frame contains - and standard European television uses a rate of 25 frames per second. Large storage devices are required, therefore, to store this data.

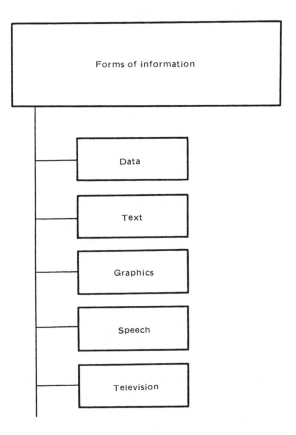

Fig. 1.4. Forms of information transmitted and processed by advanced computer networks.

The third and perhaps most serious problem is the existence of hundreds of millions of analog television receivers that are not suitable for reception of digital data. Accordingly, complete conversion of television to digital principles will require a long time.

The conversion of various forms of analog data to digital principles has created an important basis for integrating all forms of information relating to human daily life and activity. As a result, the premises have been created for the development of computer networks that incorporate (Fig. 1.4) all types of information employed in the national economy.

At the same time, the development of computer network theory and the manufacture of the necessary hardware have made it possible to undertake the creation of universal local-area networks that provide input, storage, transmission, processing, and delivery of highly diverse forms of information. This, in turn, has yielded the following:

- a reduction in the cost of information services;
- expanded service, including electronic mail, videoconferencing, expedited voicegram delivery, etc.;
- sharp reductions in the number of service personnel;
- enhanced reliability of data storage and processing;
- enhanced fidelity of data transmission;
- unification of hardware;
- possibility of obtaining all forms of information at unified subscriber locations directly at worksites.

In addition, present-day local-area networks provide a high degree of accessibility, configurational flexibility, and simplicity of servicing and expansion.

The universality of local-area networks, which comprise the bottom rung of the modern data-processing industry, can be characterized by the diagram shown in Fig. 1.5 [16]. It is evident from the figure that a local-area network intended for an institution or organization handles three groups of tasks, associated with computation, communications, and word processing.

It is hard to enumerate all the tasks that are handled by local-area networks. The main ones are the following:

- shared use of computers for calculations;
- creation of a broad spectrum of data banks and information retrieval systems;
- transmission (and temporary storage) of data via electronic mail;
- acquisition, ordering, and storage of data regarding the activity of the organization;
- preparation and editing of letters, reports, and documents;
- exchange of documents without preparation of hard copy;
- report-writing, bookkeeping, and inventory control;
- research and development;
- preparation and transmission of drawings, diagrams, and other graphics;
- control of robots, machines, and automatic machine tools.

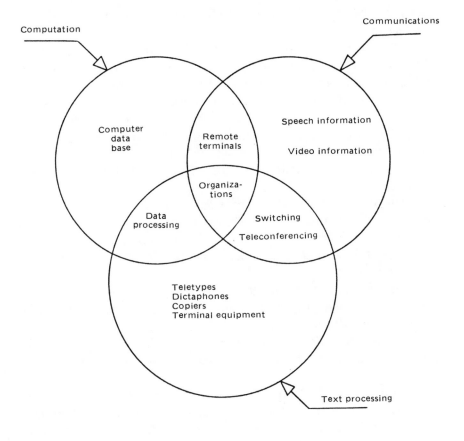

Fig. 1.5. Integration of communications, computation, and word processing.

In contrast to remote-processing systems, computer networks involve large numbers of computers. Therefore, new information tasks are commonly executed in such networks. These include, in particular, the following:

Resource allocation. A group of interrelated application processes (or programs) can reside in several different computers and can interact without user involvement. Moreover, all the data that may be required in the course of executing the application processes are taken by the processes from the appropriate data bases in any computers of the network. This operation also proceeds without user interference.

Electronic mail. This is intended for transmission of any messages between users, including texts, drawings, diagrams, figures, tables, and voicegrams. The messages may be transmitted to the addressee either immediately or at a specified time. If the addressee is not "home" and the message is to be transmitted in shortest possible time, then attempts at transmission may be repeated at specified time intervals. In addition, messages may be stored in one or more "mailboxes" and transmitted to the users on request ("general delivery").

The unit of transmitted information in electronic mail is the document. A document is understood to mean any information that has the structure required by electronic mail, in particular the addressing rules and limiting size. Documents may be text, graphics, voicegrams, etc.

Documents are transmitted by sending messages from the sender to the recipient. Constraints are imposed on a document of arbitrary content, depending on the nature of the mail service and the available external devices. These constraints include, in particular, the following: page size, symbols used, and the form of these symbols.

Four types of electronic mail can be distinguished in accordance with the types of documents used: text, mosaic graphics, geometrical graphics, and half-tone images. The first type, called **Teletex,** is intended only for transmission of text-containing documents. The remaining three types encompass **Videotex,** which deals with transmission of graphics. In the simplest case the graphics include only mosaic image elements, each point of which has two half-tones: black and white. The second case covers true geometrical graphics: drawings and diagrams. Finally, in the third case, the image becomes a half-tone, thus enabling figures, photographs, and naturalistic representations to be transmitted.

Electronic mail performs a large number of functions, including the following:

— I/O of documents to the network;
— transmission of documents to mailboxes;
— detection and correction of errors upon transmission;

TABLE 1.1
Types of addresses in local-area networks

No.	Type of address	Intended recipient
1.	Individual	One particular subscriber
2.	Group	A specified group of subscribers (whatever the necessary criteria)
3.	Global	All network subscribers

— use of priorities in transmission;
— transmission of acknowledgements of receipt of documents;
— delivery of documents to several or all addresses;
— provision of information regarding addresses;
— change of mailbox addresses.

Electronic mail can operate for a specified period of the day or round the clock.

Network conferences. These are employed in discussing management, scientific or production problems of any type. All the users/participants are located at the terminals at their worksites. Information transmitted by any one of them is displayed on the terminal screens of all the other participants. Text, drawings, diagrams, and figures can be accompanied by the spoken comments of the person who has "taken the floor." In the course of the conference, the participants can perform simple calculations and obtain information from various data bases. All the presentations, together with the graphics, are "protocoled" and sent to one of the data bases.

In a computer network, information can be transmitted in accordance with three types of addresses, as shown in Table 1.1. An **individual address** is required to transmit letters or directions. Instructions or notices require a **group address**. A **global address** is most frequently employed to transmit the following:
— laws, regulations or techniques;
— declarations concerning procedures and orders of the organization or enterprise;
— management messages related to network operations;
— information regarding changes in the list of network subscribers or new network resources;

15

Table 1.2

Parameters characterizing computer networks

No.	Parameter	Characteristics
1.	Cost	Expenditures for creation and operation of basic network software and hardware
2.	Reliability	Error detection and correction, minimization of faults
3.	Maintainability	Recording, localization, and elimination of malfunctions
4.	Protection	Methods of preventing unauthorized access
5.	Loss	Methods of guaranteeing delivery of information blocks
6.	Connectedness	Size of information blocks, maximum distances between systems, transmission rate
7.	Availability	Controlled access to resources, multiplexing, multichannel feature
8.	Conversion	Ensuring compatible operation of subscribers operating at different rates

— listing of available external devices and their location;
— date and time of day, etc.

Computer networks are characterized by many parameters, the principal ones are given in Table 1.2. The first three characteristics (cost, reliability and maintainability) are basic. The next two parameters (protection, loss) define guarantees associated with the information. Finally, the last three parameters (connectedness, availability, and conversion) describe the interaction service with application processes.

1.2
MODEL OF AN OPEN NETWORK

In 1947, a specialized international agency was set up under the aegis of the United Nations [17]. This agency, which came to be

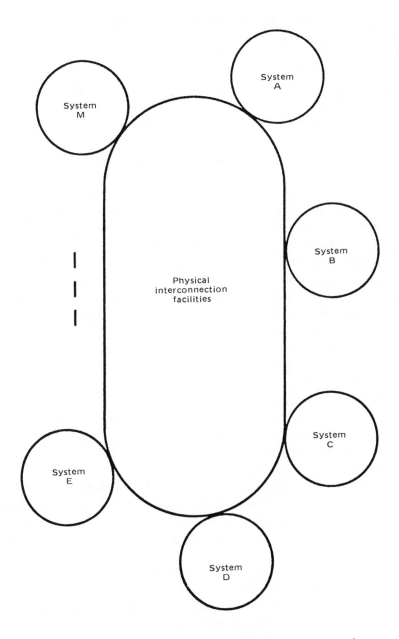

Fig. 1.6. Overall structure of model of computer network.

known as the **International Standards Organization** (ISO), was entrusted with the task of developing standards in all fields, including electrical engineering and electronics. In 1977, the ISO began work on computer network standards. Technical Committee 97, dealing with standards in the field of computers and data processing, created Subcommittee 16 for this purpose.

To provide a common basis for coordinating network development, the ISO issued **Standard 7498** [18], which defined the **Basic Reference Model of Open Systems Interconnection.** The model is flexible in the sense that it permits networks to evolve in accordance with the progress of theory and technology. Moreover, the Model provides for a gradual transition from existing instrumentation to new standards. In considering the Model, let us first familiarize ourselves with the basic concepts which it introduces.

A basic concept of the Model is that of **system**, this being a self-contained entity that is capable of information processing. A system consists of one or more computers with appropriate software, external devices, data-transmission facilities, and operating personnel. If a system satisfies the requirements of the Model, it is called **open.**

An **application process** is an important system component which supports information processing. An application process in a system may be provided by a human operator at a terminal console, a program or a group of programs. The principal parts of application processes are not considered in the Basic Reference Model. The only things analyzed are those parts of the processes that interface with sets of programs that support the execution of interaction functions of application processes in the network.

Physical interconnection facilities (Fig. 1.6) constitute the core of a computer network, via which the systems interact with one another. A physical medium, as well as hardware and software, supporting the necessary modes of information transmission, is employed to create this core. The Basic Reference Model does not consider the structure or characteristics of physical interconnection facilities; it only sets up certain requirements. The task of the Model is to provide (Fig. 1.7) a clear description of the **open systems interconnection environment** in the computer network between the principal parts of the application processes and the physical interconnection facilities. This environment is defined by Standard 7498 of the ISO.

The complexity of the interconnection functions performed by

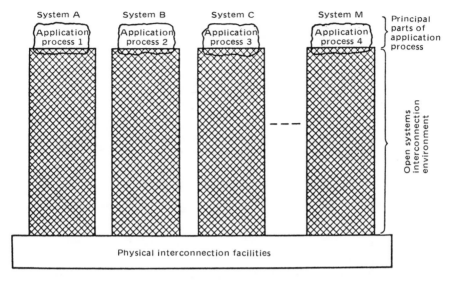

Fig. 1.7. Open systems interconnection environment.

the systems in a network requires that they be divided into groups. These are called **subsystems.** Subsystems in a system (Fig. 1.8) are arranged one above the other logically and are numbered in order beginning with the one that is connected directly to the physical interconnection facility. The Basic Reference Model assumes that each system contains seven subsystems (Fig. 1.8).

The concept of subsystem enables us to define an important network characteristic, known as **layer.** A layer is made up of the subsystems of all systems of the network that have the same rank or number. The following requirements are met in dividing a network into layers:

1. The number of layers should not be so large as to render difficult the description of the entire Model.

2. The number of layers should be enough that the functions performed by each layer describe only one clearly defined task.

3. Boundaries between layers are drawn in such a way that the description of the interface between them is simple, and the number of connections between two adjacent layers is minimized.

4. Layers should be described in such a way that rearrangement of one layer does not require modification of the functions of another.

19

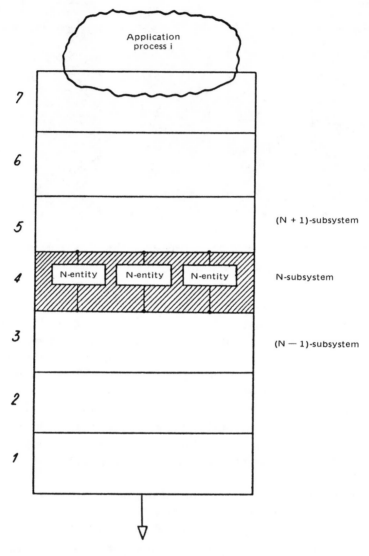

Fig. 1.8. Hierarchy of subsystems.

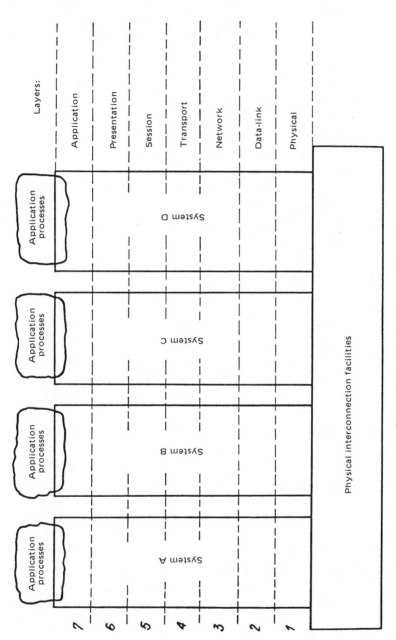

Fig. 1.9. Layers of computer networks.

The names of the layers defined by the Basic Reference Model are shown in Fig. 1.9. The parameters and characteristics referring to any of the layers are named in accordance with these designations. For example, the subsystem on the transport layer is called the transport subsystem.

As follows from Fig. 1.7, all seven layers of the **open systems interconnection environment** lie between the principal parts of the application processes and the physical interconnection facilities. A very important layer is the application layer, which interfaces directly with the principal parts of the application processes. All the remaining layers are intended to service the application layer.

The application layer is the uppermost in the layer hierarchy. The lowest, or physical, layer furnishes it with service such that the different systems interact physically with one another. Layers 1-6 provide the successively increasing service that is needed to support interaction of application processes.

Layers 5-7 are oriented toward the application processes to be executed. The four lowest layers (1-4) support end-to-end transmission (via the physical interconnection facilities) of the information that is exchanged by application processes. These layers are determined by the type of physical interconnection facilities employed.

Each subsystem contains (Fig. 1.8) one or more active elements, called entities. Two or more entities of the same layer, in one or more systems, can interact with one another by transmitting the necessary information to one another.

Entities interact via **logical channels,** called **connections,** that link them. For this, the software facilities of the network operate so as to create the illusion of a physical channel connecting these entities. Connection of N-layer entities is supported by functions executed by the $(N - 1)$-layer and which thus create an N-connection. Therefore, the connection of N-layer entities (or N-connection) is run at the $(N - 1)$-layer. Connections that are run at all layers (dashed lines in Fig. 1.10) are logical. Only connections that are run in physical interconnection facilities for entities of the lowest layer (dot-dash line in Fig. 1.10) can be real (or physical).

An important function of connections is that of furnishing entities with the capability of establishing dynamic agreement regarding interaction prior to initiating data transmission. Standard 7498 defines this type of interaction of entities at all layers. However, in a

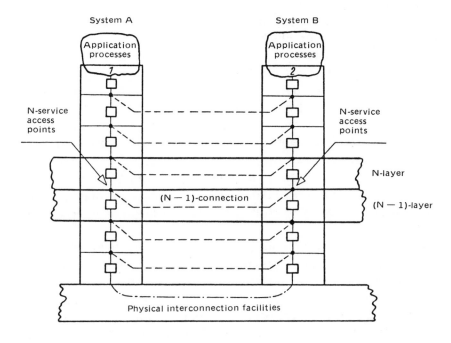

Fig. 1.10. Connections in a computer network.

number of instances, e.g., in the case of data transmission at the data-link layer, and in such application processes as telemetry and banking, preliminary organization of connections can be eliminated. In these transmission methods, interaction between entities does not involve any preliminary agreements between them. The sending entity sends data blocks to the recipient entity as soon as necessary, without the recipient's preliminary agreement. Correspondingly, an addendum to the Basic Reference Model is being developed to describe forms of data transmission without the establishment of connections.

N-entities employ connections as follows: In order for N-entities to interact, they request the (N − 1)-layer service (Fig. 1.10), via service access points, to establish connection between N-entities. The (N − 1)-layer entities establish an (N − 1)-connection. For this, in turn, the (N − 1)-layer entities request connections from the (N − − 2)-layer. This continues until the next successive connection is the one furnished by the physical interconnection facility. It is on this level that the systems interact directly with one another.

Messages transmitted between application processes are divided into parts, called **data blocks.** For convenience, this division can be effected in different layers. As a result, data blocks are transmitted between entities. These blocks contain two types of information. The first type, called **data,** comprises information that is received by entities from the next higher-lying layer. The second form of information is defined by the information and instructions that are exchanged by entities upon data transmission. This information and instructions are called **control information.** Data and control information are transmitted between entities of the same layer in data blocks that are called **N-protocol data units.** Data and control information are transmitted between entities in adjacent layers in **interface data units.**

Standard 7498 describes primarily the components of abstract open systems and some issues related to their organization. The Basic Reference Model of Open Systems Interconnection is formulated on this basis. Then, a detailed precise description of the operation of abstract open systems is developed within the framework defined by the Model. This specifies the types of service and interaction protocols of open systems.

Aside from the application layer, each N-layer of the open systems interconnection environment provides certain types of **service** to the adjacent above-lying $(N + 1)$-layer. The most important forms of this service are as follows:

— transfer of data blocks;
— reception of data blocks in the same sequence in which they were sent;
— error detection and correction in data blocks;
— acknowledgement that data blocks have been received and that they are error-free;
— control of data-block flows;
— dumping of data blocks that contain errors;
— **multiplexing** (mapping of several N-layer connections into one $(N - 1)$-layer connection);
— **splitting** (mapping of one N-layer connection into several $(N - 1)$-layer connections).

Entities on the same layer interact (Fig. 1.10) via **service access points.** Connections linking entities terminate at these points. Via these access points, the N-layer requests service from the (N − 1)-layer, while the latter furnishes this service to the N-layer. Each service access point has its own address. Entities can be connected to different access points. This interconnection between entity and service access point is provided by a special layer function called the **address function.**

The set of rules and formats that defines the interaction of N-layer entities in executing the functions of the layer is called an **N-protocol.** In the general case, a layer may have more than one different protocol. Protocol data units are transmitted between entities in the layer in accordance with the protocol. These blocks contain information transmitted from the upper-lying layer as well as information needed to control the layer operation. Since the Basic Reference Model has adopted seven layers (Fig. 1.9), a hierarchy of seven sets of protocols is correspondingly specified.

The layered structure of the open systems interconnection environment permits different protocols to be developed independently. Here, however, standards for the types of service provided by one layer to another must be defined at service access points. These standards are called **interlayer interfaces.** Figure 1.11 gives a list of protocols developed or being developed by Technical Committee 97 of the International Standards Organization.

The functions performed by layer protocols in different systems are customarily combined into groups called **services.** Two of the most important services are shown in Fig. 1.12. The **transport service** supports the execution of tasks associated with transmission of data files or arrays across the communications subnetwork. It encompasses the transport, network, data-link, and physical layers. The **user service** is located above it. This service resides on the application, presentation, and session layers and supports connection of application processes to the transport service.

In a computer network two types of **control** can be distinguished: application control and systems control. **Application control** supports connection between the principal parts of application processes and the open system interconnection environment. The task of **systems control** is to support the execution of the protocols of all seven layers in the given system. For this purpose, a **primary systems control process** resides on the application layer; while a **satellite systems control process,** linked to the primary one, resides on each layer. The satellite process on the N-layer of the system performs **N-layer con-**

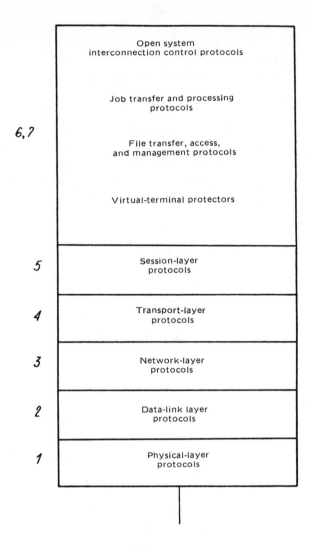

Fig. 1.11. Protocol hierarchy

trol for the system. The task of these forms of control is to support procedures of information exchange between application processes residing in different systems. This task is defined by the architecture of the open systems interconnection environment. Other, local control functions in systems are not dealt with by the Basic Reference Model.

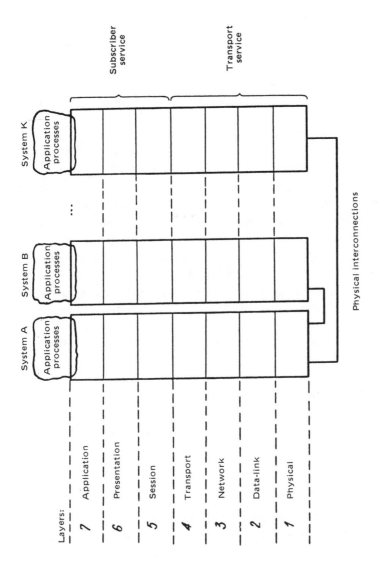

Fig. 1.12. Service of a computer network.

Layers:

7 Application
6 Presentation
5 Session
4 Transport
3 Network
2 Data-link
1 Physical

System A
System B
System K

Application processes

Subscriber service

Transport service

Physical interconnections

Application control is directly related to application processes. Therefore, it includes functions that specify the following:

— initialization of elements that represent application processes;
— initiation, maintenance, and termination of application processes;
— allocation of resources to application processes and freeing up of these resources;
— detection and prevention of simultaneous use of a resource by more than one program, as well as elimination of deadlock situations;
— assurance of data integrity and execution of necessary operating intervals;
— control of data security;
— servicing of control points and restoration of the process of execution of application processes.

Application control is performed by application-layer entities.

Systems control is intended to control all processes of the open systems interconnection environment. Its most important functions are the following:

— activation, maintenance, and deactivation of interaction resources distributed in open systems;
— loading of programs that support interaction of systems;
— establishment, maintenance, and elimination of connections between entities;
— initialization and change of parameters of open systems;
— recording of states in the process of operation;
— error control;
— reconfiguration and restarting;
— assembly of statistics.

Systems control is performed by entities of all layers.

1.3.
PROTOCOL HIERARCHY

In conformity with the seven layers of the open systems interconnection environment, a hierarchy of seven protocol groups is introduced. **Protocols** are designated in the same way as the layers. In instances in which a pair of systems interacts directly via physical interconnection facilities (Fig. 1.13), all the protocols describe the connection of the entities of these systems.

28

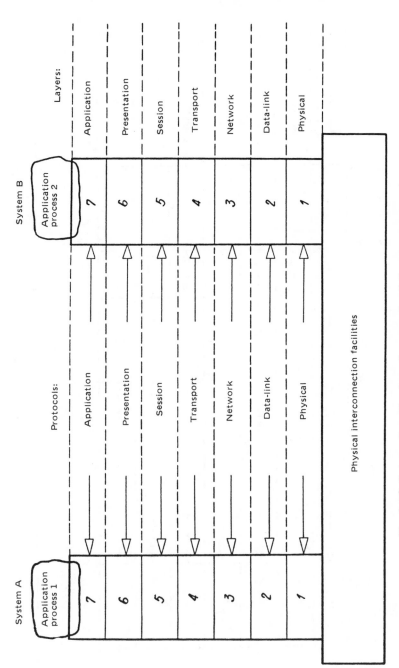

Fig. 1.13. Points of application of protocols of directly connected systems.

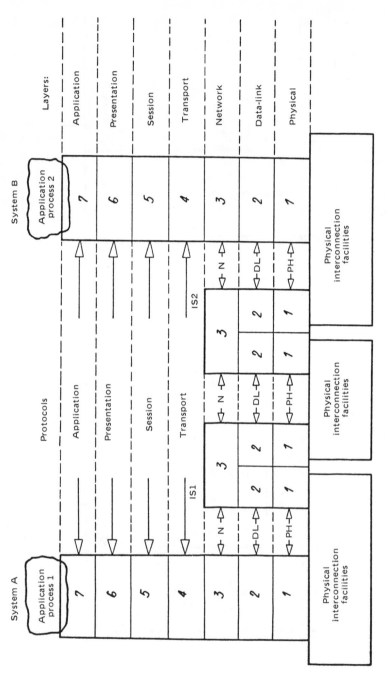

Fig. 1.14. Interaction protocols for systems linked via intermediate systems.

If, however, the systems in question (e.g., systems A and B in Fig. 1.14) are not connected directly by physical interconnection facilities, then they interact via one or more intermediate systems which provide retranslation of information. The points of application of the lower-layer protocols are altered in these cases. On layers 1-3 the network (N), data-link (DL), and physical (PH) protocols describe the interaction of those systems that are directly connected by physical interconnection facilities. In Fig. 1.14, there are three pairs of such systems: A and IS1; IS1 and IS2; and IS2 and D. On the upper layers (application, presentation, session, and transport) the points of application of the protocols are the same as in Fig. 1.13, i.e., as before, these protocols define direct interconnection (via intermediate systems) of the entities of systems A and B.

1.4.
LAYERS OF OPEN SYSTEMS INTERCONNECTION

The functions of any layer are specified by the forms of data processing and transmission that are chosen. After the processing model has been set up, the necessary protocol data units and procedures to support their transmission are described. The requirements on the types of service to be furnished by the next lower-lying layer are formulated on this basis. Thus, layer control protocols are set up. The task that layer protocols must handle, and the manner in which they do so, will be considered below.

The **application layer** handles the task of *supporting the various forms of interconnection of application processes* residing in one or more systems. The protocols that handle this task are combined into general complexes that describe sets of information processes to be executed. These complexes are called **functionally oriented.** In turn, they are controlled by a special protocol, called **context control** [19]. The **context control protocol** supports the execution of operations associated with the operation of the set of remaining upper-layer protocols in the network. It describes three principal functions. The first of these is identification of the necessary protocol from the set of available ones in the network. The second function is that of choosing the requisite protocol. The third function is that of replacing protocols in the process of interaction.

The context control protocol can provide users with the following types of functionally oriented protocols:
- terminal control;
- interaction control;
- file control;
- task control;
- system control;
- network control;
- data integrity;
- other protocols.

The **terminal control protocol** is one of the most important in the network. It furnishes convenient and efficient facilities required to support interfaces with users. The **interaction control protocol** makes it possible to interconnect application processes so that they can interactively exchange information. Control and servicing of remote data files, access to such files, and transfer of files between information processes are described by the **file control protocol.**

The **system control protocol** manages all the layers of the system. It incorporates system description and evaluation functions and assembly of statistics dealing with the operation of the system and with data exchange.

A distinctive part is played by the **data integrity protocol.** It detects errors that arise in data transmission, resolves contentious situations that arise in transmission, extracts processes from deadlocks, and manages restart operations to eliminate errors resulting from faults.

The "other" protocols include, in particular, electronic-mail and message-transmission protocols. The **electronic-mail protocol** is intended for transmission of documents between users or terminal operators. The task of the **message-transmission protocol** is to reliably exchange large data files between application processes in different systems. Transmission begins with establishment of a connection that enables the sender and recipient to interact. Messages are transmitted in the form of sequence of small data blocks. As a rule, receipt of an error-free message is acknowledged back to the sender.

In a computer network, application processes are distributed over many systems. Therefore, the application-layer entities of different systems must interact with one another. For this, two or more application processes form groups of interacting application processes.

The functions executed by the application-layer protocols include the following:

— description of forms and methods of interaction of application processes;

— execution of forms of operation (task control, file transfer, system control, etc.);

— user identification;

— indication of the possibility of access from the network to specified application processes of a system;

— transmission of requests for connection to other application processes;

— delivery of requests to presentation level for necessary methods of information presentation;

— control of data exchange by application processes;

— determination of availability of application processes;

— synchronization of interacting application processes;

— determination of quality of service (message delivery time, permissible error rate, etc.).

The presentation layer performs the task of *presentation and conversion of data to be transferred between application entities.* To understand the purpose of the presentation layer, some definitions are introduced. **Semantics** will be understood to be the meaning of the data transferred between application processes. **Syntax** will be understood to be the structure (or form of presentation) of this data. The presentation layer deals only with data syntax. The semantics, in contrast, is known only to the application processes.

The need for syntax conversion stems from the fact that different types of computers use different operating systems and a wide variety of data presentation forms. For example, one computer may operate with 8-bit words, another with 32-bit words. Computers also use different forms of data presentation in operating with external devices or peripherals. Therefore, in an open computer network in which a wide variety of computers can be employed, the number of presentation types may become very large.

The task of the presentation layer is to provide facilities which allow different systems to exchange data flows regardless of their local presentation type. For this purpose, the presentation layer provides services which allow one, when establishing a connection between application entities, to first determine an arbitrary set of syntaxes (contexts) and then, in the course of interaction, to switch

33

from one context to another. Thus, at each point in time the interaction takes place within the framework of a predetermined context. Interaction is in accordance with the only one presentation-layer protocol which is capable of operating with any type of syntax of the data transmitted.

The protocol makes it possible to establish the syntax of the information transferred between systems but not the syntax used within systems. If there are differences between the system's local syntax and the syntax of the information transferred between systems, syntax conversion or mapping is necessary. This mapping is performed entirely within the presentation layer, but the protocol standards do not specify their specific place of execution.

The presentation layer provides the following services:
— connection establishment;
— connection termination;
— content management;
— information transfer;
— dialogue control.

These services are provided partly by the presentation layer and partly by the session layer facilities. When the application layer issues a service primitive for information transfer or dialogue control, this request is redirected to the session layer.

The execution of the above functions by the presentation layer proceeds in four **phases** (or stages), shown in Fig. 1.15.

The initial phase is the *establishment of a P-connection.* In this phase a presentation entity issues a request for session establishment to a session entity, and the user data sends a request for the establishment of a P-connection between the application entities. In the event of successful establishment of a P-connection (provided that the corresponding session has also been established), the phase of *context management* begins. This phase involves the determination and selection of contexts. Once the context has been selected, the phase of *data transfer and dialogue control* begins. In this phase the transmission of data between the application processes and interaction management is initiated.

Here, if necessary, data conversion and encryptation are performed. When it is necessary to change the context, in order to continue the interaction of application processes, a return to the context management phase takes place (Fig. 1.15). The last phase is the *completion phase.* In this phase the interaction between the application entities terminates.

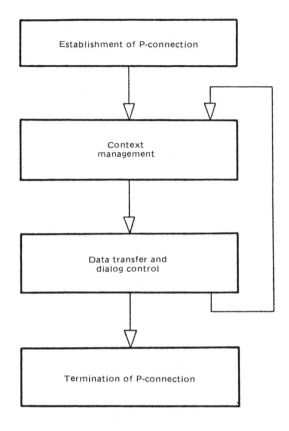

Fig. 1.15. Phases of data presentation.

Along with data, computer networks are being used to an ever increasing extent for the transmission and processing of speech. Optimal forms of speech presentation, therefore, are becoming increasingly important. Speech transmission calls for relatively high rates. At the same time, special forms of speech encoding allow these rates to be substantially reduced. Here, it should be borne in mind that the loss of up to 5% of the information transferred does not result in speech distortion [20]. However, packets must arrive in the same order in which they were sent.

The **session layer** executes the task of *organizing and conducting dialogue between application processes.* It furnishes the user with the illusion that the application process is being executed in a single powerful processor rather than in several processors in different locations.

The initiator of a session is an application entity which requests a session and specifies the address of the partner to a presentation entity. Then the sending presentation entity addresses a session entity, initiating an interactive session. In the recipient system, the process is entirely reversed. The session entity proposes to the presentation entity that it take part in a session. In turn, the presentation entity proposes a session to the application entity.

The session layer supports execution of two basic groups of functions:
— servicing of sessions;
— support of interactive mode of data transmission.
The task of the first group of functions is to establish and subsequently eliminate the connections over which the data are transmitted. The second group ensures data flow control.

The principal functions executed by the session layer are as follows:
— establishment of session connection;
— data exchange;
— interaction control;
— synchronization of session connection;
— information regarding exceptional situations;
— mapping of session connections onto transport connections;
— termination of session connection.

Establishment of a session connection permits presentation entities to initiate an interactive session. In the process of establishing this connection, a dialogue is conducted between the entities, during which the parameters of the connection are chosen (transmission rate, need for acknowledgement, and so forth). The **data exchange** that follows can be either expedited or normal.

Interaction control makes it possible to determine whose turn it is to perform session-interaction operations. Either of the partners in a session can decline to perform some operation when offered the possibility. The standards specify three modes of interaction of entities during sessions: full-duplex (dialogue), half-duplex (dialogue), and simplex (monologue).

In full-duplex mode, both partners can transmit data to each other simultaneously. Before using half-duplex, however, the partners must stipulate which will transmit data first. In the simplex mode, one partner becomes the sender throughout the session, while the other is the recipient.

Synchronization of the session connection makes it possible to establish and subsequently determine the points of synchronization of the process of interaction of entities during a session. When necessary, it makes it possible to return to any of the previous stages of the session. When various types of faults occur during operation, *information regarding exceptional situations* is issued.

The session layer utilizes the service furnished by the transport layer. Therefore, *mapping of session connections onto transport connections* must be provided. The essentials of this mapping are as follows. Data pertaining to different sessions can be consecutively transmitted over the same transport connection. Therefore, measures must be adopted to identify these sessions. At the same time, a given session can be conducted consecutively over several transport connections. This is done to enhance reliability, since if one of the transport connections is interrupted, the data can be transmitted over another.

Termination of a session connection enables presentation entities to terminate sessions in such a way that not a single data block still in transit is lost. Naturally, this requires a preliminary declaration by the initiating entity that the session has been completed and requires informing the partner of the desire to terminate. A number of necessary procedures are carried out, after which the session is ended.

It should be pointed out that, for interacting application processes residing in the same system, the session layer is the lowest one. The transport, network, data-link, and physical layers are only required to support interaction of application processes in different systems.

The **transport layer** performs the task of *furnishing application entities with end-to-end connections.* To perform this task, the transport layer transmits data between systems via all the available physical interconnection facilities in the network (Figs. 1.12 and 1.13). Therefore, the transmission in question is customarily called **end-to-end transmission,** in contrast to the analogous processes of other lower-lying layers.

In setting up the transport layer, it must be made completely independent of the type and nature of the interacting application processes. The connections furnished by the layer are **transparent,** i.e., they can handle any codes in use and all possible methods of organizing interaction on the session layer. Several transport connections may be used consecutively between a pair of session entities, for reliable operation. These and all other transport connections operate independently of one another.

For efficient data transmission, the transport layer provides several classes of service. These classes comprise various combinations of service parameters and categories. In this way, all the diverse data-transport requirements on the part of the various application processes can be taken into account. Classes of service are characterized by sets of parameters; these include capacity, transmission time, time for establishment of connection, permissible error rate, and so forth.

The service furnished by the transport layer is divided into two groups: control and data transmission. These groups include, in particular, the following:

— establishment and dissolution of transport connections;
— support of interaction between session connections and transport connections;
— control of sequencing and integrity of data blocks transmitted over transport connections;
— error detection and partial correction; notification regarding nonrecoverable errors;
— restoration of connection after the appearance of a fault;
— consolidation or deconsolidation of transmitted data blocks;
— flow control for transport blocks;
— assignment of priorities in block transmission (normal and expedited);
— acknowledgement of received block;
— dumping of blocks from transport connection in deadlock situations.

By executing these functions, the transport layer can adapt the system to any mechanism of data transmission over particular physical interconnection facilities. Moreover, the transport layer can restore data blocks that were lost on layers 1-3. If the physical interconnection facilities provide several paths for delivering data blocks to the recipient system, then, in the event that one of the network connections fails, the transport layer can select other paths. It does so in such a way that the application process is unaware of the switch.

Assembly of several messages into one, disassembly of one message into several, consolidation or deconsolidation of blocks, and assignment of priorities in block transmission are performed to ensure optimum operation of the layer entities. Control of block sequencing and integrity ensures that the recipient receives the blocks in the same order in which the sender issued them. Thus, it is guaranteed that all blocks have arrived without damage. Notification regarding nonrecoverable errors is required because, in practice, not all errors can be corrected by the level entities.

The layer operates on the basis of the following three alternating phases:

— *establishment of transport connection:* choice of types of service; decision as to whether multiplexing is needed; determination of optimum block size; identification of connections;

— *data transmission:* organization of block sequences; assembly into blocks; segmenting of blocks; multiplexing and splitting of connections; flow control; error detection and correction;

— *termination of connection:* notification of reason for termination; identification of connection to be terminated.

The transport layer utilizes two data-transmission strategies, carried out on the network layer: diagrams and virtual circuits (or connections). A **datagram** is a data block that is transmitted by the transport layer without prior organization of a connection. The sequence of data blocks may not necessarily arrive at the recipient in the same order in which it was sent. Upon arrival, therefore, the sequence of blocks must be ordered. Since there is no flow control in datagram transmission in a communications network, when critical states arise, the data blocks are discarded and then must be transmitted again upon request. The absence of a connection also requires that a datagram contain complete information regarding the sending and recipient entities.

A **virtual circuit** is a connection between a sending transport entity and a recipient transport entity, furnished by the network layer. Data blocks transmitted over virtual circuits do not contain explicit addresses of the sender and recipient. These are included in the circuit numbers. As a result, in this case each block has an abridged address field as compared to a datagram. Some effort and expense is required to make possible the organization of virtual circuits. However, the inherent shortcomings of datagram transmissions (absence of block flow control, loss of blocks, alteration of the transmission sequence) are eliminated.

Comparison of datagrams and virtual circuits reveals that in both cases the transport and network layers together perform virtually the same task of transmitting data over logical channels connecting application processes. The only difference involves the location of the functions of ordering the sequence of transmitted data blocks, monitoring the loss of blocks, and controlling the flows so that network lockouts do not occur. When datagrams are employed, these functions are performed by the transport layer. In the virtual-circuit method, the functions are performed by the network layer.

The **network layer** performs the task of *data retranslation, effected via one or more systems.* Performance of this task ensures that transport entities are independent of the routing and switching arrangements in the physical interconnection facilities. The channels created in these facilities interconnect the sender and recipient systems.

The basic types of service furnished by the network layer are as follows:

- organization of network connections run via physical interconnection facilities;
- identification of endpoints of network connections;
- transmission of data blocks;
- error detection and notification;
- flow control for data blocks;
- elimination of network connections;
- sequencing of the delivery of data blocks.

An important function that is frequently employed in computer networks is **information routing**, i.e., choice of subsequent paths for data blocks in accordance with their destination addresses. The following functions are performed on the network level to provide this routing:

- establishment of a group of network connections in one data-link connection;
- delivery of ordered sequences of blocks independently of their routing;
- assignment of switching and routing priorities;
- combination of several data-link connections into one network connection;
- notifcation of successful delivery of block sequences.

— detection and correction of errors upon transmission over network connections;
— segmenting and combination of data blocks;
— flow control;
— choice of type of service.

In transmitting data blocks, the network layer corrects many types of errors that appear. These include: distortion of data, loss of data blocks, duplication of blocks, violation of block sequences, and failure to transmit blocks to their destination. Duplication of blocks occurs when, after a block has been transmitted, an arriving instruction is erroneously interpreted as a signal that the block has been lost. In this case the block is transmitted a second time, i.e., unnecessary duplication occurs. Network data blocks are also customarily called **packets.**

The complexity of the network layer frequently requires that it be partitioned into hierarchical groups, called **sublayers.** Logical analysis and implementation of the tasks handled by the layer are thus simplified. For example, subtasks associated with support of interaction between two computer networks and of transmission control within each network may be segregated into separate sublayers.

The **data-link layer** serves *to transmit data blocks via physical connections.* As a result, the network layer is "ignorant" of the types of physical connections employed in the network. The data-link layer furnishes facilities for establishing, maintaining, and dissolving data-link connections between network entities. Within specified limits, each of these entities can dynamically control the transmission rate of data blocks over these connections.

The data-link layer provides the following types of service:
— transmission of data blocks;
— identification of endpoints of data-link connections;
— organization of block transmission sequences;
— error detection and control;
— notification regarding errors that cannot be corrected on the data-link layer;
— control of flows over physical connections;
— choice of quality-of-service parameters.

The last form of service includes the mean time between errors, transmission delay, capacity, and so forth.

Data-link blocks can be of various sizes. The size can be greater, the lower the frequency of appearance of errors in the physical connection and the greater the capacity of the layer for detecting and correcting these errors. Data-link blocks are frequently called **frames.**

The primary functions performed by the data-link layer are as follows:

— utilization of physical connections (initialization of requests for connection, control of activation and deactivation of these connections;

— establishment and dissolution of data-link connections;

— error detection and correction in data-link connections;

— data flow control in these connections;

— organization of transmission sequences for data-link layer blocks;

— assurance of transparency of connections.

An important function that is frequently performed at the data-link layer is **information selection,** i.e., the procedure of selecting data blocks received by the system in accordance with their destination addresses. This is necessary when more than two systems are connected to one physical connection. In this case, each system receives data blocks that are addressed to all the systems. At the data-link layer, only the data blocks addressed to the given system are chosen.

When necessary, the data-link layer can be partitioned into sublayers that comprise self-contained groups of functions. For example, the layer can be divided into a sublayer of physical connection control and a sublayer of control of access to the physical connection.

The **physical layer** serves to *interface systems to the physical interconnection facilities.* To do so, the layer specifies the mechanical, electrical, functional, and procedural characteristics that describe access to physical connections. Bit sequences are transmitted via these connections, which link data-link entities. *Transparency of the physical connection* is ensured, i.e., the connection must be capable of transmitting arbitrarily encoded information that utilizes any symbol sets. To utilize the connection efficiently, it may be made to simultaneously handle information that is being exchanged by several systems. Physical connections can be either permanent or temporary. In the latter case, they are dynamically created and then eliminated. A connection may link a data-link entry to one or more such entities.

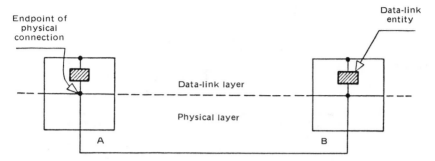

Endpoint of physical connection

Data-link entity

Data-link layer

Physical layer

A

B

Physical connection

a

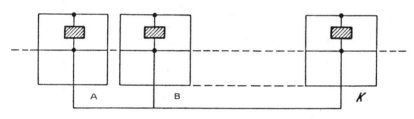

A

B

𝐾

Physical connection

b

Fig. 1.16. Types of physical connections.

Bit sequences may be transmitted over physical connections in full-duplex, half-duplex, or simplex mode.

Two types of physical connections, point-to-point and multipoint, should be distinguished. A **point-to-point connection** (Fig. 1.16a) is one that links two systems (A and B). If a physical connection supports interaction (Fig. 1.16b) between more than two systems (A, B, ..., K), it is called a **multipoint connection.**

The physical layer provides the following forms of service:
— establishment of temporary or permanent physical connections;

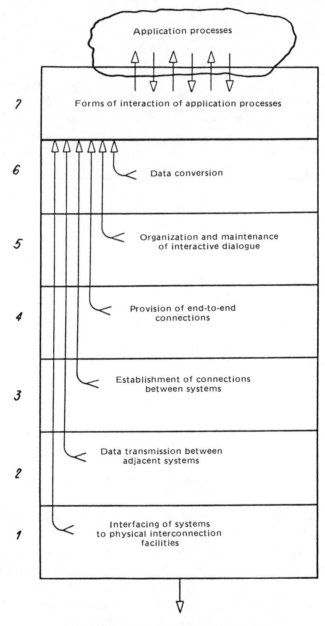

Fig. 1.17. Structure of layer service.

— physical endpoints of connections;

— identification of physical connections;

— organization of bit transmission sequences;

— notification regarding receiver failure;

— establishment of quality-of-service parameters.

The physical layer is involved in detection of a certain class of events that interfere with normal network operation (collision of frames transmitted simultaneously by several systems, break in the line, loss of power, loss of mechanical contact, etc.). Information regarding such malfunctions is transmitted to the data-link layer entities.

The principal functions performed by the physical layer are as follows:

— establishment and dissolution of physical connections;

— transmission of bit sequences in synchronous or asynchronous mode;

— monitoring of multipoint connections.

This last function is required because, at any point in time, data from only one of the associated systems can be transmitted over a multipoint connection. Therefore, it is necessary to **monitor** the connection (or link), i.e., to determine whether transmission of a bit stream (from any source) is taking place.

Thus, layers 1-6 provide increasing levels of service furnished to application processes (Fig. 1.17). As a result, all the necessary forms of interaction of application processes distributed over the network and residing in different systems can be carried out.

CHAPTER 2

SYSTEMS AND CLASSES OF LOCAL-AREA NETWORKS

Systems are the basic components of computer networks. The tasks that networks handle determine the type, structure, and characteristics of the systems. In turn, the types of systems and physical interconnection facilities divide networks into classes.

2.1.
TYPES OF SYSTEMS

Two types of systems (Fig. 2.1) can be distinguished: subscriber systems and gateway systems. A **subscriber system** is one that furnishes application processes to users or that utilizes the processes for user needs. A system whose purpose is to support data transmission between subscriber systems will be called a **gateway system.** In accordance with these definitions, the primary systems in a computer network are subscriber systems. It is on the basis of them that the network is constructed. Gateway systems are auxiliary and are frequently absent altogether in computer networks.

Subscriber systems can be subdivided (Fig. 2.1) into four types, depending on the functions that they perform. A **host system** is one that furnishes users with one or more information and computing resources. These may include the following: data banks, information retrieval services, job-execution services, mathematical models, etc.

A **terminal system** is one that contains one or more terminals and organized procedures of interaction (via the communications subnetwork) with the information and computing resources of the host systems. Systems which are entrusted with controlling all or part of a computer network will be called **management systems.**

Mixed systems are combined systems that perform the functions of two (or, rarely, as many as three) of the above types of subscriber systems.

Gateway systems whose purpose is to support interaction between two or more networks are called **internetwork gateways.** A gateway system whose function is to combine communications subnetworks in a single computer network will be called an **intersubnet gateway.** This type of system also includes systems that perform routing and switching functions for subscriber systems of a network.

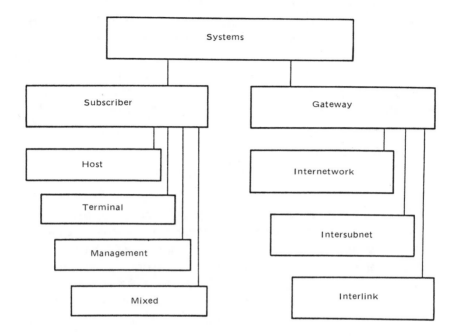

Fig. 2.1. Classification of systems.

They will also be referred to as **communications systems.** If a gate-way system connects two or more channels that differ in terms of their parameters or characteristics, it will be called an **interlink gate-way.**

Internetwork, intersubnet, and interlink gateways execute func-tions of converting information from one group of standards (or pro-tocols) to another. These groups are defined by the connected com-puter network, communications subnetworks or channels. There-fore, these systems are frequently called **interface systems.** Communi-cations systems sometimes constitute an exception. When there is only one such system in the communications subnetwork, it may not necessarily perform information conversion but may deal only with switching and routing functions.

Subscriber systems are implemented in one or more computers. The largest computers in the network are dedicated to the execution of host-system functions. Mini- and microcomputers are frequently employed as terminal and management systems. Microcomputers are becoming more and more widespread. When a microcomputer is intended for a single user, it is referred to as a **personal computer.**

Gateway systems do not require large amounts of computer power, and therefore they can be implemented using mini- or microcomputers. Recently digital logic modules (diode arrays, programmable logic arrays) have begun to be extensively used to create gateway systems. The result has been the appearance of processorless gateway systems.

2.2.
BASIC SYSTEM HARDWARE

Technical progress in microelectronics, resulting in the appearance of microprocessors, has been a major achievement that has influenced the development of computer architecture. A basic feature of this architecture is that information processing is decentralized and distributed over a large number of processors. As a result, universal single-processor computer structures are being replaced by multiprocessor distributed batch **computer installations.** Such installations may include the following:

— an I/O processor;
— a data-link processor;
— a decimal-data processor;
— a memory-allocation processor;
— a central processor;
— a trunk-interface processor;
— a computer-channel control processor;
— a buffer-storage control processor;
— a FORTRAN processor, etc.

It has even become possible to dynamically alter the architecture of a computer installation during operation. Systems programs are developed for this purpose; they specify the processor to which each task is to be entrusted at each stage. As a result, specialization of the processors is temporary rather than permanent. This specialization depends on the nature of the task to be handled by the installation.

The era of general-purpose computers, all designed to be able to execute any type of information and computing task, is coming to an end. Now, more and more frequently, supercomputers for host systems, multimicroprocessor communications systems, and mini- and microcomputers for terminal systems are appearing. Computers at the **worksites** of designers, engineers, managers, and so forth are becoming especially popular.

Progress in hardware and software has made possible the creation of a new generation of computers, known as **fifth-generation computers.** Such computers are under development in all advanced countries, including Japan [21], the USA [22], and Europe [23]. The intended goal is that of designing computers and data-processing methods that can approximate the capabilities of the human brain. A more immediate aim is that of creating series of computers, ranging from ultralarge to small computers, *specially designed for operation in computer networks.* It is assumed that fifth-generation computers will appear at the beginning of the 1990's.

It is projected that the computers in question will be high-performance machines using large data bases and will be capable of training and logical reasoning. In fifth-generation computers particular emphasis is paid to methods of communication with users. Such computers should understand speech, text, and graphics. In addition, they should deliver processed information in user-convenient form, i,e., they should be able to speak, write, and draw.

Modern computer systems are set up in such a way that each unit becomes self-contained and has its own internal control. This permits better organization of data processing, simplifies the documentation accompanying the system, and enables the software requirements to be more clearly defined.

Advances in microelectronics have not only altered the architecture of large computer installations but have also led to the appearance of small and ultrasmall computers. An example of the latter is the Radio Shack "pocket computer" [24]. A TRS-80 pocket computer is 1.6 X 7 X 17.5 cm is size and weighs only 170 g. Its cost is on a par with an inexpensive radio. The computer has a built-in 57-key keyboard covering all the letters of the Latin alphabet, numbers, and special symbols. The machine uses the BASIC language and has a built-in two-line liquid-crystal display with a capacity of 24 symbols. The on-line storage is 1.9 kbytes. There is a built-in battery pack capable of 300 hr of operation.

As for microcomputers, their performance is increasing rapidly, as is the capability and assortment of external devices. For example, Alpha manufactures a microcomputer that includes the following [25]:

— an on-line storage up to 1024 kbytes;

— hard disks up to 280 Mbytes;

— a common disk storage of up to 2400 Mbytes per processor;

— capability of attaching up to 24 terminals or printers to one processor. The computer operates with BASIC, PASCAL, and LISP.

Motorola manufactures 16-bit 68000 microprocessors with a clock frequency of 12 MHz [26]. An increase to 20 MHz is planned for the near future. The Zilog Corporation manufactures the 16-bit Z9000 processor. In terms of its capabilities, this microprocessor is fully on a par [27] with large minicomputers such as the PDP-11/70. The microprocessor has a virtual memory capability.

The Philips Corporation has also begun to develop microcomputers. It has developed a 16-bit computer [28] whose microprocessor employs two LSI circuits. A characteristic feature of this microcomputer is that it can operate with the instructions of a minicomputer and can have 4 Gbytes of virtual memory. It employs 32-bit addresses for this purpose.

The Intel Corporation has produced some interesting developments [29]. It has developed the iAPX-432 microprocessor family, which is oriented specially toward the use of the Ada language. A characteristic feature of this language is its orientation toward programming of tasks intended for multifunctional, shared-use application processes.

Under the control of the iMAX operating system, these microprocessors can perform multiprocessor processing of a wide variety of user tasks. There may be up to four main processors in a complex. In addition, on-line and read-only memory units, as well as auxiliary I/O processors, can be connected to the common bus of the complex. The I/O processors support connection of external devices and channels. It is typical of the iAPX-432 that it can multiply 32-bit numbers more rapidly than the IBM 370/148.

An important feature of the microprocessor complex under consideration is that all microprocessors and memory devices connected to the common bus interact via special protocols, exchanging packets with one another. As a result, the complex is essentially a small local-area network. Packets are from 1 to 16 bytes in length, and are transmitted either to one addressee or to all addressees simultaneously (broadcasting mode).

Zilog has developed [129] a VLSI circuit that comprises a 32-

bit microprocessor. This processor, known as the Z80000, has a six-stage data-processing pipeline with direct addressing to 16 Mbits of memory. The processor performance is 1.5 million op/sec. The processor has a hash memory that forms part of the integrated circuitry.

Minicomputers are also witnessing further development. An example of an advanced minicomputer is provided by the P4500 system manufactured by Philips [30]. This computer has up to 1024 kbytes of on-line storage and disks with a capacity of up to 600 Mbytes. The access time to on-line storage, for a word size of two bytes, is 600 nsec. The computer has a multiprocessor architecture.

A new type of computer, known as the **supermini,** has also appeared. Computers of this type are intermediate between minicomputers and large computer installations. An example can be provided by the DPS-6 supermini manufactured by Honeywell Information Systems [31]. This computer operates with 16- or 32-bit words. It has an on-line storage of up to 16 Mbytes and a disk storage of up to 1 Gbyte. It can operate with 64 channels.

Technological advances have led to the creation of new storage devices, and this in turn has resulted in lower cost of data-storage hardware. For example, MOS storage devices have appeared that contain 1,884,160 bits with random access on a single 5 X 5-mm plate [32]. The integrated circuit formally contains 1 Mbits of storage; in addition, the chip contains 704,512 reserve bits and 128 kbits for parity checking. The reserve cells are employed in the event that any of the primary cells malfunction.

Recent years have witnessed extensive efforts aimed at creating devices for long-term information storage. The capacities of ordinary magnetic disks have increased. **Floppy disks,** employing plastic plates with a magnetic coating, have appeared. Cheap and simple **hard disks** have also been extensively developed. In contrast to floppy disks, hard disks employ a magnetic layer deposited on a hard nonremovable metal plate.

Videodisks constitute a new stage in the development of large storage. Here, information is entered onto and then read from a plate 25-35 cm in diameter (generally on both sides). Videodisks were initially read-only memory devices. Subsequently, however, it proved possible to develop video devices capable of becoming large high-speed external computer storages. The cost of a videodisk is now comparable to that of a good ballpoint pen. Videodisks are thus becoming an efficient basis for the creation of mass archival memories.

Information is recorded onto and read from videodisks in different ways. One method [33] involves laser-beam scanning of indentations or "bits," in a silvered disk. Another method involves the use of a metallic needle with a microscopic diamond tip. The needle picks up electric charges created on the surface of the disk. The latter method is simpler, but it can be employed only in read-only memory devices where there is no rerecording of information.

Videodisks have a number of major advantages over other electronic storage devices. These include the following:

— high rate of sampling of information (up to 2000 Mbit/sec);
— possibility of rapid rerecording of information;
— high recording density, hundreds of times greater than the density for magnetic tape;
— compactness of storage;
— long information storage times (10-20 years, as compared to 6 months for tape);
— large storage capacity.

Regarding this last characteristic, it should be pointed out [34] that videodisk systems employing disks with a capacity of up to 500,000 Mbytes each are currently under development.

An example is a videodisk developed by RCA [59]. This disk is 35.56 cm in diameter, and it rotates at 1800 rpm. Information is recorded onto and read from this disk at a rate of 50 Mbit/sec. The amount of information that can be stored on one removable disk is 100,000 Mbits. RCA is currently developing not only individual videodisk devices but also entire installations of these devices.

Philips has created [35] four videodisk devices that operate as external computer storages. Each side of a disk can accommodate 10,000 Mbits, the equivalent of 25 reels of tape. Exxon Enterprises has also begun to sell videodisk units [60]. Here the disk capacity is 7500 Mbits, while the disk-drive interface corresponds to the IBM standard for peripherals.

The 3M Corporation has also begun to manufacture high-capacity videodisks [36]. Each side of the 3M disk, 305 mm in diameter with a 35-mm central hole, can accommodate 1600 Mbits of data, roughly equivalent to the capacity of 2000 floppy disks 216 mm in diameter. The disk rotates at 900 rpm. Information is entered onto the videodisk by the user, by means of a semiconductor diode laser that burns in pits I μm in diameter. Recordings cannot be erased. Therefore, the disks can be used to create large computer archival storages.

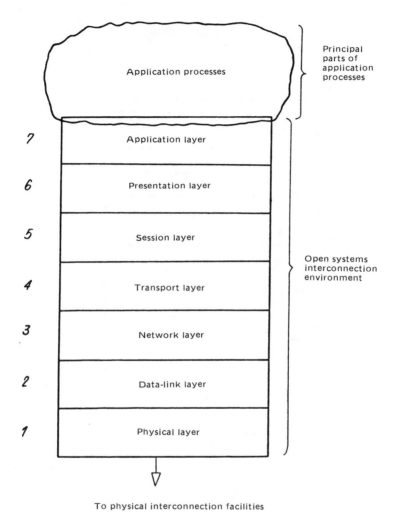

Fig. 2.2. Overall logical structure of subscriber system.

2.3.
SUBSCRIBER SYSTEMS

Figure 2.2 shows the overall logical structure of a **subscriber system**, corresponding to the Basic Reference Model of Open Systems Interconnection. The system consists of two major components: the principal parts of the application processes and the seven-layer open

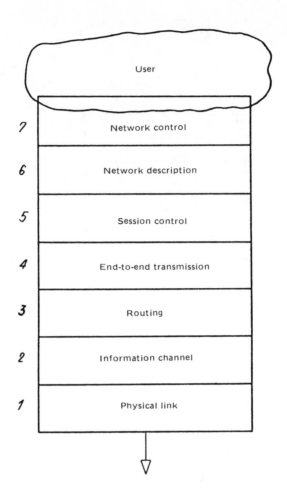

Fig. 2.3. Structure of DEC subscriber system.

systems interconnection environment. The seven-layer environment is described by the Basic Reference Model. As regards the application processes, as noted above, the Model defines only the parts of them that interact directly with the application layer. The Model does not consider the principal parts of the application processes. Each layer of the subscriber system is named in conformity with the Basic Reference Model (Fig. 1.9).

Figure 2.3 shows an example of the distribution of functions over the layers of a subscriber system, as employed by the Digital Equipment Corporation [37]. These functions correspond to the Basic Reference Model, as implemented in the company's DNA network architecture.

To support interaction in the same network between subscriber systems manufactured by different companies, more and more use is being made of virtual forms of information representation and processing. In a network there are two methods of supporting interaction between each terminal and all the available application processes. In the first method, the presentation layer provides q standard forms of data representation for the q types of terminals employed. As long as the number of commercially manufactured terminals was small, this method was widely employed. As the diversity of terminals increased, however, the complexity involved in using this method increased rapidly. This led to a search for other methods of supporting interaction between terminals and application processes. The result was the concept of **virtual terminal,** defined by a **virtual terminal protocol.** The concept of virtual terminal involves the introduction of an abstract terminal that has a standard set of specified characteristics. It is most common to consider three classes of virtual terminals, with the following forms of data presentation:
- page;
- stream;
- graphic.

Each of these classes of terminals has its own particular characteristics. Thus, page-type terminals specify the page format and description and define the way in which data is entered into storage.

Introduction of the virtual terminal concept enables each application process to interact with many types of actual terminals. For this purpose, the information in all the physical (real) terminals must be represented in the manner required by the concept adopted. If a real terminal does not meet these standards, then the characteristics of the terminal must be converted to the adopted virtual terminal.

In data storage, transmission, and processing, the concept of **file** is extensively employed. A file is a data set that has its own name and that resides in one of the systems. A file can have an arbitrary structure defined by the user. In this case it is entered into storage and then can be found only as a single entity. At the same time, a file can have a standard structure such that not only the entire file but also certain parts of it can be selected from storage.

A unified standard form of representation of a data set is called a **virtual file.** This form, defined by a **virtual file protocol,** describes the following:

- the nature of formating of file-control instructions;
- transfer of files and instructions;
- code-conversion procedures.

Use of this standard form enables different systems to perform the following operations with files:

- open a file (provide space for it in storage);
- enter a file;
- read a file;
- erase a file;
- request a file;
- close a file (eliminate its place in storage).

The concept of virtual file can be implemented in two ways. The first way (the preferred one) involves the development of software that executes the standard forms prescribed by the virtual file. In the second case, the system employs local files (with their own standard) that are mapped into virtual files by special programs.

The third standard form of data representation is the **virtual job,** described by a **virtual job protocol.** It includes the following functions:

- control of job structure;
- formating of instructions;
- formating of data.

As a result, the following operations can be implemented:

- transfer of job;
- transfer of results obtained from a job;
- requesting of information on job execution status;
- generation of information on job execution status;
- cancelling of a job (when the job becomes unnecessary or errors are detected);
- communication between operators.

The software of subscriber systems specifies the information and computing resources of the network and the forms and methods of data processing. Regardless of the computers on which they are based, all the subscriber systems in the network must in effect perform the same functions, defined by the protocols of layers 1-7. In this connection, it is advisable to develop a software package that describes these protocols in a language that is comprehensible to the largest possible number of types of computers in use.

Therefore, attempts are under way to develop languages that can conveniently, rapidly, and efficiently describe all the functions (Fig. 1.7) of the open systems interconnection environment. Then, given the availability of translators from this language for all the types of computers in the network, it becomes possible to utilize a unified software package, and to modernize it and develop it simultaneously for all users. This approach is a highly efficient one, but, unfortunately, it is still a long way from implementation.

At the same time, attempts to develop convenient languages for this purpose have already appeared. An example is provided by the C language [41], which was proposed by Bell Laboratories; in terms of its complexity, it is intermediate between assembly language and high-level language. Since a language requires certain support facilities, a machine-independent standard network software package known as SNOE (Standard Network Operating Environment) has been developed for C.

Figure 2.4 shows the software structure of a subscriber system employing SNOE. The figure also gives the percentages of the individual software groups. SNOE was developed specially for use in computer networks and is employed in the computer operating system environment.

SNOE supports the execution of an extensive set of tasks, including the following in particular:

— application-process control;
— standard representation of data;
— support of interaction of application processes;
— common message I/O;
— memory control;
— access to lists;
— organization of timers and traffic signals for flow control;
— time and date reckoning.

The SNOE network package has a standard interface with computer operating systems. As a result, SNOE programs can be employed in any computer operating system connected to SNOE. This greatly simplifies the process of "tuning" the network package for a particular operating system.

Usually, several different operating systems are employed in the subscriber system of a local-area network, employing different types

57

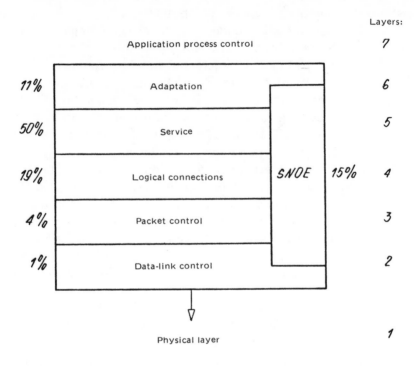

Fig. 2.4. Software structure of subscriber system.

of computers. This makes the implementation and utilization of complex information resources considerably more complicated. Therefore, local-area networks have begun to employ operating systems that are the same for all computers. This greatly simplifies the creation and operation of software, as well as network control and diagnostics. The most widely employed operating system is the UNIX system, which was developed by the Bell Laboratories [151] and which has been incorporated by Western Electric into various machines in various versions. In the USA in 1983 alone, the UNIX operating system was installed in 150,000 computers [148]. It is currently in use [11,49,138-144] in IBM computers (370, 3033, 4300, Series/1) and DEC computers (VAX-11, PDP-11, LSI-11). It is employed by the following: Amdal 470, Data General, Hewlett-Packard, Intel 8086, Zilog 8000, Honeywell Level 6, Univac 11000, Motorola 68000, etc. American Telephone and Telegraph (AT&T) is currently preparing to produce the UNIX operating system on the basis of VLSI technology.

A new personal computer, the IBM XT/370, has appeared [148]. A feature of it is that it uses the VM/CMS operating system. CMS, or Conversational Monitor System, operates under the control of the well-known VM/370 system. CMS is regarded as a rival of the UNIX operating system. CP/M operating systems are also widely employed in microcomputers [50]. Operating systems intended for use in computers of different types are called **machine-independent.**

All previous computer operating systems were created for particular machines with a specified array of hardware: disks, tapes, input devices, printers, etc. In contrast, the **UNIX operating system** is independent of both the physical structure of the computer and of the types of hardware it employs.

UNIX is a universal interactive operating system with time-sharing. It operates with extremely simple files, since, in this case, a file can be any set of bits, without a special format. As a result, the UNIX user can easily create and control files. In earlier operating systems, to describe a file the user had to write a special program, specifying all the characteristics of the file: size, structure, code, format, etc. This program also had to describe the type of hardware used to transmit and receive the file, as well as a considerable amount of other information.

Because UNIX is independent of the computer hardware, the user need not indicate the physical device from which information is taken or the device to which it is transmitted. He numbers the information storages that he is manipulating and specifies only the numbers of the ones between which data are transmitted.

The UNIX operating system is written in C, requires a modest amount of on-line storage (around 100 kbytes), and can operate with virtually any modern computer. The instruction set employed in UNIX supports execution of application processes not only in one but in several computers forming part of a network. Therefore, UNIX is becoming more and more widely used in various local-area networks. The first such networks were set up at Bell Laboratories. In these networks all the various computers operate under the control of UNIX.

Network software packages written (for any computers) in a UNIX environment are beginning to appear on the market. For instance, 3 Com, Interlan, and Plexus have developed [38,143] network software packages that operate under the control of UNIX System III. These packages are intended for 16- and 32-bit machines of various manufacture.

A new version of UNIX, called System V, is coming into use on a large number of different computers. National and Zilog are developing [151] semiconductor circuitry for installing this powerful version of UNIX in their 16-bit microprocessors.

Thus, the use of the same operating system in all the computers of a local-area network opens up a new approach to the problem of network software development. It becomes possible to create a unified network software package. Then, the necessary modules of this package can be incorporated into each subscriber system in the network, in accordance with its specialization. Processes of logical development and reconstruction of the network are also simplified. When one of the protocols changes, a new module of the software package is written, and this module replaces the corresponding old one in all subscriber systems simultaneously.

The UNIX operating system was not created specially for use in computer networks. Even more alluring, therefore, is the prospect of creating a unified operating system that is specially intended for local-area networks and is employed in all subscriber systems of these networks. The University of California, which has developed UNIX Version 4.2 BSD, is proceeding along these lines [151]. The new functions incorporated into UNIX make it possible to create software for specific subscriber systems, by combining software modules using logical "connectors." Similarly, Plexus Computers has expanded the instruction set of UNIX to support operation in a network [151]. This makes it possible to control remote files via the communications subnetwork.

In realistic settings, it is convenient to implement subscriber systems in the form of two units. The structure of such a system is shown in Fig. 2.5. It consists of a subscriber and a station. Here, the **subscriber** is the basic part of the system, implemented in a computer which executes all application processes and part of the open systems interconnection environment. The **station** is the device that interfaces the computer to the physical interconnection facilities and implements the functions of the remaining part of the interconnection environment. Both parts of the interconnection environment are connected by an **intrasystem link,** which supports the interface between the user and station. The station is constructed on the basis of one or

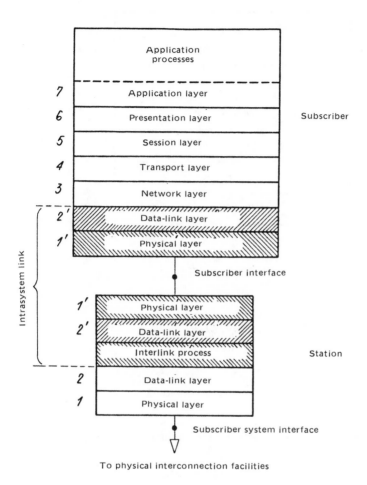

Fig. 2.5. Subscriber system consisting of two units.

more microprocessors. At the same time, it can also be created on the basis of a **processorless logic device,** this being a device employing programmable logic arrays, gate arrays or other discrete components, without any kind of processor.

Implementation of subscriber systems in two units is advantageous for two reasons. First, the station unloads the computer, freeing it from auxiliary routines associated with data transmission. Second,

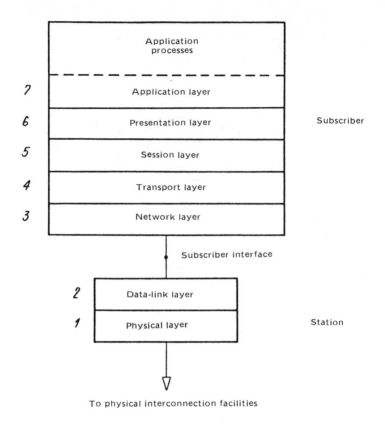

Fig. 2.6. Simplified structure of two-unit subscriber system.

the presence of a station between the physical interconnection facilities and the computer makes it possible to have subscriber interfaces that are independent of the characteristics and parameters of these facilities. As a result, the subscriber interface can be chosen to be convenient from the standpoint of the computer, so that the computer can be connected to various types of physical interconnection facilities. For this, it is necessary only to modify the station.

Synthesis of subscriber systems in the form of two devices (subscriber and station) requires the use of a connecting channel or bus. In turn, a channel (or bus) requires that both the subscriber and the station support the interfacing with this channel (or bus) and control of it. Therefore, additional data-link and physical layers are incorpo-

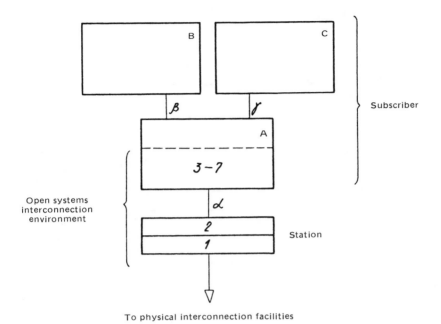

Fig. 2.7. Logical structure of multicomputer subscriber system.

rated into the subscriber and station. They are not defined by the Basic Reference Model, since the Model does not deal with the details of hardware interfacing inside a system. An interlink process is incorporated into the station to support data conversion from the subscriber interface standard to the subscriber-system interface standard, and vice versa.

Since layers that support subscriber interface are not considered by the Model, they are frequently omitted in diagrams. Then the logical structure of the subscriber system shown in Fig. 2.5 assumes the simplified form shown in Fig. 2.6.

Frequently a subscriber is realized in several computers. For example, Fig. 2.7 shows a subscriber system in which the subscriber consists of three computers (A, B, and C). Here, the functions of layers 1-2 are performed by the station, while the functions of the remaining layers are performed by computer A. The application processes in this system reside in computers B and C, and, in part, in A.

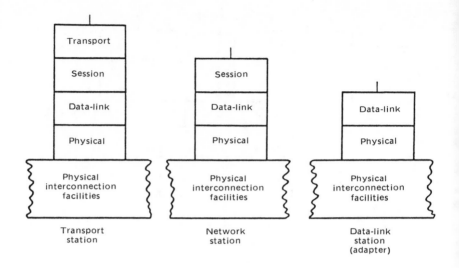

Fig. 2.8. Forms of logical structure of station.

Interaction between computers associated with the execution of application processes, the presence of channels β and γ, and control are not considered by the Basic Reference Model. These functions are defined by the operating system that controls the three-computer installation. In the Model, this part of the system is defined only as the region of existence of application processes.

In Figs. 2.5-2.7, the station implements only the data-link (2) and physical (1) layers of the open systems interconnection environment. The remaining layers (7-3) are implemented by the subscriber. In addition, to unload the subscriber more completely, the network (3) and transport (4) layers are more and more frequently entrusted to the station. As a result, the following types of stations are created: **transport, network,** and **data-link.** The logical structure of these stations is shown in Fig. 2.8. The auxiliary data-link and physical layers that are required (Fig. 2.5) to interface the station and the user are omitted here, in order to simplify the figure. This procedure will frequently be resorted to in what follows. It should be borne in mind that a data-link station is frequently an **adapter.**

Attempts are under way to standardize the physical connection at the subscriber interface, but this problem has yet to be resolved.

TABLE 2.1.

Physical subscriber interfaces

Designation	Type of interface
GOST 25007-81	S1 interface of data transmission system
GOST 18145-81	Circuits on S2 interface between DTE and DCE
V.24	Characteristics of DTE-DCE exchange circuits
V.35	Data transmission at 48 kbits/sec using circuits of 60-108 kHz group band
X.21	Interface between DTE and DCE for executing synchronous operations between them
X.21 bis	Use of DTE with interface to V-series modems in data network
RS-232-C	Interface between DTE and DCE that employ serial exchange of binary data signals
RS-422-A	Electrical characteristics of balanced digital interface circuits
RS-423-A	Electrical characteristics of unbalanced digital interface circuits
RS-449	Universal serial interface between DTE and DCE, employing serial data exchange
IEEE-488	Bus proposed by Hewlett-Packard
IEEE-796	Bus proposed by Intel
IEEE s-100	Bus for supporting microprocessor interaction, proposed by Intel
Unibus	Bus proposed by DEC
Q - bus	Bus proposed by DEC

Remarks:
V and X refer to standards of the International Consultative Committee
on Telegraphy and Telephony (CCITT);
RS refers to the standards of the Electronic Industries Association (EIA);
IEEE refers to the standards of the Institute of Electrical and Electronics
Engineers:
GOST refers to the All-Union State Standard of the USSR.

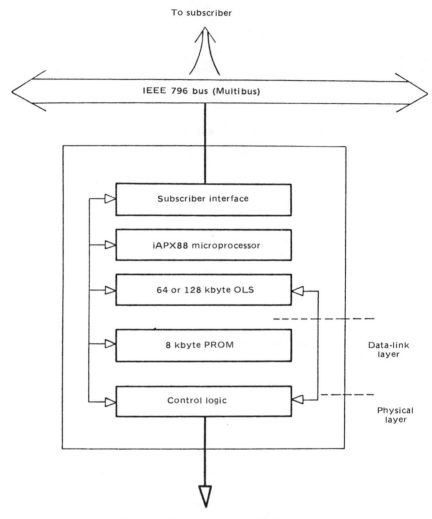

To subscriber

IEEE 796 bus (Multibus)

Subscriber interface

iAPX88 microprocessor

64 or 128 kbyte OLS

8 kbyte PROM

Control logic

Data-link layer

Physical layer

To physical interconnection facilities

Fig. 2.9. Structure of station.

Therefore, the standards that are most frequently employed in practice (Table 2.1) will be cited. The extent to which these standards are employed is evidenced by the fact [150] that, e.g., Multibus is employed by more than 200 organizations in more than 1250 items.

Stations have various forms of technical implementation:
— on the basis of one minicomputer;
— on the basis of one or more microcomputers;
— processorless stations based on the use of discrete logical structures.

The form of implementation of a station depends on the number (Fig. 2.8) of layer functions executed in it (two, three, or four), and also on the rate at which data blocks should pass through the station.

Figure 2.9 gives an example of the structure of a station providing for implementation of the functions of four layers [38,39]. The Exxon/101 station, manufactured by Excelan, has a subscriber interface in the form of the IEEE 796 bus. The station employs a 16-bit Intel microprocessor with a high operating speed (8 MHz) and direct addressing to an on-line storage (OLS) with a capacity of up to 1 Mbyte. A two-port OLS provides storage for programs defined by the lower-layer functions and buffering of frames. The microprograms reside in a programmable read-only memory (PROM). It is assumed that the station will be universal in the sense of being able to operate with physical interconnection facilities of various types.

Support of the entire range of tasks and forms of data processing requires various types of computer networks, including various types of physical interconnection facilities. From the economic standpoint, it is necessary that a given subscriber be capable of operating in different networks. There is considerable promise, therefore, in developing standard units which can be used to assemble stations to operate with particular subscriber interfaces and physical interconnection facilities. In this case, a station (Fig. 2.10) will consist of three parts: a subscriber-interface board, a protocol implementation unit, and an interface board for physical interconnection facilities.

Given a set of subscriber interface boards, it is possible to choose one that will support one of the interfaces shown in Table 2.1. Similarly, a set of interface boards for physical interconnection facilities makes it possible to connect the station to different types of such facilities. By incorporating two standard internal interfaces (1, 2) into the station, all the sets of boards can be connected to one common protocol implementation unit.

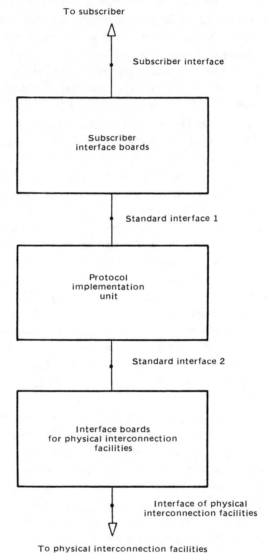

Fig. 2.10. Station unit

By changing its software, the protocol implementation unit can be made to implement functions of the different levels employed in particular computer networks. Hence, by selecting the necessary interface boards, it is possible to obtain a station intended for different subscribers in different networks.

An example of a station with standard units is provided by Interlan [40]. The Interlan station can operate in four types of networks and can have four subscriber interfaces: Unibus, Q-bus, Multibus, and IEEE S-100. As a result, given eight types of units, 16 different station structures can be obtained.

The host systems of a local-area network determine the network's principal information and computing resources. Of no less importance, however, are terminal systems. The characteristics of the terminal system and of the associated terminals determine whether the users can obtain the information they require in the most convenient form. Multiterminal subscriber systems are widely employed in networks. At the same time, developments in microprocessor technology, as well as the extensive assortment of currently available VLSI and LSI circuitry, have given ever greater prominence to **personal terminal systems,** oriented toward a single user.

A personal system has one or more built-in microprocessors, and correspondingly performs a number of operations associated with processing of data, text or graphics.

For example, Motorola manufactures [42] a **radio terminal,** this being a portable personal terminal system intended for users whose motion is confined to an area about 5 km in radius. The radio terminal is connected to the network via a digital radio link at a single frequency of 800 MHz. Up to 1500 terminals can operate at this frequency in a local-area network.

The radio terminal is constructed as a rectangular box only 197 X 102 X 33 mm in size. The box, weighing 793 g, contains the following:

— two 8-bit microprocessors;
— an 80-kbyte on-line storage;
— a 160-kbyte ROM;
— a two-line liquid-crystal display with a capacity of 54 symbols;
— a 59-key keyboard;
— a radio transmitter/receiver;

— a 4800 bit/sec transmit/receive modem;

— a built-in antenna;

— a nickel-cadmium rechargeable battery pack.

When necessary, data can also be transmitted over telephone lines.

Work is being conducted with the aim of creating three-dimensional and pseudo-three-dimensional images in terminal systems. For example, Texas Instruments has developed [43] a terminal system whose display can imitate three-dimensional images. The system generates complex 15-color image groups, each of which is perceived as a pattern lying at the appropriate depth. This imitation of depth is achieved through the use of 36 images that move relative to one another. In this manner, an illusion of motion of certain objects in the pattern relative to other objects can be created.

An important issue in terminal systems is that of dispensing with mechanical keyboards that furnish a fixed set of symbols. There have been a number of developments along these lines. For example, Solid State Technology has developed [44] the Proteus subscriber system, which reproduces a set of "keys" on the screen. From the available set, which runs to 64,000 keys, the user can set up on the screen the keys required for his particular work. These may comprise letters, symbols, instructions, linguistic operators, queries to a host or information system, etc. By pointing to the necessary key on the screen, the user can enter the appropriate information into the terminal system.

Terminal systems can be universal, capable of being used by various specialists in organizations. Recently, as a result of decreasing costs of computers and terminals, specialized terminal systems (worksites), intended for only a certain type of work or for a natural group of specialists such as managers, designers, engineers, accountants, etc., are becoming more and more widespread.

A typical example of a system that performs a particular group of functions is a **facsimile terminal system,** used to transmit graphics from one user to another in a computer network. For instance, Fairfield has developed [45] a facsimile terminal system that transmits graphics over a network at a rate of 9.6 kbits/sec. This rate can be lowered for low-speed channels. At 9.6 kbits/sec, a page of text can be transmitted in 15 seconds at a resolution of 25 X 80 points per square centimeter.

One of the subscriber systems in a network is always entrusted with network control. This system, called a **management system** or

Table 2.2.
Functions of Management System

No.	Group of functions	Functions
1.	Information-gathering	— Monitoring of network components — Information on channel loading — Connection time — Error recording — Loading of network resources — Reports on network operation
2.	Diagnostics	— Self-testing — Testing of component operation — Monitoring of packet transmission — State display — Generation of artificial load
3.	Restoration of operations	— Repeat establishment of connections — Repeat loading of programs
4.	Configuration control	— Incorporation of new subscribers — Network directory service — Establishment of backup channels — Mandatory disconnections of physical interconnections — Isolation of malfunctioning logical components
5.	User service	— Display of dynamic state of network — Assistance in unclear situations — Information on available network resources

network control center, performs various functions, the major ones of which are listed in Table 2.2. For reliability, the management-system computer frequently has a backup machine.

2.4.
GATEWAY SYSTEMS

Figure 2.11 shows the logical structure of a gateway system. It consists of E-layer components 1-P, united by an E-process. The E-layer components in the system can be either the same or different. In the former case, the components perform the same functions but for different data-block flows. In the second case, the components

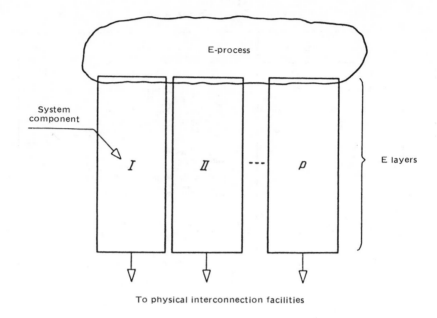

Fig. 2.11. Overall logical structure of gateway system

perform different sets of layer procedures. In contrast to the application processes of the subscriber systems, E-processes are not accessible to network users.

Components 1-P interact only via the E-process. At other points, on the layers of the open systems interconnection environment, the components are not connected to one another and operate in self-contained fashion. Each component has its own physical interconnection facilities. As was shown earlier, gateway systems are divided into internetwork, intersubnet, and interlink gateways.

An **internetwork gateway** implements all seven $(E = 7)$ layers of the open systems interconnection architecture (Fig. 2.12a). Here, the system components are united by means of an **internetwork application process,** and the system is employed to support interaction between two or more networks. For example, Fig. 2.12a shows an internetwork gateway intended for combining two networks. Since an internetwork gateway links only different networks, in general its components perform different layer procedures. On some layers,

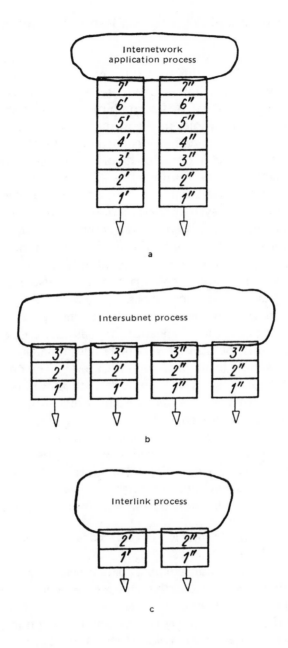

Fig. 2.12. Internetwork (a), intersubnet (b), and interlink (c) gateways.

however, these procedures (assuming identical protocols) may coincide.

For E = 3 is obtained from Fig. 2.11 the **intersubnet gateway** shown in Fig. 2.12b. In this system the components are united by an intersubnet process. An intersubnet gateway is intended for creating a communications subnet or for combining several communications subnets into a larger whole. In the former case, the intersubnet gateway is called a **communications system** and is used for switching and routing of data blocks in one subnetwork. In the latter case, it is employed for switching and routing of data blocks transmitted between different subnetworks. Such a system is called a **gateway system** proper. In a gateway system, the functions performed by the various components are always different. In a communications system, however, they may be either different or the same, depending on the protocols adopted in the communications subnetwork.

In most cases, intersubnet gateways are also responsible for management tasks. These include assembly of statistics regarding operation, diagnostics in the environment of the system, reloading or replacement of software, indication of malfunctions, etc. In these cases (Fig. 2.13), the upper layers (4-7) and a management application process appear in the intersubnet gateway. The procedures executed on the upper layers may coincide with those implemented on the same layers of the subscriber system. Frequently, however, simpler protocols are employed.

Figure 2.12b shows an **interlink gateway.** Here E = 2 and the components are united by an interlink process. The system is intended for connecting two data links. Therefore, the components of an interlink gateway always perform different layer procedures.

The principal functions performed by gateway systems are as follows:
- support of transmission of data blocks between networks, subnets, or data links;
- assembly and disassembly of data blocks (if different block sizes are employed in the networks, subnet, or links);
- data flow control;
- notification regarding overflow and malfunctions;
- restoration of transmission after malfunctions;
- monitoring of interaction of networks, subnets or links;
- determination of the state of the interconnected networks, subnets or links.

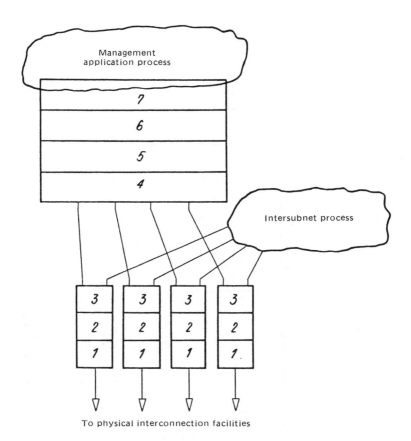

Fig. 2.13. Intersubnet gateway with upper layers.

Interaction between networks, subnets, and links can be supported either with or without establishing network connections. In the latter case, self-contained units, or **datagrams,** are employed. In the former case, **virtual circuits** are employed. The datagram method is simpler and involves less processing time for the blocks in a gateway system. The virtual-circuit method provides higher reliability of interaction and is more convenient, the more similar the characteristics and protocols of the connected networks, subnets, or links.

It should be pointed out that, in addition to their independent value, gateway systems can also be used as part of subscriber systems.

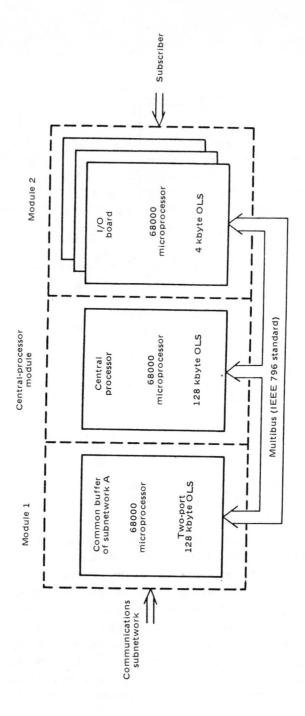

Fig. 2.14. Physical structure of bridge.

Such a case is shown in Fig. 2.5. Here, the interlink gateway functions as a station that is part of a subscriber system. It performs the usual functions associated with data conversion upon transmission of data blocks between different types of links (subscriber and station).

The logical connection between different types of gateway systems has resulted in the development of universal devices that can function in different ways. An example can be provided by a device manufactured by Bridge Communications, called a **bridge** [46]. This device can function as a station of a subscriber system or as an intersubnet gateway.

The structure of this bridge is shown in Fig. 2.14. It consists of three modules, implemented using Motorola 68000 microprocessors. This high-speed microprocessor operates with a 10-MHz clock frequency and has a two-port on-line storage of up to 256 kbytes. Module 1 is employed for interfacing with the communications subnet. Module 2 provides interfacing with the subscriber in conformity with the Multibus standard (IEEE 796) or with a second communications subnet. The central-processor module supports interaction of modules 1 and 2. The set of modules shown in Fig. 2.14 provides a station. This device is manufactured under the designation CS/1. If in Fig. 2.14 module 2 is replaced by a second module 1, the result is a device designated GS/1, which performs the functions of an intersubnet gateway.

CS/1 bridges (stations) support establishment of virtual circuits between subscribers on the basis of their addresses. They supervise transmission, correct errors, provide repeat connections and transmissions, and control data flows. The CS/1 bridge has a capacity of up to 1 Mbit/sec. A large number of virtual circuits can run simultaneously through a bridge. Each I/O board (Fig. 2.14) supports data transmission at a rate up to 9.6 kbits/sec. Up to 16 boards can be installed. The GS/1 bridge (intersubnet gateway) supports interaction of two or more communications subnetworks at a rate of around 1 Mbit/sec.

The assortment of gateway systems that are available for various computer networks is becoming more extensive. Gateway systems are now being manufactured commercially by Xerox, Bridge Communications, and Bolt Beranek and Newman [47].

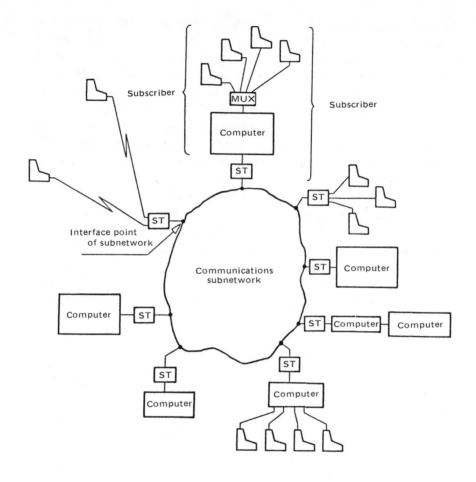

Fig. 2.15. Structure of computer networks.

2.5.
CLASSIFICATION OF NETWORKS

Figure 2.15 shows the structure of a computer network. As noted in Chapter 1, the core of the network is the communications network. Each **subscriber system** consists of a subscriber and a station. As stated previously, a **subscriber** may comprise a group of computers, a single computer, remote or local terminals, external storage devices, etc. A **station** is the part of the system that interfaces

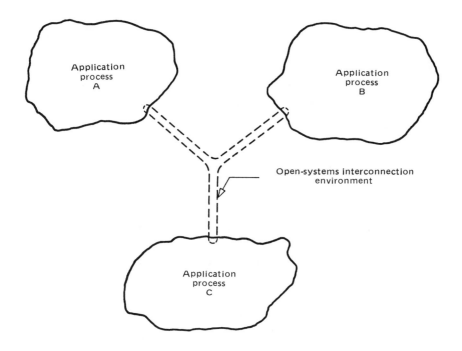

Fig. 2.16. Interaction of application processes.

the subscriber with the communications subnetwork. The points of connection of subscriber systems to the communications subnetwork (interface points of the subnetwork) are described by the standards adopted for the subnetwork.

The interaction of the application processes residing in the subscriber system may be represented as shown in Fig. 2.16. Here, the **open-systems interconnection environment** connects the principal parts of the application processes, providing them with all necessary forms of information exchange. As a result, the application processes are combined into a single entity in the logical sense.

The resources that make up the open-systems interconnection environment can be created in two ways. One way (Fig. 2.17) involves the addition, to the principal parts of the application processes, of devices or programs that implement protocols of all the layers (1-7). Then one or more communications systems, connected by

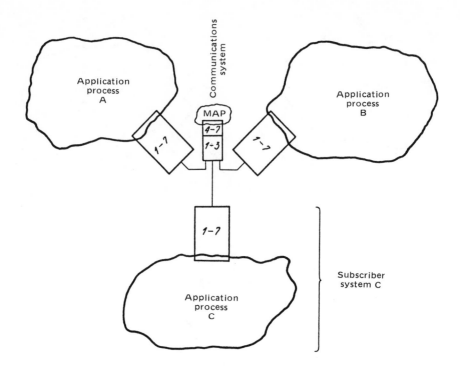

Fig. 2.17. Interaction of application processes via communications systems.

channels, are installed between subscriber systems. Layers 4-7 and the management application process (MAP) of these systems are not involved in exchange between subscriber systems. They are intended for network control purposes. Therefore, layers 4-7 of the communications system and the management application process, shown in Fig. 2.17, are segregated into separate groups. One or more communications systems support interaction between subscriber systems, routing and switching information.

The second way of creating the interconnection environment (Fig. 2.18) involves the addition of interaction resources to the principal parts of the application process, as in Fig. 2.17. Then, however, all the subscriber systems are interconnected directly, without using communications systems.

In conformity with the above schemes, and in accordance with the transmission mechanism for data blocks, local-area networks can be divided into two classes:

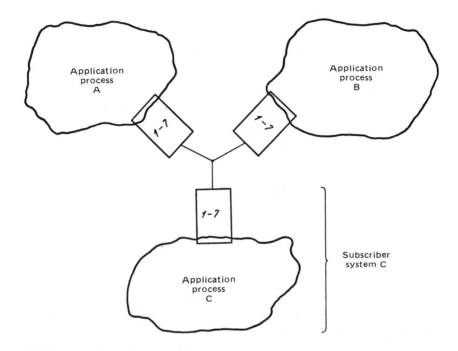

Fig. 2.18. Direct interaction of application processes.

— *with information routing;*
— *with information selection.*

In a **network with information routing** (Fig. 2.17), interaction between subscriber systems is supported by **routing**, i.e., a process in which the transmission paths of data blocks are determined on the basis of their destination addresses. This distributed process is performed by all the communications systems in the network. In a **network with information selection** (Fig. 2.18), subscriber systems interact on the basis of a process of **selection**. Here, each subscriber system receives all the data blocks that are transmitted in the network. The system examines their addresses and processes the data blocks addressed to it, discarding the other blocks.

Any of the classes of computer networks that have been considered should be able to support the following three types of interaction:

1. subscriber system/terminal;
2. terminal/terminal;
3. subscriber system/subscriber system.

81

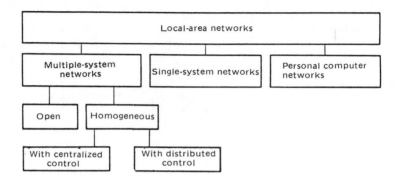

Fig. 2.19. Classification of computer networks.

Interaction of the first type is the simplest to perform. As for interaction of the third type, in setting up a network it is implemented after the other two because of its complexity.

The second type of classification of local-area networks is based on the number and types of subscriber systems employed. This classification is shown in Fig. 2.19. An example of a multisystem network is given in Fig. 2.15. This figure shows the network in which there are eight subscriber systems. Multisystem networks can be divided into open and homogeneous networks. An **open network** conforms to the Basic Reference Model of Open Systems Interconnection and therefore supports interaction of computers of any manufacture. Naturally, the constituent computers in an open network must execute a set of standard network protocols. In conformity with the Model, an open network always has distributed control. Therefore, it does not contain a central system that controls data transmission in the network.

A **homogeneous network** is characterized by the fact that it includes only computers of a certain type. The architecture and protocols of the network are defined by the standards adopted for these computers. An example of a homogeneous network is the Soviet network of Unified System computers, based on the concept of Remote Network Processing of Unified System computers. A second example is DECNET, which includes only computers manufactured by the Digital Equipment Corporation.

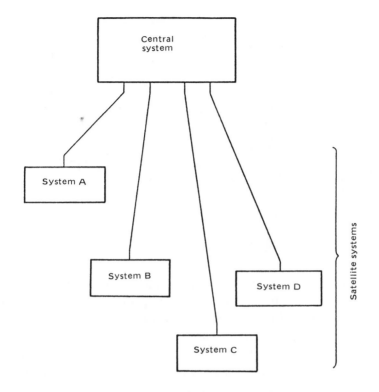

Fig. 2.20. Computer network with centralized control.

Homogeneous computer networks can be divided into two groups, depending on whether or not they have a central subscriber system. The first group includes **networks with centralized control**. Each of these networks has a **central system** that controls the operation of the entire network. An example of a structure with centralized network control is shown in Fig. 2.20. Here, the central system controls the operation of a network in which there are five systems. For this purpose the application process of the central system organizes data-transmission sessions, performs network diagnostics, assembles statistics, and performs bookkeeping. In a network with centralized control, authorization must be obtained from the central system in order to transmit a data block from system A to system D. When the central system malfunctions, the entire network ceases operation.

Networks with centralized control are simple in terms of sup-

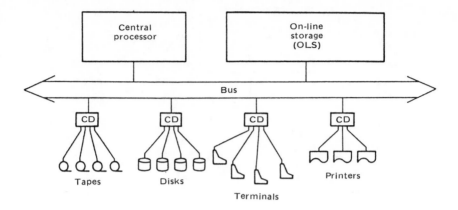

Fig. 2.21. Structure of computer.

porting interaction functions between systems and are based on the fact that the primary information and computing resources reside in the central system. However, they are very unreliable and not very suitable in instances in which the information and computing resources are uniformly distributed over a large number of network subscriber systems. In the main, therefore, networks with decentralized control are employed in practice. Networks with centralized control are employed only in networks involving small numbers of subscribers.

A second group of homogeneous local-area networks comprises **networks with distributed control** (Fig. 2.19). There is no central system in these networks, and all the necessary control functions are distributed among the network systems. However, a special subscriber system, or an application process in such a system, is employed for diagnostics, assembly of statistics, and a number of other network management functions. Needless to say, no authorization is required for two systems to exchange data blocks in this case.

Before considering **single-system networks**, the typical structure of a single-bus computer should be recalled. This structure is shown in Fig. 2.21. The core of the computer is a bus, to which are connected the central processor, on-line storage, and, via control devices (CD), peripherals such as tapes, disks, terminals, and printers. The bus usually runs to 20-30 meters in length. If the computer components must be separated by distances of hundreds of meters or kilometers, then the computer becomes a single-system network.

84

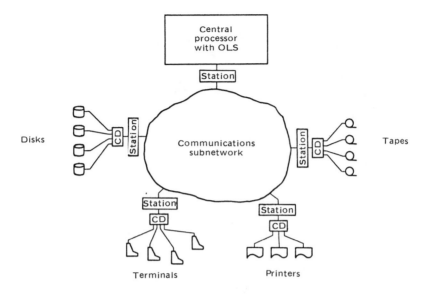

Fig. 2.22. Single-system computer network.

Figure 2.22 shows the structure of a single-system computer network. Here the bus is replaced by a communications subnetwork and a set of stations. Needless to say, when this is done, the operating system of the computer and all the software it contains remain virtually unaltered.

Strictly speaking, a single-system network is not described by the Basic Reference Model of Open Systems Interconnection. However, the stations implement the lower protocol layers of this Model. As for the environment of the higher layers, they are defined by functions executed by the operating system and software of the computer. **Asymmetrical forms** of interaction of components (central processor, disks, etc.) are employed in this case.. For instance, the mode of interaction between the processor and the disk is not the same as that between the disks and the processor. In multisystem networks, as a rule, the interaction of systems displays **symmetrical forms,** in which subscriber system A deals with subscriber system B in the same way in which B interacts with A.

It should be pointed out that computer networks with information selection can be of either the multiple-system or the single-

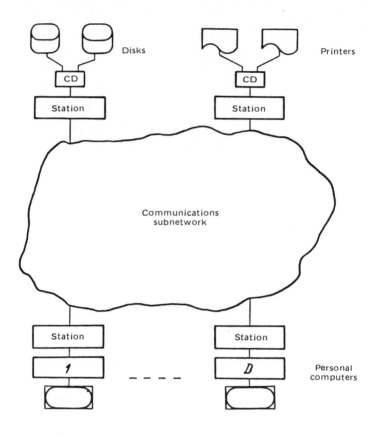

Fig. 2.23. Personal computer network.

system variety. Networks with information routing are always multiple-system networks. This stems from the fact that this class of networks cannot have less than three systems: two subscriber systems and one communications system.

Personal computer networks (Fig. 2.19) are intermediate between multiple-system (Fig. 2.15) and single-system (Fig. 2.22) networks. Figure 2.23 shows the general structure of a personal computer network. It can be seen that, although a personal computer network is a multiple-system network, its principal task is that of furnishing the personal computers with access to common disk storages,

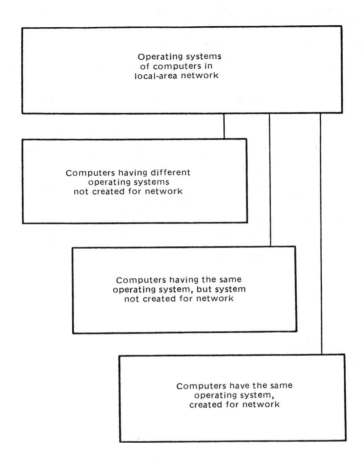

Fig. 2.24. Types of operating systems.

printers, and other external devices. In this respect, a personal computer network is similar to a single-system network. On the other hand,
although there are no complex distributed application processes in
the network, certain procedures involving interaction between personal computers are performed, e.g., electronic mail or file transfer.
In this respect, personal computer networks are similar to multiple-
system networks.

In comparison to networks of other types, the interaction functions performed by personal computer networks are very limited.

87

However, their simplicity and low cost have resulted in their widespread dissemination. In 1982, 12,000 personal computer networks were in operation worldwide in various countries [48]. According to predictions [48], the number of such networks will amount to 110,000 in 1987, containing or connecting around 920,000 personal computers.

Local-area networks can be divided into three types in terms of the operating systems employed in the computers (Fig. 2.24). In the overwhelming majority of networks, the computers employ the same operating systems used in self-contained operation. This is due to the fact that networks are based on computers developed prior to the appearance of these networks. For example, the local-area Experimental Computer Network of the Academy of Sciences of the Latvian SSR comprises primarily Unified System and SM computers. The former employ the OS 6.1 operating system, while the latter employ a completely different system, the OS TS.2.

CHAPTER 3

COMMUNICATIONS SUBNETWORKS

Various types of switching nodes have been employed in data transmission for a long time. Because of the conversion to microprocessor technology and very large-scale integrated circuitry, the reliability of switching nodes has increased considerably, and they are becoming small, inexpensive, unserviced units. The idea of multipoint connections has also been known for a long time and was employed to connect terminals to computers. Its use to support interaction among users of equal status has provided the impetus for the creation of a new class of networks.

3.1.
GENERAL CHARACTERISTICS OF SUBNETWORKS

A **communications subnetwork** is an ensemble consisting of a physical medium, software, and hardware that support data transmission between a group of subscriber systems. This type of subnetwork is an important component of computer networks. The principal requirements which it must meet are as follows:
- high reliability of transmission of data blocks;
- low cost of transmission;
- high transmission rate;
- durability and longevity of hardware;
- low information loss;
- minimum service personnel;
- transmission of arbitrarily encoded data.

Until now, communications subnetworks have been used chiefly to transmit data between subscribers such as computers and terminals. In parallel to these there are television, telephone, telegraph, and teletype networks. Each of these networks is intended for a certain type of information. The last few years have witnessed the wholesale conversion to digital data transmission. This has opened up the possibility of creating **integrated communications subnetworks,** to which various types of subscribers can be connected.

Any communications subnetwork is intended (Fig. 3.1) for supporting various types of interaction between subscriber systems. The points of connection of the systems to the network are called the **interface of the communications subnetworks.** This interface is the

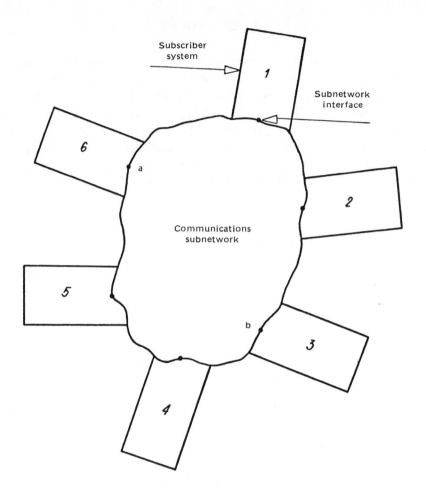

Subscriber system

Subnetwork interface

Communications subnetwork

Fig. 3.1. Overall structure of computer networks.

same for all subscriber systems. Recently, however, additional functions associated with conversion of nonstandard interfaces to the interface of the communications subnetwork have begun to be incorporated into such subnetworks. These subnetworks are called **intelligent.**

Originally, information that was furnished or required by computers and terminals was transmitted via communications subnet-

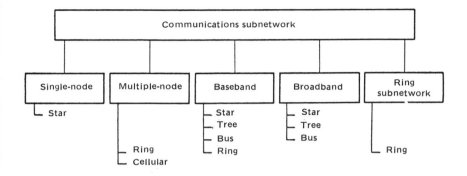

Fig. 3.2. Types of local communications subnetworks.

works. Now, more and more frequently voicegrams, speech, graphics, and even television are being transmitted via such subnetworks. Naturally, any subnetwork must support various types of data transmission, including interactive transmissions, files, messages, and large data arrays. Four principal characteristics determine the communications subnetwork: traffic, transmission reliability, establishment time for an end-to-end connection (via the subnetwork), and rate of transmission of data blocks.

In accordance with the definition of a communications subnetwork, five types (Fig. 3.2) can be distinguished: single-node, multiple-node, baseband, broadband, and ring. This classification is determined by the way in which data blocks are delivered from the sending subscriber system to the recipient system. As for the topology, the above types of subnetworks can have the same forms. For instance, it can be seen from Figure 3.2 that multiple-node, baseband, and ring subnetworks may all be ring-shaped.

In considering the five types of subnetworks (Fig. 3.2), bear in mind that each one has its advantages and shortcomings. Therefore, none of them can be regarded as optimal. Each one displays good qualities in a certain range defined by the requirements of the subnetwork.

Two notions of transmission rate should be distinguished in a communications subnetwork. The first of these is the physical **channel transmission rate.** It is defined as the number of bits transmitted per second over a particular channel. The second rate is the **end-to-**

TABLE 3.1

Factors affecting end-to-end rate

No.	Factor	Characteristic
1.	Topology	Link length determines signal propagation time; repeaters, splitters, and other link components introduce additional delays
2.	Number of subscriber systems	The more systems, the more time lost in matching their operation in network
3.	Structure of station	Efficiency of structure, number and arrangement of buffers, degree of hardware implementation of functions, and microprocessor response after operating speed of station
4.	Amount of traffic	Number and frequency of transmissions increase time spent in transmission control
5.	Number of errors	Time lost in verifying, re-requesting, and repeat transmission of data blocks
6.	Utilization efficiency of data blocks	The more information bits packed into a data block, the fewer the number of blocks required
7.	Extent of control operations	Minimization of interrupt processing, transmission messages, assembly/disassembly makes it possible to reduce time losses
8.	Subscriber interface	Transmission quality and rate between station and subscriber also determine possible loss of speed

end rate. It is characterized by the number of bits per second transmitted between a given pair of interface points of the subnetwork (e.g., between points a and b in Fig. 3.1). This rate is the primary one, since it determines the transmission of data blocks through the entire subnetwork. It is this rate that primarily determines the operating speed of a communications subnetwork.

For example, in one local-area network [11] the physical channel transmission rate is 3 Mbit/sec. Measurements have shown, however, that the end-to-end rate amounts to only 0.6 Mbit/sec.

Many factors cause the end-to-end rate to be less than the channel rate; the principal ones are indicated in Table 3.1. Analysis of the factors indicates the extent to which it is possible to enhance the end-to-end rate.

It should be pointed out that the end-to-end rate does not entirely determine the operating speed of a communications subnetwork. A second important time factor is the **end-to-end transit time** for a data block through the subnetwork. Indeed, it is easy to imagine a subnetwork with rapid data transit, e.g., at an end-to-end rate of 1 Mbit/sec. If, however, the subnetwork is not optimally set up, a data block may take an inordinate amount of time to transit through it (e.g., 0.5 sec).

An important characteristic of a communications subnetwork is the **physical medium** it employs, which may be:
— the "ether" (open air);
— a light guide;
— coaxial cable;
— twisted pair;
— flat cable, etc.

On this basis, a **data link** (or channel) - an aggregate of a physical medium and channel hardware, interconnecting two systems - is created. Examples of data links employed in communications subnetworks will be considered below.

An **infrared link,** which employs the "ether" (or "open air"), is a new type of link in networks. It is convenient when high transmission rates over short distances are required. Equipment manufactured by Datapoint provides a good example of such a link. The transmitter has a power of only 1 μW but provides line-of-sight transmission of digital data at a rate of 2.5 Mbit/sec over distances up to 3 km, using noncoherent infrared signals.

Another example of an infrared link is provided by a portable terminal manufactured by Siemens. This terminal, which is about as large as a medium-size book, provides an on-line connection to a computer from various points of the shop floor. A radio link, which would be sensitive to the electromagnetic fields of the electric-arc welding equipment in use, would not have been feasible in this case. Therefore an infrared system was employed.

A shortcoming of infrared links is that only line-of-sight data transmission is possible. This property becomes an asset, however, in that infrared transmission does not disturb the frequency bands of radio or video links. The range of infrared links is short; therefore large numbers of such links can be set up in a given locality.

Microwave links permit data to be transmitted over considerable distances, up to 15-20 km (line-of-sight). The transmission rates run as high as 20 Gbits/sec.

Light-guide links, in which the physical medium is supertransparent glass fiber, are high-speed, reliable, and efficient under large data flows. The simplest type of light guide consists of a quartz core 50-70 μm in diameter, surrounded by a thin glass film whose index of refraction is substantially less than that of the core. Thus, light waves are reflected inside the glass fiber and do not escape. Frequently the quartz core is coated with plastic. Light guides of this type are cheaper but less reliable. In contrast, glass fiber is more expensive, is unaffected by humidity or temperature, and does not age.

The capacity of light-guide links is very high. The theoretical limit amounts to tens of trillions of bits per second, and rates of 2.41 Gbit/sec have already been attained in practice [51]. In such links the light source is provided by a microlaser or light-emitting diode; semiconductor photodiodes are employed as receivers.

The advantages of light-guide links include: reliability, absence of "cross-talk" interference in a light-guide bundle, and lack of sensitivity to interference from electrical power systems and networks. Light guides are of small size and weight and give good protection against unauthorized access. At the same time, extensive deployment of light-guide links is constrained by limited mass production of supertransparent glass and quartz fibers.

An example of a light-guide link is the 200-Mbit/sec link developed by IBM [52]. A monolithic optical receiver with a silicon photodiode on a ceramic substrate was developed for this link. The transmission rate over an optical link depends on the quality of the glass fiber and on the response of the associated electronics. The rate has already attained 2 Gbit/sec in a number of cases [51].

The use of coaxial cables in communications subnetworks is increasing rapidly. Such cables are customarily divided into broadband and baseband types, depending on the transmission rate. **Broadband cable** provides transmission rates of 300 - 500 Mbit/sec at distances up to 50 km. The operating rate of **baseband cable,** as a rule, is limited to 50 Mbit/sec.

At moderate transmission rates, communications subnetworks utilize inexpensive twisted-pair and flat cables. High-quality **twisted pairs** can provide transmission rates to 3-5 Mbit/sec; frequently, however, the rate falls substantially short of this limit.

The choice of physical medium depends on many factors, in-

TABLE 3.2.

Choice of physical medium

No.	Data to be transmitted	Type of medium	Maximum distance (km)	Maximum rate (Mbit/sec)
1.	Computer data	Twisted pair	0,1	0,1
2.	Computer data and limited amount of speech	Baseband coaxial cable	2,5	100
3.	Computer data, speech, and television	Broadband coaxial cable	100	400

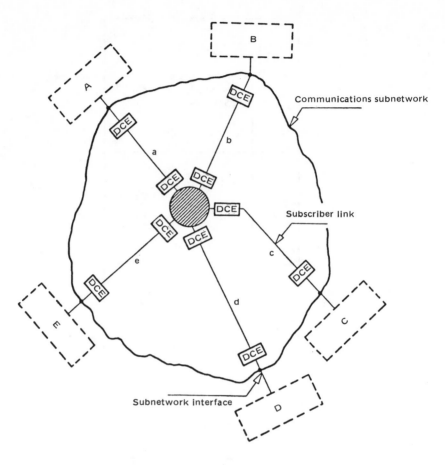

Fig. 3.3. Single-node communications subnetwork.

cluding cost, transmission rate, reliability, etc. Recommendations on the choice of three types of physical medium are given in [53]. These recommendations are listed in Table 3.2. Here, the choice is governed by the types of information to be transmitted between users.

3.2.
SINGLE-NODE COMMUNICATIONS SUBNETWORKS

A **single-node communications subnetwork** (Fig. 3.3) consists of one communications system (shaded circle in the figure) and of a group of **subscriber links,** each of which connects a subscriber system

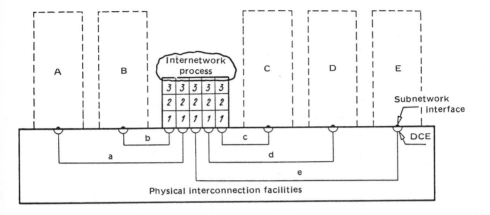

Fig. 3.4. Logical structure of single-node subnetwork.

to the communications system. Hence the name of the subnetwork under consideration. Each link terminates with **data circuit-terminating equipment** (DCE), to which the subscriber systems (dashed rectangles A-E) are connected from outside the subnetwork. The points of connection of the subscriber systems to the DCE determine the **interface of the communications subnetwork.** Naturally, a single-node subnetwork (Fig. 3.3) can have only one shape, namely a star shape.

Figure 3.4 shows the logical structure of a single-node communications subnetwork, corresponding to Figs. 2.12b and 3.3. It consists of a communications system and five (a-e) groups of two-point physical connections. Each group of connections (as in Fig. 3.3) terminates in data circuit-terminating equipment (DCE), depicted by a semicircle. A group of physical connections with a pair of DCE at the ends of the connections comprises a link. Subscriber systems (A-E) can be connected to the subnetwork at interface points.

A communications system implements the protocol of all seven layers of the open systems interconnection environment. However, **basic control,** associated with transmission between subscriber systems, utilizes the protocols of only the three lowest layers, i.e., the network, data-link, and physical layers. Subnetwork **management,** in contrast, utilizes the protocols of all seven layers (Fig. 2.13).

In a communications system, the functions of the network (3),

97

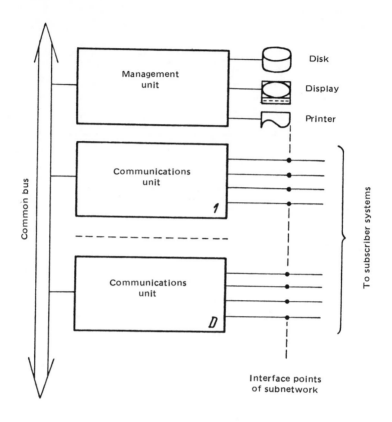

Fig. 3.5. Structure of communications system.

data-link (2), and physical (1) layers are directly related to the links. Above them is an internetwork process that is common to them all. This process provides routing of information and performs functions of connecting links for transmission of packets over them.

As a rule, modern communications systems consist of a group of virtually identical microprocessor units (Fig. 3.5). One of them specializes in management functions (assembly of statistics, system diagnostics, operating reports). The remaining units (1-D) perform functions associated with information routing and switching. The number of communications units employed depends on the size of the communications network. When necessary, when the size of this subnetwork is to be increased, the requisite number of communications units can be added to the communications system.

The communications-system units are interconnected by a bus (or, for reliability, by two common busses). An interesting idea involves the use of a single coaxial cable, rather than a multiple-wire bus. This stems from the fact that a bus is a complex entity, which controls data exchange between microprocessors. Its malfunctioning leads to serious consequences. Coaxial cable, in contrast, is a highly reliable passive element.

Operator control (issuing of instructions, loading and reloading of programs, diagnostics, etc.) of a communications system can be carried out where the system is located. The management unit has a display and a printer for this purpose (Fig. 3.5). At the same time, a communications system can be managed from any other location that is convenient for the purpose. Then the display and printer are unnecessary, and operator control of the system is effected in remote fashion.

An example of a multimicroprocessor communications system is shown in Fig. 3.6 [54,55]. It consists of identical microprocessors connected to two ring busses. The structure of this system can incorporate up to 64 microprocessors. Two of them are for management (type M), while the other 62 are communications microprocessors (type C). Each microprocessor has from 64 to 256 kbytes of on-line storage, and a set of controllers. Microprocessors of type M have controllers that support connection of one or two floppy disks to each of them. The disks are not involved in basic control. Programs are loaded from them, and the operating statistics of the communications system are entered onto them. In contrast to type M microprocessors, type C microprocessors have link-interaction controllers. In addition, of course, the processors of different types have different software.

The type M microprocessor (primary and backup) are required to manage the communications system. In executing management functions, they interact with the control operator of the communications subnetwork.

Microprocessors of type C control the links and provide packet routing. Depending on the transmission rate, each processor can interact with up to 16 links. The transmission rate over two links is 64,000 bit/sec, while over 16 links it drops to 50 bit/sec. Micropro-

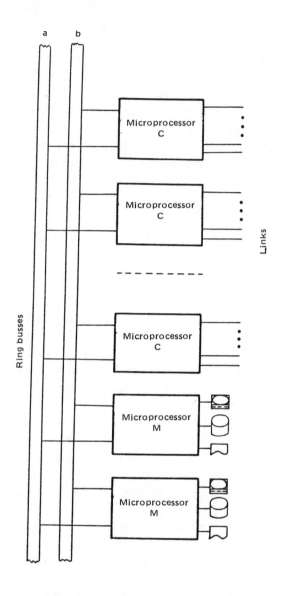

Fig. 3.6. Communications system with ring busses.

TABLE 3.3.

Generations of single-node communications subnetworks

Generation	Method of switching control	Signal type
1	Mechanical	Analog
2	Microprocessor	Analog
3	Microprocessor	Digital

cessors of type C perform functions defined by the protocols of the three lowest layers (network, data-link, and physical).

All the microprocessors interact with the primary and backup ring busses. Modest communications systems can employ simple but relatively slow busses, each of which transmits data at 100 kbit/sec. Large communications systems employ high-speed busses, operating at 8 Mbit/sec.

The first star-shaped subnetwork that came into widespread use in various organizations was the institutional telephone system. It consists of an **automatic branch exchange** ("PABX"), connected to telephone sets by subscriber links.

From the standpoint of the mode of switching control and the shape of the switched signals, PABX's have undergone three phases of development, shown in Table 3.3. In the first phase, PBAX's employed mechanical devices. In the second phase, these devices were replaced by microprocessors. This increased the reliability and operating speed, and made it possible to furnish new types of telephone service, such as call forwarding, redialing, signaling at stipulated times, etc. Basically, however, the network remained unaltered and provided transmission of analog data.

The third phase witnessed a radical alteration of the structure of local communications, involving a changeover to digital principles. Analog-to-digital and digital-to-analog converters, providing digital data transmission, appeared in the networks. As a result, efficient transmission over the network of data exchanged by computers and terminals, in addition to speech, became possible. In this manner, PABX's have become communications systems with extensive functional capabilities.

101

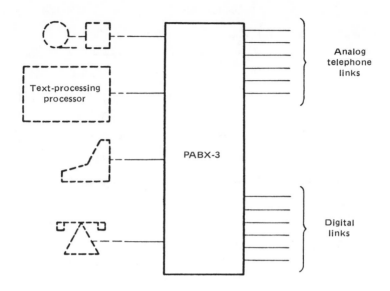

Fig. 3.7. Switching node.

As a rule, third-generation PABX's include not only a communications system but also interface converters. The latter are required because PABX's more and more frequently perform packet switching. Telephone sets and most terminals, however, operate with bit streams rather than packets. Therefore, PABX's require interface converters that assemble bit streams into packets and break out the packets into bit streams. In addition, these converters must provide control of packet flows. It is preferable to convert analog speech signals to digital form, and vice versa, in the telephone sets themselves, but this conversion can also be performed by special PABX units.

Figure 3.7 shows an example of the structure of a communications subnetwork with a third-generation PABX. This installation, which includes a communications system and interface converters, was developed by the Intercom Corporation and is called an IBX. It is intended for complete integration of speech and data transmission. The IBX installation provides 4096 asynchronous and synchronous digital and analog links for subscriber systems. Each link is based on twisted pairs. Two link interfaces are employed, RS-232C and RS-449. Transmission rates are as high as 56 kbit/sec. The IBX interface converters provide analog-to-digital conversion and conversion of lower-layer protocols.

102

The number of manufacturers of third-generation PABX's is increasing rapidly. For instance, Mitel manufactures the SX-2000 Superswitch system, which has up to 2,000 ports and switches up to 10,000 links at rates up to 2 Mbit/sec [56]. For small single-node communications subnetworks, Northern Telecom has developed the SL-1 system [56]. It can switch up to 400 links.

Single-node communications subnetworks have a number of advantages over other types of subnetworks. The major ones are:

— low cost of incorporation of subscriber systems into the network;
— possibility of utilizing available links and link components of institutional PABX's;
— use of standard communications sytems;
— possibility of simultaneous data and speech transmission;
— use of a simple physical medium (twisted pairs).

At the same time, single-node subnetworks have certain shortcomings. A major one is that they contain a vulnerable point (in terms of reliability), namely the node. This means that all the node components must be appropriately backed up, while the diagnostic routines should be able to locate faults and activate backup components rapidly. Other shortcomings of single-node subnetworks are the following:

— limited data transmission rates;
— large overall length of the links.

3.3.
MULTIPLE-NODE COMMUNICATIONS SUBNETWORKS

In contrast to single-node subnetworks (Fig. 3.3), **multiple-node communications subnetworks** (Fig. 3.8) have several communications systems. In addition to subscriber links, therefore, such subnetworks require **trunks** (or **backbones**), that interconnect the communications system. The interaction of these systems via the trunks is determined by the **internal subnetwork interface.** Multiple-node subnetworks can be of differing topology (Fig. 3.2). For instance, Fig. 3.8 shows a ring-shaped multiple-node subnetwork. In addition, multiple-node subnetworks can be cellular (Fig. 3.9). This shape is most frequently employed when it is convenient or advantageous to employ simple or unserviced types of communications systems, each of which switches a small number of links.

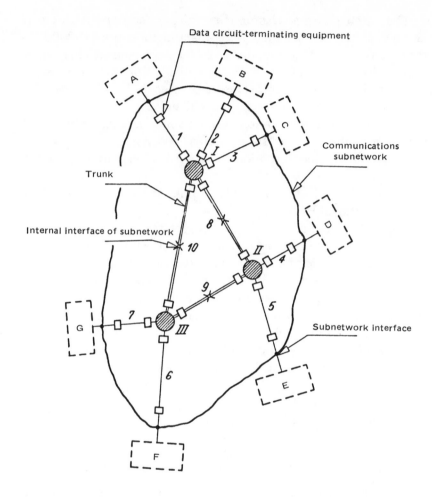

Fig. 3.8. Multiple-node ring communications subnetwork.

Figure 3.10 shows an example of the logical structure of a multiple-node communications subnetwork, corresponding to the arrangement in Fig. 3.8. In the case of basic control, each of the communications systems implements three layers of the basic-control protocols, namely the network, data-link, and physical layers.

In contrast to single-node networks, multiple-node subnetworks (Fig. 3.10) employ two types of links: trunks (8-10) and subscriber links (1-7). Therefore, the standards for interfacing with these links

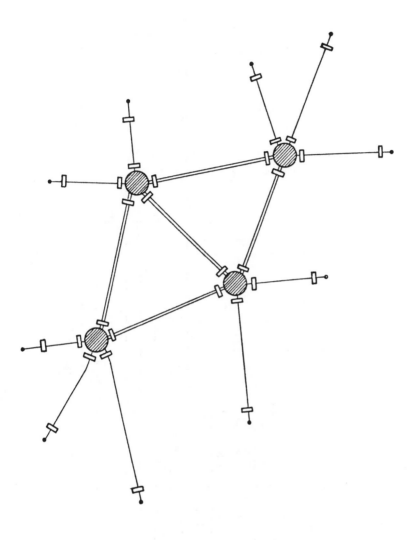

Fig. 3.9. Cellular subnetwork.

(1, 1′) for link control (2, 2′) and for transmission of data blocks
(3, 3′) may be different. To unify the hardware and network software, however, it is desirable that the standards in a multiple-node
subnetwork be the same as in a single-node one. This makes it possible, when necessary, to add a second, third, etc., communications
system to a single-node subnetwork, thus converting the subnetwork
to a multiple-node one.

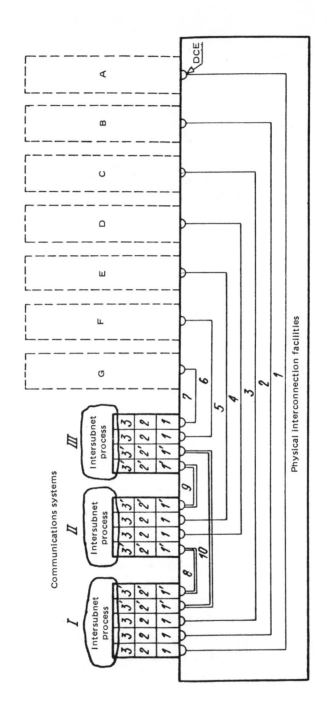

Fig. 3.10. Logical structure of multiple-node subnetwork.

In a single-node communications subnetwork, the (single) communications system may have operator service, and then the subnetwork management is located there. In a multiple-node subnetwork, operator servicing of each of the communications sytems is too much of a luxury. Therefore, the subnetwork must have a single center which provides all remote operator servicing of communications systems. This center is set up on the basis of a communications subscriber system.

An example of a small multiple-node communications subnetwork is the one developed by the French company Télécommunications Radioelectriques et Téléphoniques [145,146]. The hardware of this subnetwork consists of COMPAC microprocessor communications systems and an EMACOM-3 management system. The subnetwork supports packet transmission.

Each communications system in this subnetwork comes in the form of a small desktop unit and provides routing of packets over eight links. The use of two or three such units increases the number of links to 16 and 24, respectively. The system has an external storage in the form of two compact cassettes. The software for the communications system is loaded locally (from a cassette) or remotely from the management system.

The management system performs the function of controlling the multiple-node subnetwork. The system consists of a desktop unit with a built-in display. It performs a considerable number of functions, including the following:
- automatic control and monitoring of the subnetwork;
- remote support of operation of communications system, including remote loading of software;
- remote diagnostics and measurement;
- gathering of statistics and prepartion of reports on subnetwork operation;
- restoration of operation after malfunctions and breakdowns;
- remote reconfiguration of the subnetworks.

In analyzing multiple-node communications subnetworks, certain positive features should be pointed out. These include, in particular, the following:
- distributed structure of the subnetwork, which fits well into the topology of subscriber systems;
- possibility of employing simple unserviced communications systems;

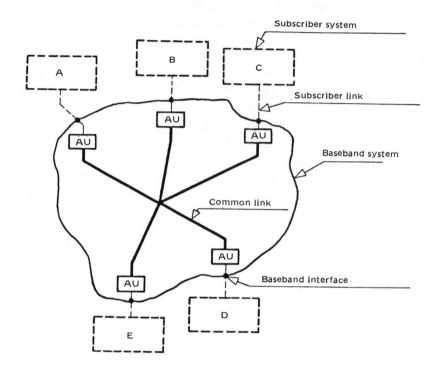

Fig. 3.11. Star baseband system.

— capability for handling data and speech simultaneously;
— use of simple twisted-pair lines.

At the same time, multiple-node subnetworks have a number of shortcomings, e.g.:

— large numbers of communications systems and links;
— limited transmission rates;
— relative complexity of data routing and transmission control.

3.4.
BASEBAND SYSTEMS

A **baseband (broadcast) subnetwork** is a communications subnetwork in which the physical medium provides simultaneous transmission (to within signal propagation over the physical medium) of data blocks to all subscriber systems connected to it. In the physical

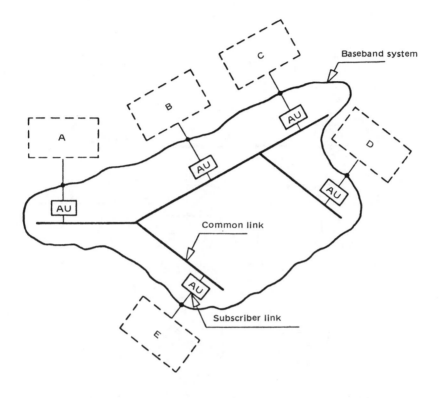

Fig. 3.12. Tree baseband system.

medium, there is no segregation of frequency bands for transmission, i.e., the medium is utilized entirely (monopolistically). Therefore, systems of this type are frequently called **baseband transmission systems.** Transmission is in digital form. A baseband system (Fig. 3.2) can have four forms: star, tree, bus, and ring.

The core of a **star baseband system** is a **common link** (Fig. 3.11), which consists of branches that depart from a single point and terminate in data circuit-terminating equipment. This equipment is referred to as **access units** (AU) to the physical medium. Each access unit is connected to a subscriber system via a link called a **subscriber link.** The boundaries of the baseband system are determined by the points of the **baseband-system interface.** As the name indicates, a

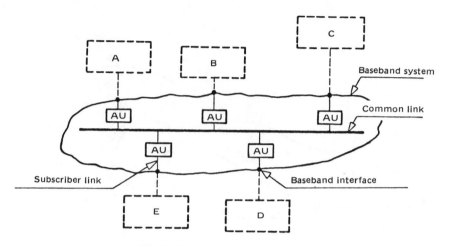

Fig. 3.13. Bus baseband system.

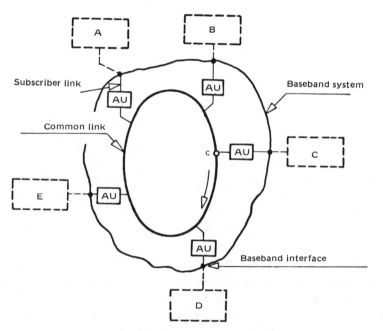

Fig. 3.14. Ring baseband system.

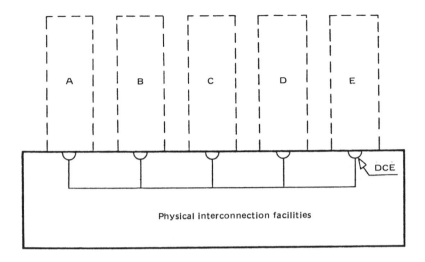

Fig. 3.15. Logical structure of baseband system.

tree baseband system is one in which the common link is tree-shaped (Fig. 3.12). A system of this type is employed when large numbers of subscriber systems at relatively great distances from one another must be connected.

In a **bus baseband system,** the common link is in the form of a bus. Its structure is shown in Fig. 3.13. It is simple and convenient, and therefore can be employed for most networks. However, bus systems are inferior to tree systems in instances involving large local-area networks, e.g., municipal information and computing networks.

A **ring baseband system** (Fig. 3.14) is in the shape of a ring, to which all the subscriber systems of the network are connected. This system has the feature that, when data blocks are transmitted by system C, the ring must be logically broken at point c and converted into a bus.

The transmission principle is the same in all baseband broadcast systems. Any transmitted data block is received almost simultaneously (to within the signal-propagation delay) by all subscriber systems. Then each subscriber system inspects the received data blocks, selects the one addressed to it, and eliminates the rest.

Figure 3.15 shows the logical structure of the physical interconnection facilities making up a baseband system whose structure cor-

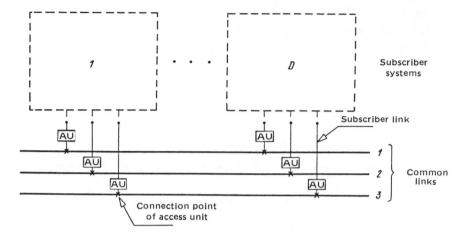

Fig. 3.16. Group of baseband systems.

responds to Figs. 3.11-3.14. It contains a group of multipoint connections, at whose boundaries there is a group of data circuit-terminating equipment (DCE), called access units (AU). In considering the structure of the system, it should be pointed out that the multiple-node and single-node communications subnetworks contain one or more communications systems, linked by groups of physical connections. In the case of basic control, the communications systems perform the functions of the network, data-link, and physical layers. Each baseband system, although it does not perform the functions of the open systems interconnection environment and is made up only of groups of physical connections, also supports the necessary data exchange between subscriber systems. However, a baseband system delivers transmitted data blocks to all subscriber systems connected to it, rather than to a single addressed system (as in the case of nodal communications subnetworks).

A given computer network may employ not merely one but several identical or different baseband systems for data transmission. This occurs when it is necessary

— to increase performance and reliability of data transmission;
— to provide transmission of different kinds of information.

For example, a network may contain several baseband systems, one used to transmit television frames, another for telephone conversations, and the rest for data exchange between computers and terminals.

Figure 3.16 shows an example of a computer network that employs three trunk baseband systems. As usual, each of the systems consists of a common link, access units, and subscriber links. A subscriber system can be connected to one, more than one or all the baseband systems. The list of baseband systems via which the system can transmit data is determined by the structure of the network, the necessary transmission reliability, and the planned traffic.

It is fairly simple to physically connect an **access unit** to a common link based on flat cable or twisted pairs. Certain difficulties arise when the physical medium is provided by coaxial cable. In this case, two methods of connecting the access unit to the common link are employed in practice.

The first method, called **destructive,** involves cutting the coaxial cable of the common link at the point of connection of the access unit [154]. Then a tee connector is inserted at this point.

The second method, called **nondestructive,** involves puncturing the coaxial cable with a special blunt needle at the required point. The needle penetrates to the center conductor of the cable and thus provides the necessary contact. The base of the needle is insulated so that shorting to the cable braid does not occur.

It should be noted that the destructive method yields a more reliable contact between the access unit and the coaxial cable. However, repeated cutting of the coaxial cable entails a loss of reliability of the system, since a break in the common link at even one point causes the communications network to cease operation. In addition, repeated cutting of coaxial cable introduces noise because of the appearance of a variety of reflections at the cut points. Therefore, more and more manufacturers are avoiding the destructive method that was widely employed earlier, when relatively few taps were required.

The nondestructive method preserves the integrity of the entire common point, thus enhancing the reliability and operating quality of the baseband system. Use of this method also means that new access units can be connected, and unnecessary ones disconnected, during operation of the network, without affecting its normal operation.

A baseband system (Fig. 3.17) consists of access units and a physical medium. It is the job of the **access unit** to support interaction between subscriber links and the physical medium of the system and to execute a variety of functions associated with data transmission via this medium. Therefore, the access unit has three mod-

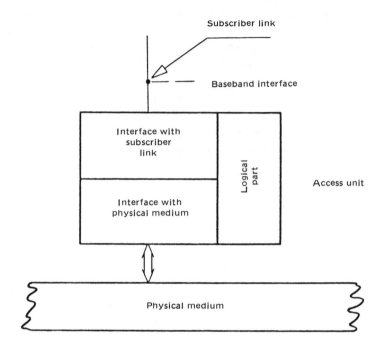

Fig. 3.17. Structure of access unit.

ules. Two of them support interfacing between the subscriber link and the baseband system. Their structure is determined by the type of subscriber link and physical medium employed.

The third module of the access unit is the logical part, which performs the following functions:

- self-diagnostics of faults and sending of fault signals to the subscriber system;
- disconnection of access unit (when faulty) from the physical medium and connection to the medium;
- reception and preprocessing of signals from the physical medium;
- transmission of signals to the physical medium;
- monitoring of the physical medium to determine whether it is busy.

The access unit is usually in a hard-to-reach place next to the

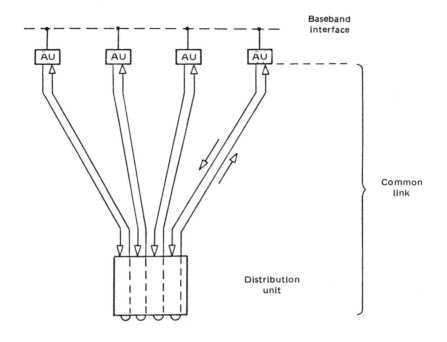

Fig. 3.18. Star baseband system employing light guides.

physical medium, e.g., coaxial cable. Therefore, it is manufactured in the form of a closed box to be installed under the floor or in a wall. This installation requires that the access unit be reliable and be suitably powered from the subscriber system. The common link of the baseband system may become an antenna that admits noise into the access unit and subscriber system. To avoid this, the circuits of the access unit and of the common link are electrically isolated. This is done by using isolation transformers.

The common link (Figs. 3.11-3.14) has one or more **segments,** i.e., parts that do not contain any repeaters (or amplifiers). Segments are coupled by means of repeaters that restore the signal shape, which is distorted as the signal travels over the common link. Coaxial cable is being more and more frequently used as the common link in baseband systems. At low rates (not exceeding a few hundred bit/sec), however, twisted-pair or flat cable can be employed.

Recently, there has been particular interest in the use of **fiber** optics in baseband systems. Star systems are the most suited to the use of light guides [57]. Figure 3.18 shows the structure of such a system. Here, in contrast to Fig. 3.11, the common link consists of pairs of light guides, while a light distribution unit is installed at the center of the star.

Subscribers operate only with electrical signals, but light rays are transmitted over light guides. In addition to their customary functions, therefore, the access units in Fig. 3.18 perform operations involving conversion of electrical signals to light, and vice versa.

The light source and converter must be connected precisely to the end section of the light guide. At present, therefore, each light guide transmits in only one direction. Hence, each "spoke" of the star common link in Fig. 3.11 is represented by two light guides in Fig. 3.18.

By mixing the light signals, the distribution unit can transmit light received over one of the spokes to all of the spokes that depart from it. The number of spokes, and hence the number of subscriber systems that can be connected, may run into the hundreds. Naturally, if there are E subscribers in the system, the light source must have sufficient power to be picked up by the E light receivers after the light has been divided into E parts in the distribution unit. Light guides are also employed in trunk baseband systems. Because of technical difficulties associated with the development of taps to access units, however, the number of such systems does not exceed ten at present.

Baseband systems provide an effective means of connecting large numbers of subscriber systems and have the following major advantages:

    — capability for simultaneous transmission of data and speech;
    — high transmission rates;
    — simplicity of running and installing the system;
    — high operational reliability;
    — possibility of connecting new systems without halting the network;
    — small overall length of all the system links.

At the same time, these systems display a number of shortcomings:

    — high cost of physical medium;
    — substantial noise in the system when the number of access units is large;

— relatively complex forms of transmission control.

3.5.
BROADBAND SYSTEMS

For data transmission, computer networks frequently employ the techniques of standard cable television, which yield a particularly high throughput. Since the performance and the transmission rate are high in this case, **frequency bands** are segregated in the physical medium. Therefore analog signals, rather than digital signals, are transmitted via the physical medium (which is provided, as a rule, by broadband coaxial cable).

A frequency band can perform the same functions as the physical medium of the baseband system considered in the preceding section, i.e., those of transmitting information from a sending subscriber system to all the other subscriber systems in a network. If interaction between this frequency band and the requisite number of **access units** is provided, a communications network that is called a **multipoint frequency link** is obtained.

When necessary, **frequency subbands** can be set up in a frequency band, each subband having a limited throughput and supporting connection of two subscriber systems. By combining a subband with access units, a **point-to-point frequency channel** can be established.

A **broadband system** will refer to a group of communications subnetworks based on a unified physical medium, in which a set of logical point-to-point and multipoint frequency channels is created through the use of frequency-division multiplexing. Within each frequency channel in the system, information is transmitted by modulating the carrier frequency. The term "broadband system" (or **broadband channel**) refers to the wide range of the transmitted frequencies.

Schematically, broadband systems appear similar to baseband ones (Figs. 3.11-3.13). They also consist of a physical medium and access units. At the same time, as previously indicated, the structure of a broadband system differs markedly from that of a baseband system. The principal difference is that broadband systems form a group of communications subnetworks, whereas baseband systems form only one. Hence, a baseband system can be used as the basis for one communications subnetwork, whereas a broadband system can provide the basis for a set of them.

117

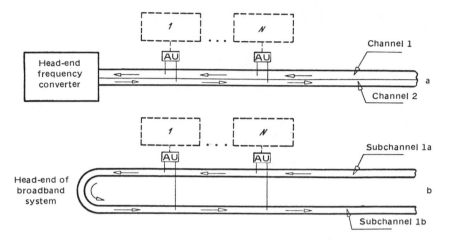

Fig. 3.19. Two types of broadband systems.

Thus, in a broadband system with k frequency channels, k signals can be transmitted simultaneously. The number of frequency channels can run to the hundreds. Since broadband systems form a set of point-to-point frequency channels, they generally have a **channel switch.** This switch handles the connection of free point-to-point channels to subscriber systems which need to conduct data transmission sessions.

As shown earlier (Fig. 3.2), baseband systems can have four configurations: star, tree, bus, or ring. In the case of broadband systems, the ring configuration is not employed because of the presence of large numbers of frequency channels operating in parallel.

Every broadband system contains large amounts of unidirectional hardware (amplifiers, splitters, repeaters, etc.). Therefore, the frequency channels in such a system transmit in only one direction.

There are two methods of transmission in a broadband system (Fig. 3.19). In the first method, pairs of frequency channels are established, and data is transmitted over them at different frequencies (only one pair of channels is shown in Fig. 3.19a). Here channel 1 assembles the data blocks to be transmitted to subscriber systems. Conversely, channel 2 breaks out the received data blocks to these systems. Since the channels operate at different frequencies, the system has a **head-end frequency converter.** This converter serves to transmit the blocks received from channel 1 to channel 2.

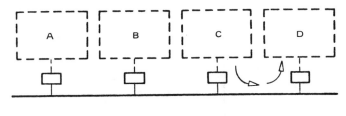

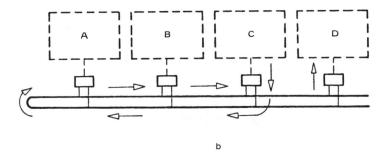

Fig. 3.20. Transmission paths of data blocks in baseband system (a) and in band of broadband system (b).

In the second transmission method, the cable makes a loop (Fig. 3.19b) in the **head end** of the system and thus runs past all access units twice. One part (subchannel 1a) assembles data blocks, while the other part (subchannel 1b) breaks out the blocks. This type of broadband system will be called a **loop broadband system.**

In comparing the two methods, note that, in the first case, the length of the expensive broadband system (together with channel elements such as repeaters, splitters, etc.) is halved. At the same time, the throughput of the system is also halved, since half of it assembles, while the other half breaks out, the same data blocks. Therefore, the choice of method depends on economic factors and on the necessary system throughput.

In a broadband system, therefore, all information is transmitted through a head-end frequency converter or through the system head

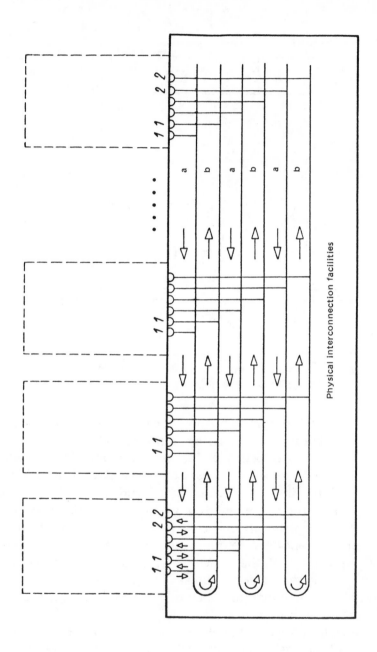

Fig. 3.21. Logical structure of loop broadband system.

end. As a result, the data-block paths in a broadband system are twice as long, on average, as in a baseband system. Figure 3.20 shows the transmission paths from subscriber system C to subscriber system D in both a baseband system (a) and in a multipoint frequency channel of a broadband system (b). In the second case, the blocks pass through the head end of the system, and therefore their path is much longer.

The logical structure of broadband systems is fairly complicated. This stems from the fact that such systems involve large numbers of parallel groups of physical connections. The structure depends (Fig. 3.19) on the transmission method in the system. Thus, for the method shown in Fig. 3.19b, the logical structure of the broadband system has the form shown in Fig. 3.21. In the loop system shown here, three groups of connections are created through the use of frequency-division multiplexing. Any group consists of two parts (a and b), interconnected by loops.

Each group of connections in a broadband system can be employed in two ways. Thus, if more than two subscriber systems are connected to points 1, ..., 1, the group of connections will define a multipoint channel. If, however, two subscriber systems are connected to points 2, ..., 2, the group of connections will define a point-to-point channel.

If the method shown in Fig. 3.19a is used to create a broadband system, then the logical structure of the system is somewhat modified. In this case (Fig. 3.22), parts a and b of the connection groups are not interconnected by a loop but are connected to head-end frequency converter. Otherwise the logical structure remains the same as in the case of the transmission method with a loop in the front end of the system.

In general, access units in a broadband system have the same structure (Fig. 3.17) as in a baseband system, but a number of new functions appear. For instance, in a broadband system the access units must transmit analog signals to the physical medium. However, the interaction between access units and subscribers is digitally based. Therefore, the access unit performs appropriate digital-to-analog and analog-to-digital signal conversion. In a broadband system, moreover, access units must frequently operate in alternation (not simultaneously) with different point-to-point frequency channels. Therefore, these units must incorporate the possibility of changing the frequencies of the transmitted and received analog signals.

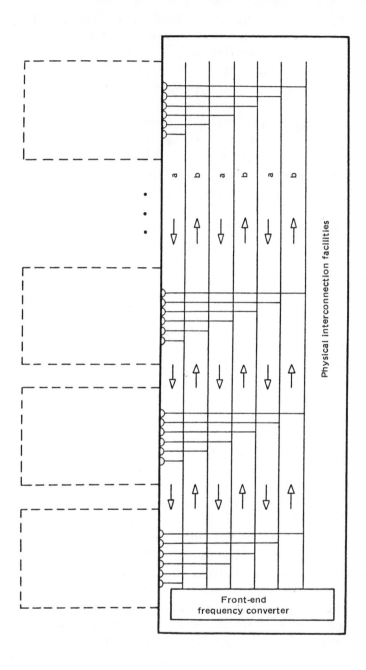

Fig. 3.22. Logical structure of broadband system with head-end frequency converter.

Physical interconnection facilities

a b a b a b

Front-end
frequency converter

122

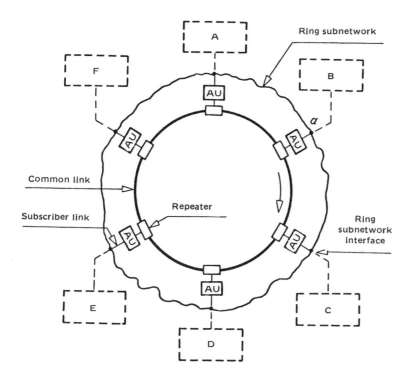

Fig. 3.23. Ring subnetwork.

Most frequently, the physical medium in a broadband system is provided by a broadband coaxial cable. Light guides are currently not employed, since fiber optics cannot yet meet the requirements of this application.

The merits of broadband systems include their universality and high throughput. By segregating separate bands and subbands, transmission can be provided for extensive groups of subscribers from terminals and computers to standard television equipment. Also among the merits of broadband systems are the unified physical transmission facilities. However, broadband arrangements are very expensive, cumbersome, and complex in operation. Therefore, broadband systems are employed only in large local-area networks with a wide range of types of subscribers.

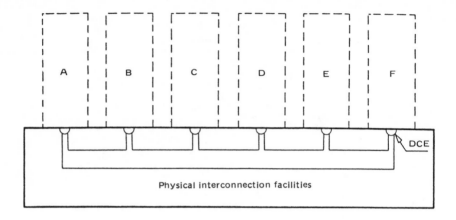

Fig. 3.24. Logical structure of ring subnetwork.

3.6.
RING SUBNETWORKS

A **ring subnetwork** (Fig. 3.23) is a communications subnetwork in the form of a ring containing **repeaters** at points at which subscriber systems are to be connected. Each repeater has a small delay that is needed by the subscriber system to enter data and to read the information passing it via the ring. An **access unit,** connected via a subscriber link to the subscriber system, is connected to the repeater. Since each repeater has a delay, the transmission time for a data block around the ring depends on the number of subscriber systems that are connected.

Figure 3.24 shows the logical structure of the ring subnetwork corresponding to the arrangement in Fig. 3.23. A characteristic feature is the presence of a ring that passes through units of special data circuit-terminating equipment (DCE). Each of these units contains an access unit and a repeater. The repeater must have a delay adequate for the subscriber system to determine frame addresses and to receive or transmit packets.

Figure 3.23 shows a ring subnetwork with distributed control. An example of such an arrangement is Ringnet, developed by Prime Computer Corporation. However, the complexities entailed by distributed control have led to the development of ring subnetworks employing centralized control. For this purpose, a device called a

124

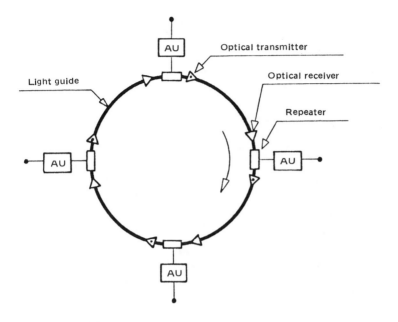

Fig. 3.25. Ring subnetwork employing light guides.

monitor is added to the rings. An example of such a ring subnetwork is the Cambridge Ring.

In most cases, ring subnetworks are based on twisted pairs, or flat or coaxial cables. However, fiber optics is being more and more widely employed in such subnetworks. This stems from the fact that there is no need for light couplers or taps in this case.

Figure 3.25 shows an example of a light guide-based ring subnetwork. In contrast to Fig. 3.23, in this case there are two new types of components, namely optical transmitters and receivers. An optical transmitter converts electrical signals to light signals and feeds the latter to the light guide. An optical receiver, in contrast, receives light signals from the guide and converts them back to electrical signals. Such arrangements tend to be unreliable because malfunctioning of one of the components causes the entire network to cease operation. Therefore, attempts are under way to develop optical switches that can disconnect malfunctioning parts from the ring.

Several ring subnetworks are often employed to enhance operating reliability, and sometimes to increase throughput, in computer

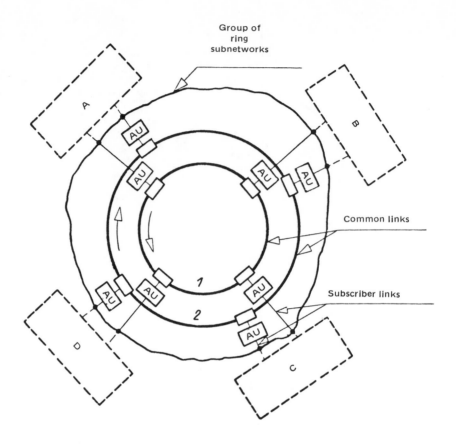

Fig. 3.26. Group of ring subnetworks.

networks. Frequently two communications subnetworks are employed, the information in them being transmitted in different directions around the ring subnetwork. An example of such a network is shown in Fig. 3.26. The network contains two ring subnetworks (1, 2), to which subscriber systems A-D are connected.

A principal liability of ring subnetworks is that the ring arrangement of repeaters is unreliable. Developers of communications subnetworks have proposed two ways of eliminating this unreliability. The first way involves installation of an electronic switch in parallel with each repeater (Fig. 3.27). In the event of a malfunction, the switch creates a bypass around the repeater.

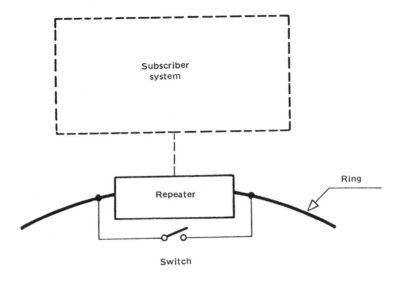

Fig. 3.27. Repeater with shunting switch.

The second way involves the establishment of a **channel center** [58] at the geometrical center of the communications subnetwork (Fig. 3.28). All the links of the ring subnetwork feed into it, forming loops that come out of the center. Only the repeaters and the subscriber-system connection points remain in their previous location. Electronic switches, which disconnect loops without breaking the ring, thus removing repeaters and the associated subscriber system, are installed at the channel center.

In comparing Figs. 3.27 and 3.28, note that the ring links are much longer in the second case. However, reconfiguration of the switching of these links becomes much simpler in the case of Fig. 3.28.

It should also be noted that, in a ring subnetwork, the operation of all the repeaters must be synchronized. Timing of the motion of frames around the ring is employed for this purpose. This is done as follows:

- when the ring begins to operate, a designated principal repeater is timed, and all the other repeaters are to be synchronized to it;

127

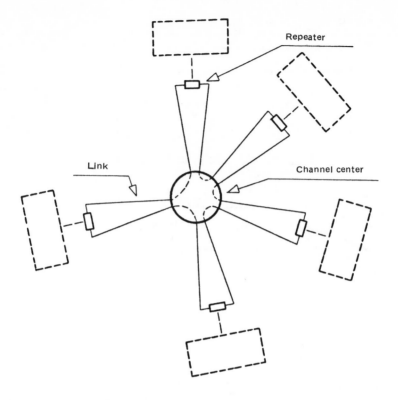

Fig. 3.28. Ring subnetwork with channel center.

— the remaining repeaters are adjusted with respect to time;
— automatic frequency control of the repeaters is employed during operation.

Ring subnetworks constitute a simple type of communications subnetwork. They provide the following:

— ease of connection of subscriber systems;
— simple control of data transmission;
— low network cost.

However, ring subnetworks also possess major shortcomings, including, in particular, the following:

— lack of reliability, stemming from the fact that malfunctioning of one ring element causes the entire network to cease operation;
— the greater the number of subscriber machines connected to

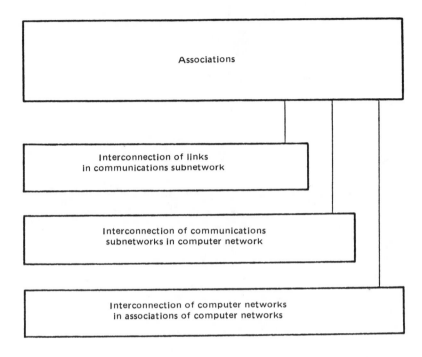

Fig. 3.29. Types of interconnections.

the network, the greater the transmission time around the ring;

— difficulties associated with speech transmission;

— need for synchronization of all the repeaters in the rings.

3.7.
LINK, SUBNET, AND NETWORK INTERCONNECTIONS

The diversity of data-processing tasks calls for a flexible approach to the design and implementation of computer networks. In this respect, various types of interconnections, or ties, become important. These interconnections can be divided into three groups, shown in Fig. 3.29.

Interconnection of links in a communications subnetwork is necessary when a need arises for connecting two links of different types in series. For example (Fig. 3.30), an infrared link is to be

129

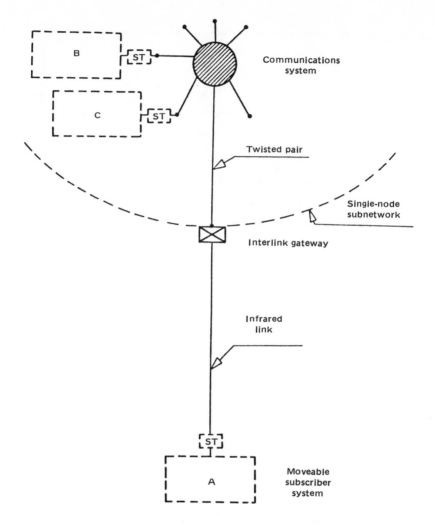

Fig. 3.30. Structure of interaction of two links.

added to a twisted pair in a single-node subnetwork. The infrared link is required because a moveable terminal system is installed in a large area. An associative **interlink gateway** is set up between two different links to connect them.

Figure 3.31 shows a second example of interconnection of links in a communications subnetwork. Usually, subscriber systems at small distances (up to 50 m) can be connected to a baseband system. In

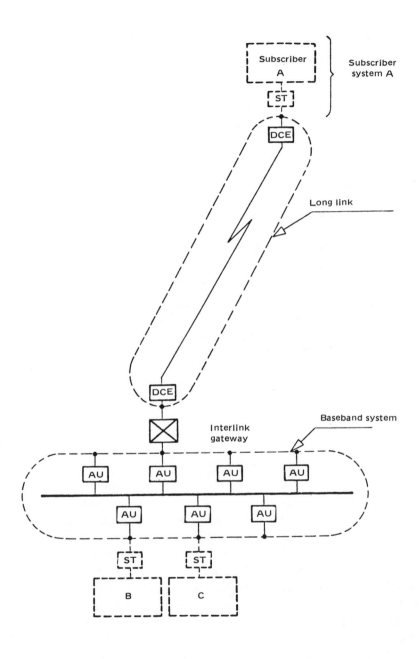

Fig. 3.31. Interconnection of baseband system and long links.

131

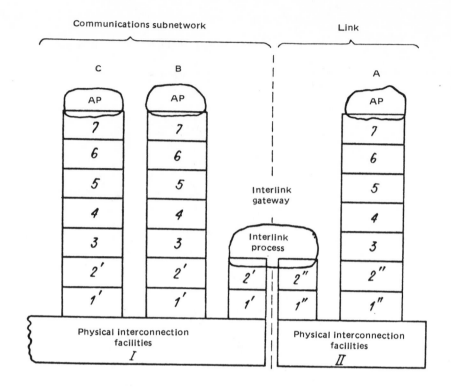

Fig. 3.32. Logical structure of interaction between links and communications subnetwork.

this case, however, it becomes necessary to connect a subscriber system at a greater distance (more tham 50 m). To do this, a long link is run; the link is connected to the system by an interlink gateway.

Figure 3.32 shows the logical structure of interaction between a link and the rest of a communications subnetwork via an interlink gateway. Here, physical connection facilities I are the core of the subnetwork, while physical facilities II are the core of the link connected to it. In Fig. 3.30, physical facilities I form part of a single-node subnetwork, while facilities II form part of an infrared link. Similarly, in Fig. 3.31 physical facilities I and II form part of a baseband link and a long link, respectively.

Only three of the subscriber systems (A, B, and C) connected with the subnetwork in Figs. 3.30 and 3.31 are shown, for purposes of simplification. These systems are depicted in Fig. 3.32. The logical structure of the interlink gateway corresponds to Fig. 2.12c, while each subscriber system corresponds to Fig. 2.2. Here, the interlink process supports conversion of data upon transmission between the communications subnetwork and the connected link. The application processes (AP) of the subscriber system perform the requisite data-processing functions.

It should be noted that the protocols of the application (7), presentation (6), session (5), transport (4), and network (3) layers of subscriber system A connected via the additional link should correspond strictly to the protocols of the same layers of subscriber systems B, C, ... that operate with the communications subnetwork. Only in this case can system A become a component of a common (or combined) computer network.

As for the data-link layer (2'') and physical layer (1'') protocols of subscriber system A connected to the communications subnetwork via the interlink gateway, they differ from protocols 2' and 1' of the same layers of the remaining systems (B, C, ...) which operate with the communications subnetwork. This stems from the fact that the connected link (1'') differs physically from the remaining links (1') of the communications subnetwork. Therefore, the control processes for this link (2'') are also different from the control procedures (2') for the other links of the subnetwork.

Protocols 2'', 1'' and 2', 1' of the two parts of the interlink gateway are correspondingly defined. Here it should be assumed that the left side of the interlink gateway (Fig. 3.32) belongs to the communications subnetwork, while the right side belongs to the connected link. Both parts are joined by the interlink process.

Frequently, several local communications subnetworks of different types may be set up within one organization. To support interaction of subscriber systems connected to these subnetworks, it is necessary to create (Fig. 3.29) an **interconnection of communications subnetworks** in one computer network. **Intersubnet gateways** are employed for these purposes. These gateways may interconnect subnetworks of the same type (e.g., baseband/baseband) or subnetworks of different types (single-node/ring; multiple-node/baseband; ring/baseband, etc.).

Figure 3.33 gives an example of interconnection between the multiple-node subnetwork and a baseband system. An intersubnet gateway is employed to support interaction between the baseband

133

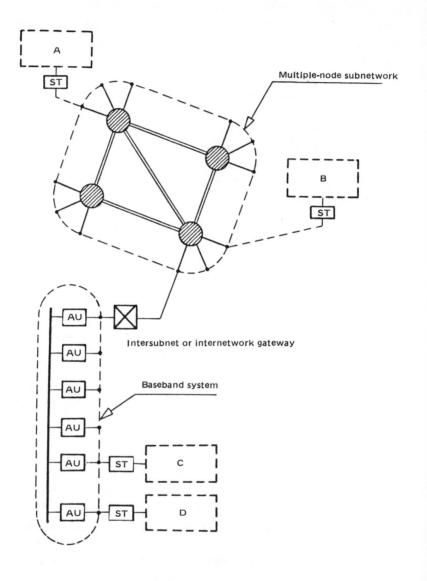

Fig. 3.33. Structure of interconnection between baseband
system and multiple-node subnetwork.

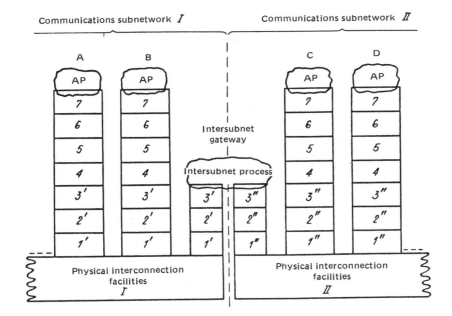

Fig. 3.34. Logical structure of interaction between two communications subnetworks via intersubnet gateway.

system and the multiple-node subnetwork. The gateway performs the necessary operations at the network, data-link, and physical layers.

Figure 3.34 shows the logical structure of two communications subnetworks connected by an intersubnet gateway. This structure corresponds to the arrangement in Fig. 3.33. The left and right sides of Fig. 3.34 represent the multiple-node subnetwork and baseband system, respectively. The form of the gateway is shown by Fig. 2.12b. Since the communication subnetworks to be interconnected are different, the protocols of the network, data-link, and physical layers of the associated subscriber systems are correspondingly different. Therefore, the multiple-node subnetwork and baseband systems are described by two separate sets of layer protocols (3', 2', 1' and 3'', 2'', 1'', respectively). Correspondingly, one half of the gateway corresponds to the protocols of communications network I, while the other half corresponds to those of subnetwork II. The network process of this system performs the necessary conversion on the data that circulate between the subnetworks in question.

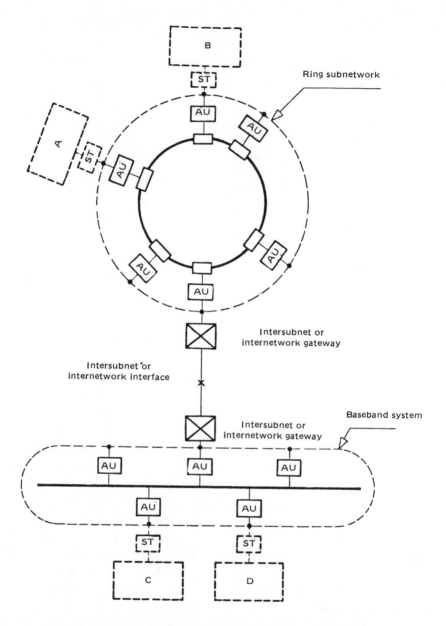

Fig. 3.35. Interconnection of two subnetworks (networks)
by a pair of internetwork (intersubnet) gateways.

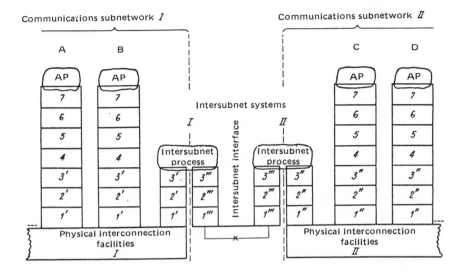

Fig. 3.36. Logical structure of interaction between two
communications subnetworks via two intersubnet
gateways.

An inconvenience of the arrangements in Figs. 3.33 and 3.34 is
that there may be substantial numbers of communications subnetworks implementing different sets of layer 1-3 protocols. To connect
them, therefore, many types of intersubnet gateways, corresponding
to the various combinations of sets of layer protocols, must be manufactured. For instance, it can readily be calculated that interconnection of just eight different communications subnetworks requires 28
types of intersubnet gateways corresponding to the resultant 28 pairs
of combinations. Frequently, moreover, an intersubnet gateway between communications subnetworks is not "adequate" for both of
them. This occurs in subnetworks where short links are employed.
Now, in baseband systems the subscriber links cannot generally be
longer than 50 m. Therefore, an intersubnet gateway cannot connect
two baseband systems whose closest points are more than 100 m dis-
tant from one another.

To avoid this, two intersubnet gateways, rather than one, are installed between a pair of communications subnetworks, and the interface between them is standardized. Then only eight different
types of such gateways are required to interconnect the same eight

types of subnetworks. This allows an intersubnet gateway with a standard **network interface** to be incorporated into the hardware of commercially designed and manufactured communications subnetworks.

Figure 3.35 shows an example of interconnection of communications subnetworks using two intersubnet gateways. Here one of the gateways belongs to a ring subnetwork, the other to a baseband system. A network interface is defined at the point of interconnection of the ring and baseband system, located between the gateways. At this point, the interface defines the rules of a common network, inter-link, and physical layer standard for all the communications subnetworks.

Figure 3.36 shows the logical structure of interconnection of local communications subnetworks, corresponding to the arrangement in Fig. 3.35. Here, in conformity with the arrangement in Fig. 2.12b, the intersubnet gateways implement the networks, data-link, and physical layers. As the figure indicates, the structure under consideration employs three sets of layer 1-3 protocols. The first set (3', 2', 1') pertains to communications subnetwork I (ring subnetwork). The second set (3'', 2'', 1'') corresponds to communications subnetwork II (baseband system). Therefore, a third protocol set (3''', 2''', 1''') is introduced to obtain a standard network interface point. This set defines the interface between the intersubnet gateways.

Only in two cases can communications subnetworks be interconnected in the form shown in Figs. 3.34 and 3.36. The first case occurs when two communications subnetworks used as a basis for creating a single (common) computer network are interconnected. The second case involves interconnection of two computer networks in which the protocols of the higher layers (4-7) of the subscriber systems are completely identical. In this case, interconnection also yields one network, based on two (or more) communications subnetworks.

When two groups of subscriber systems with different sets of higher-layer (4-7) protocols are connected to two communications subnetworks, **interconnection of computer networks** results. Schematically, this interconnection looks the same as shown, e.g., in Figs. 3.33 and 3.35. Here, however, instead of the intersubnet gateway there are one (as in Fig. 3.33) or two (as in Fig. 3.35) internetwork gateways. As for the network interface, it becomes an **internetwork interface.**

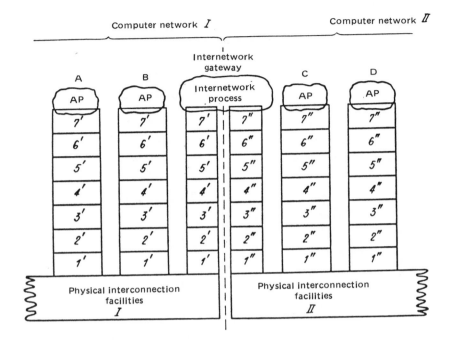

Fig. 3.37. Logical structure of interaction between two computer networks via internetwork gateway.

Figure 3.37 shows the logical structure of interconnection of two computer networks by means of one internetwork gateway. The networks are interconnected by the **internetwork gateway system** whose logical structure is shown in Fig. 2.12a. This system is an association of subscriber systems of both network I and network II. Therefore, it repeats all seven protocol layers of both networks. Computer networks are interconnected in an internetwork gateway system by an internetwork process.

When it is advisable to obtain a standard **internetwork interface** between computer networks to be connected, the procedure is as follows. The components of the internetwork gateway whose structure is shown in Fig. 2.12a are placed in the networks to be joined and are interconnected by additional **internetwork channels.** The result is a **distributed internetwork gateway.**

Figure 3.38 shows the logical structure of a distributed internetwork gateway intended for interconnecting two computer networks.

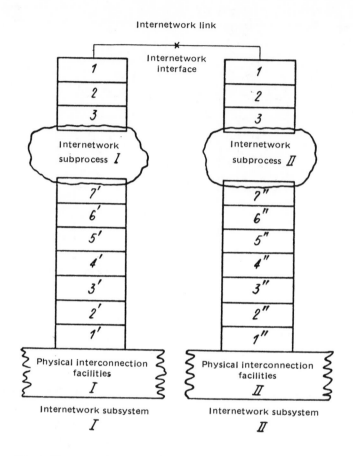

Fig. 3.38. Logical structure of distributed internetwork gateway.

Here the seven-layer parts of the system are located in the two networks. Since the parts in question are distributed in space, the internetwork process (Fig. 212a) is divided into two **internetwork subprocesses.** An additional internetwork channel is required to combine both parts into a single whole.

Thus, the structure shown in Fig. 3.38 requires that an additional degenerate single-channel communications subnetwork, defined by network (3), data-link (2), and physical (1) layers, be placed between each pair of computer networks to be interconnected. Correspondingly, the pairs of three-layer parts (1, 2, 3) shown in Fig.

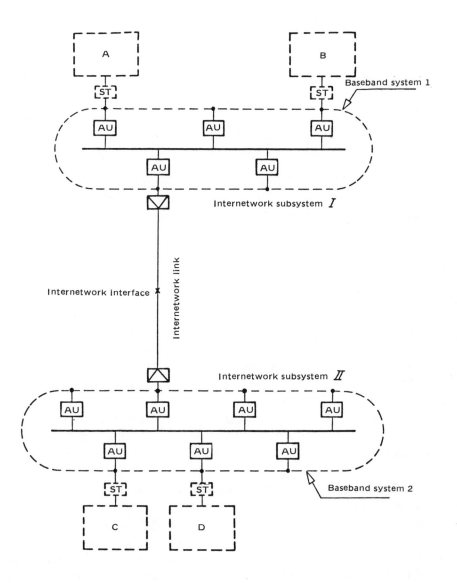

Fig. 3.39. Interconnection between two computer networks via two internetwork subsystems.

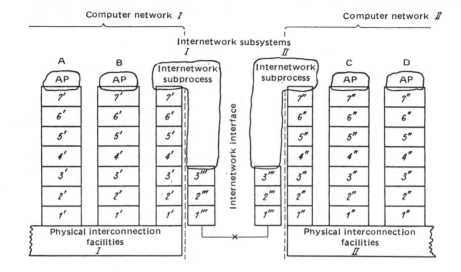

Fig. 3.40. Logical structure of interaction of computer network via two internetwork subsystems.

3.38 are introduced into the distributed internetwork gateway. Since the internetwork interface is standardized, the pairs of parts perform the same group of functions. As a result, the distributed internetwork gateway breaks down into two **internetwork subsystems.**

Figure 3.39 shows the physical structure of interconnection of two computer networks with a standard internetwork interface. Here, the networks are interconnected by means of two internetwork subsystems (I and II). The subsystems are connected by an internetwork channel.

Figure 3.40 shows the logical structure of the two-network interconnection in Fig. 3.39. Here, the networks are connected by two internetwork subsystems (I and II) which have an asymmetrical structure. Via the seven-layer component, each of the subsystems is incorporated into the network, functioning as a subscriber system. The three-layer component supports communication with the other networks.

By using distributed internetwork subsystems, it is possible to create multinetwork interconnections in which data is exchanged between any pair of networks in accordance with a common standard.

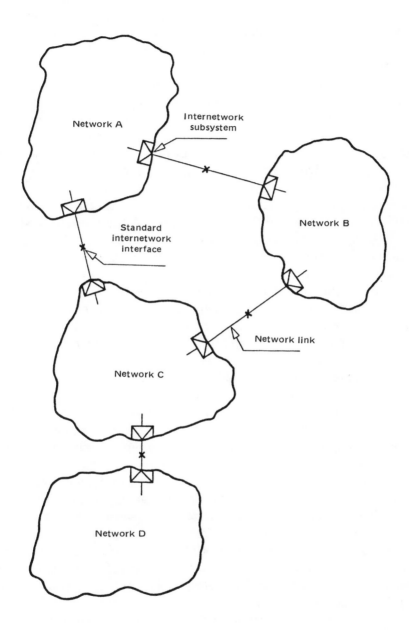

Fig. 3.41. Interconnection of four computer networks.

An example is shown in Fig. 3.41. Here four networks are connected together. The number and location of the internetwork channels are determined by economic considerations and by the internetwork traffic.

The following should be borne in mind in creating interconnections of networks. The protocols of these networks provide for various classes of service. For instance, the transport-layer protocol can have five classes of service. The zero class performs the minimum set of functions. As the class number increases, new capabilities are gradually added: error correction, multiplexing, datagram control, etc. Before a session, therefore, the interacting subscriber systems should select and utilize a class of service common to the pair. For example, say that systems A and B interact. System A has the third and first service classes, while system B uses the first class. In all sessions involving interaction of these systems, therefore, the common first class will be employed.

It should be pointed out that the reliability of interconnection of networks is always lower than the reliability of each of the networks. Therefore, the internetwork gateway should incorporate functions that enhance the reliability of interaction. These functions include, in particular, the following:
 — prevention of "looping" of data blocks;
 — monitoring of routing of these blocks;
 — provision of repeat transmission of blocks.
To obtain the requisite reliability and throughput, two networks are frequently interconnected by several internetwork channels, rather than just one.

Frequently, a given computer network is interconnected to several networks of different types. An example is shown in Fig. 3.42. This figure depicts the UCL network of University College London [59]. This is a small ring-based network. It supports interaction of subscriber systems located in the College. However, the research conducted there requires interaction with subscriber systems in other networks. Three internetwork gateways (1, 2, 3) are installed in the UCL network for this purpose.

The first of these gateways (1) connects UCL to the Catenet network (Fig. 3.42). This is a special network, utilizing the protocols of the Department of Defense of the USA. The second internetwork gateway (2) supports interaction between UCL and two other networks simultaneously: the Sernet network of the Scientific Research

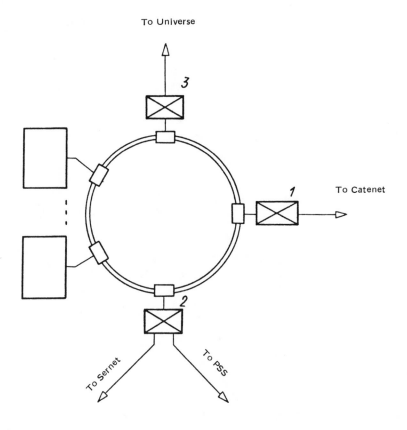

Fig. 3.42. Interconnection of UCL local-area network and other networks.

Council and the PSS data network of British Telecom (the British PTT). Large numbers of subscriber machines are connected to the PSS network in various parts of Great Britain. In addition, PSS is connected to Telenet and Arpanet in the USA.

The third internetwork gateway (3) connects UCL to the Universe network. The Universe project [60,61] is an experimental program that is intended to explore satellite interconnection of local-area networks. Therefore, Universe is a kind of switch that connects these networks via the OTS satellite.

According to this project, which is in the implementation stage,

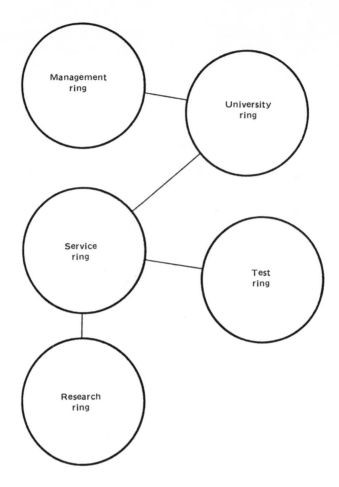

Fig. 3.43. Interconnection of five ring subnetworks.

150 subscriber systems will be incorporated into six ring subnetworks in different parts of Great Britain. Although interconnected by satellite, the PSS packet-switching data network will be employed as a backup.

Satellite communication is effected using dish antennas 3 m in diameter, located at six sites of the Universe network: University College London, the universities at Cambridge and Loughborough, the Marconi Research Center in Chelmsford, the British Telecom research laboratories at Martlesham Heath, and the Rutherford laboratory at Chilton. The satellite links operate in the 11-14 GHz range and permit data exchange with the satellite at a rate of 2 Mbit/sec. This rate offers a good match with the operating rates of the ring subnetwork, which lie in the range 2-10 Mbit/sec.

To enhance reliability, a given organization will frequently employ a combination of communications subnetworks (sometimes identical), rather than just one. These subnetworks are interconnected by intersubnet gateways. In the event that one of the subnetworks malfunctions, this arrangement permits the others to operate normally.

An example of this interconnection of communications subnetworks is shown in Fig. 3.43. The University of Kent in England has set up a network consisting of five interacting ring subnetworks [62]. This system is known as UKCNET. The internetwork gateways that interconnect the rings are based on Zilog Z80 microcomputers.

High reliability of network operation has been achieved in this manner. Only 16 faults occurred in UKCNET over a year of operation. Of these, one lasted 3.5 hr, another 2.5 hr; the rest lasted less than 10 min. The error frequency in data transmission is very low, not exceeding 1 bit in 10^{11}.

CHAPTER 4

INTERNATIONAL STANDARDS

By generalizing the experience gained worldwide in developing computer networks, it has been possible to determine the most efficient and promising architectures for data processing and transmission. In turn, this has made it possible, on the basis of the Basic Reference Model of Open Systems Interconnection, to set up a hierarchy of network protocols and interfaces. Together with the documentation describing the parameters and general characteristics of networks, these protocols and protocol hierarchies form a solid framework of international standards.

4.1.
PROTOCOL GROUPS

Three **protocol groups** can be distinguished in the hierarchy of network protocols (Fig. 4.1). The first of these groups defines the transport-service users and applies to the application, presentation, and session layers. This group is common to networks with information routing and to networks with information selection.

The two other protocol groups describe the executors of the transport service. They apply to the transport, network, data-link, and physical layers. These groups are different for networks with routing and selection. This is true because these networks employ different types of communications subnetworks. Transport protocols support transmission of data blocks through these subnetworks and therefore are closely related to communications subnetworks.

Figure 4.2 indicates the interrelationship of the protocol groups under consideration. It is evident from this figure that the protocol group of transport-service users is set up with a view to the fact that it must interact with both groups of lower-layer protocols. To match these groups with one another, a unified **transport interface** is introduced between the session and the transport layers. As a result, application processes can obtain the requisite forms of service for networks with both routing and selection.

Figure 4.3 gives an example of the arrangement of protocol groups in a subscriber system. The figure shows the connection of a Unified System computer to a baseband system or to a single-node

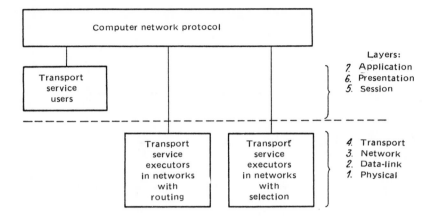

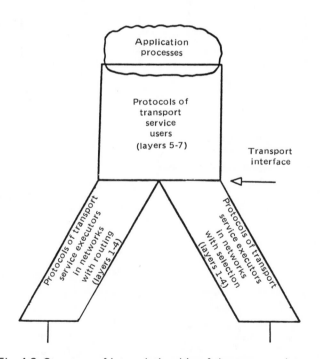

Fig. 4.1. Protocol groups of computer networks.

Fig. 4.2. Structure of interrelationship of three protocol groups.

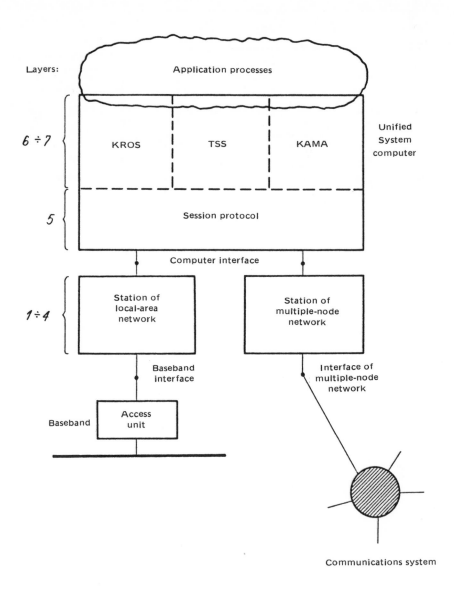

Fig. 4.3. Interaction between Unified System computer and baseband system or multiple-node subnetwork.

(multiple-node) communications subnetwork. The upper protocol group (layers 5-7) is common and resides in the Unified System computer. The session protocol must provide service for the KROS (remote job input system), TSS (time-sharing system), and KAMA (remote data control system) systems programs.

The Unified System computer has two types of stations that implement the protocols of the lower layers (transport, network, data-link, and physical). These stations are connected to the Unified System computer with the same computer interface. As a result, the Unified System computer can operate with any of the stations in the same way. One of the stations is intended for connecting the Unified System computer to a baseband system, the other to a single-node (multiple-node) communications subnetwork.

The principal international organization involved in the development of computer network protocols is Technical Committee 97 of the International Standards Organization [63].

Work aimed at the development of standards for open systems interconnection architecture, protocols, and management procedures is carried on chiefly by Subcommittees 6 and 21, which have the following working groups (WG):

Subcommittee 6: Telecommunications and Information Exchange Between Systems

WG1. Data-link layer.
WG2. Network layer.
WG3. Characteristics of physical interfaces.
WG4. Transport layer.
WG5. Architecture and coordination of layers 1-4.

Subcommittee 21: Retrieval, Transfer, and Management of Information for Open Systems Interconnection

WG1. Open systems interconnection architecture.
WG2. Computer graphics.
WG3. Data bases.
WG4. Management of open systems interconnection.
WG5. Specific application services.
WG6. Session, presentation, and common application services of open systems interconnection.

The ISO is engaged in developing protocols for the groups under consideration. These are shown in Table 4.1 [18,20]. In addition, standards are being developed for various types of physical media, including the following:

TABLE 4.1.

Protocols developed by the International Standards Organization (ISO)

Group	Protocols
I	— virtual terminal — file transfer, access, and management — job transfer and execution — interactive sessions
II	— transport service — network service — link control protocol
III	— transport service — random access to baseband system — token-passing for use of physical interconnection facilities

- broadband coaxial cable;
- narrow-band coaxial cable;
- twisted pair;
- optical light guide;
- microwave link.

The European Computer Manufacturers Association, or ECMA, is extensively engaged in the development of international standards [65-78]. The Association includes a large number of companies, including IBM, DEC, CII-Honeywell-Bull, Burroughs, Siemens, Univac, NCR, etc. The Association is developing protocols for virtually all layers. For instance, it has already prepared and approved (Table 4.2) standards for protocols of groups 1 (layers 5-7) and 3 (layers 1-4). In addition, the first standards for physical interconnection facilities have been approved.

The International Consultative Committee on Telegraphy and Telephony (CCITT) is primarily concerned with the development of

TABLE 4.2.

Standards of European Computer Manufacturers Association (ECMA)

Layer	Standard	Name
7	ECMA-85	Virtual file protocol
6	ECMA-86	Generic data presentation. Description of service and definition of protocol
	ECMA-84	Data presentation protocol
	ECMA-87	Generic virtual terminal. Description of service and protocol
	ECMA-88	Basic class virtual terminal
5	ECMA-75	Session protocol
4	TR/14	Local-area networks. Architecture and protocols of layers 1-4
	ECMA-72	Transport protocol
1-3	TR/13	Organizational principles of network layer
	ECMA-82	Local-area networks. Data-link layer
	ECMA-81	Local-area networks. Physical layer
	ECMA-89	Local-area networks. Techniques of token-passing around ring subnetwork
	ECMA-90	Local-area networks. Techniques of token-passing along trunk
	ECMA-80	Local-area networks. Coaxial-cable physical medium

the second group of protocol standards. For networks with information routing, the Committee has developed the X-series of recommendations. It has also adopted Recommendation S.70, which defines the simplest class of transport protocol. The Committee has also begun to elaborate protocols of the first group.

A number of other organizations and companies have prepared and are preparing proposals for international standards. For example, Xerox has developed the so-called Xerox Network System Protocol (XNS) [38]. A transmission control protocol has been proposed for Arpanet (and this protocol has been adopted by the Department of Defense of the USA).

153

4.2.
APPLICATION PROCESS CONTROL

On the application layer, the ISO is concerned primarily with the following protocols [63] :
- FTAM (file transfer, access, and management);
- JTM (job transfer and manipulation);
- VTSP (virtual terminal service protocol);

The basis of *file transfer, access, and management* is provided by the principle of a virtual file storage. This model provides an abstract (i.e., computer-independent) description of the structure of files and their characteristics. The procedures for organizing interconnection between users and files and for file identification are specified in detail. Various forms are employed in the classification of data sets: file trees, tables, arrays, etc.

Job transfer and manipulation is based on remote data input and output, utilizing external devices and peripherals of different computers. In this case, the user must know the local hardware and job control language of the computer in which the job will be executed. It is assumed that standardization of the job language is as yet unfeasible. What is required, however, is an abstract language for calling up the service specified by the job transfer and handling. Therefore, the model of application-process control under consideration contains several "agencies" of interacting application entities residing in different subscriber systems. Interaction is based on the "one-to-many" principle.

Virtual terminal service is intended for supporting interaction between users at terminals and application processes in different computers. The interaction is in the form of dialogue and short messages. The forms of data presentation vary considerably, depending on the type of terminal employed. Therefore, the virtual-terminal model employs various methods of mapping the abstract structure of the user data onto the specific terminal device. Correspondingly, several classes of virtual terminals are introduced: basic, graphic, etc.

The first application-layer protocol to appear was the **virtual file protocol,** developed and adopted by ECMA [71,79] . The aim of this protocol is to provide execution of standard forms of controlling **files,** i.e., data sets, each having its own name or address. By introducing a common model, called a **virtual file,** files are made independent of their modes of arrangement in computers of any type

154

TABLE 4.3.

Operation control instructions

No.	Instructions	Procedures executed after instruction has been given
1.	Connect	Establishment of connection; agreement on or choice of connection parameters
2.	Disconnect	Normal termination of connection
3.	Break	Abnormal (expedited) termination of connection
4.	Begin data	Beginning of transmission of data blocks
5.	Cease transmission	Abnormal halting of transmission
6.	Resume transmission	Continuation of transmission after it has ceased
7.	Establish control point	Establishment of point in interaction to which a return is always possible if necessary

and of the specific features of the operating systems of these computers.

The service defined by the ECMA-85 standard for virtual files is subdivided into two categories:

— rules of access to virtual files or parts of them;

— virtual file control procedures.

For convenience, two-level file addressing is employed. The first address specifies the name of the virtual storage in which the file is located. The second address describes the file name proper. Then file protection from unauthorized access is characterized. For this purpose, the protocol provides for introduction of a list of persons authorized to obtain information from the file storage. In addition, it is possible to introduce passwords to be designated at the beginning of operation with files.

Two forms of interaction are introduced by the protocol:

— requests that do not require responses;

— requests to which a response must be given.

Requests are supplied by transmitting instructions, a list of which

TABLE 4.4.

Instructions for operating with files

No.	Instructions	Procedures performed after instruction is issued
1.	Generate file	Creation of new file
2.	Find file	Search for needed file
3.	Open file	Beginning of processing of file contents: re-entry, correction
4.	Free up file	Termination of operation with file
5.	Erase file	Elimination of file
6.	Close file	Termination of operation with file
7.	Data	Transmission of data blocks
8.	End of group	Signal for termination of transmission of a group of data blocks

may be found in Tables 4.3 and 4.4.. These instructions enable the user to execute a wide variety of tasks associated with files and with the creation of data bases.

It should be pointed out that there are two ways of eliminating a connection. In the case of instruction *Disconnect*, the partner is warned in advance that operations will terminate; he can prepare for it and can receive all the data blocks that still linger in the network. The instruction *Break* involves an abnormal or emergency elimination of the connection, in which some of the transmitted data blocks may be lost. The instruction *Disconnect* is given by the user, whereas *Break* is generated by the layer program.

Establishment of **synchronization points** is important in executing any data-processing process. If there are no such points, in the event of errors, malfunctions, or unclear situations, it will be necessary to resume the entire procedure (computation, logical analysis, interaction) from the very beginning. When there is a set of synchronization points, interacting application processes can return to any of them when necessary. Then, in the event of an abnormal situation or an error, only the part of the procedure since the last synchronization point need be repeated.

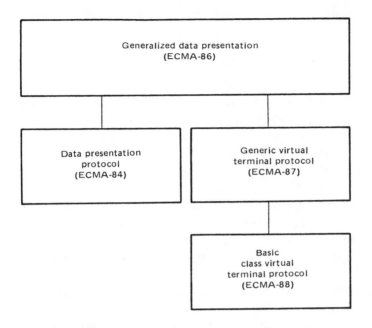

Fig. 4.4. Structure of data-presentation protocols.

FORMS OF DATA PRESENTATION

Presentation of data in a form convenient for the variety of application processes is an important and complicated problem. Its complexity stems not only from the functions performed by the application layer but also by the traditions of various organizations and computer manufacturers, who have used different approaches in developing data-processing facilities and employ different forms of describing information. Therefore, both the ISO and ECMA have devoted a great deal of attention to this issue [63,70,72-74,79].

The main principle employed by the ISO in defining the service furnished by the presentation layer is the *principle of context*. **Context** is the set of forms of data description employed in a particular transmission session. The presentation layer contains several types of contexts and permits the selection of the one required in the next upcoming session.

The main types of presentation-layer service defined by the ISO are the following:

157

– establishment and dissolution of connection on the presentation layer;

– choice of necessary contexts;

– transmission of formatted user data;

– data transmission control.

ECMA has developed and adopted four interrelated standards (Fig. 4.4). The **ECMA-86 standard** defines the basic principles of data presentation and of coordination of the structure of special-purpose (specific) standards. Examples of such standards are ECMA-84, ECMA-87, and ECMA-88.

The ECMA-86 standard provides the following:

– terminology, conceptualization, and model of the description of service associated with data presentation;

– general definition of the interaction of two application-layer entities that employ presentation service, including specific services in the form of virtual terminals and virtual files;

– indication of the mode of interaction of application and presentation entities.

The **data presentation protocol** described in the **ECMA-84 standard** defines the functions required to provide the service furnished to the virtual-file protocol (ECMA-85). At the same time, this standard may prove convenient for a number of other application-layer protocols which will be adopted subsequently.

The ECMA-84 protocol defines the following:

– the service provided by the presentation layer for application-layer entities;

– the procedure by which the service is implemented;

– the manner in which protocol entities are mapped onto the session layer (ECMA-75).

Figure 4.5 shows the form of description of data exchange. The form of description is specified by instructions of application-layer entities directed to presentation-layer entities. These instructions provide information on the types of data sets used and on the desired presentation formats of these types in data exchange. Exchange is effected via the lower part of the open systems interconnection environments, made up of layers 1-5.

The standard under consideration describes two types of data: strings of symbols (both byte and bit) and numbers (both fixed and floating-point). These types are agreed upon by the presentation en-

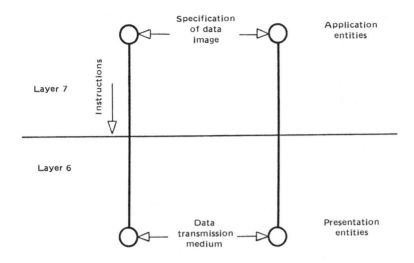

Layer 7

Instructions

Specification
of data
image

Application
entities

Layer 6

Data
transmission
medium

Presentation
entities

Fig. 4.5. Form of description of data exchange.

tities prior to utilizing the symbols at the instruction of the application entities. The agreement is made at the beginning of a session,
but it can be renegotiated in the middle of the session. The session
partner chooses the data type from among those proposed by the session initiator and confirms the agreement.

The aim of the **generic virtual terminal protocol (EMCA-87)** is
to provide a description of a model of such a terminal. The model defines the principal types of service, including establishment of connection, exchange of instructions and data, status notification, disconnection, etc. This service satisfies a wide variety of operating
modes of various types of real terminals: symbol, graphic, line, page,
special-format, etc. The concept of **terminal class**, equipped with a
certain set of requirements and characteristics, is introduced to cover
the entire set of terminals. An example of such a terminal class is
provided by the ECMA-88 standard.

The **ECMA-88 standard** defines the basic class of **virtual terminal** presentation. This class describes actual symbol terminals that
operate in line (teletype) or page (display) mode. The standard primarily describes the forms of data presentation for interaction between a terminal user of a terminal system and the resources of a

host system. Since, however, these interaction procedures are symmetrical, they can be extended to the following pairs: application-process program/application-process program and user/user.

The ECMA-88 standard defines the following:
— components of the virtual-terminal model;
— types of service furnished;
— procedures of executed functions;
— rules for using service.

Introduction of the virtual terminal model makes it possible to execute the functions required by real terminals on the basis of the adopted logical structure. The virtual terminal is described by four basic characteristics:
— image of the data, defined by the logical structure;
— manner of changing the terminal state;
— signalling method;
— control procedure.

The basic class of virtual terminal defines four classes of sets of terminal parameters:

P1: line terminal (teletype);
P2: page terminal (display, printer);
P3: full-screen monochromatic terminal;
P4: color terminal.

In each class the individual parameters are agreed upon (at the beginning of a session) or modified (during a session), e.g., screen size, code, number of colors, background color, number of levels of symbol contrast, etc. Therefore, each terminal class is characterized by a tree of possible parameters. All the necessary parameters are agreed upon in the process of moving along this tree.

4.4.
ORGANIZATION OF SESSIONS

The European Computer Manufacturers Association (ECMA) and the International Consultative Committee on Telegraphy and Telephony (CCITT) were the first to undertake the development of a **session protocol.** The Association adopted the ECMA-75 standard [66], while the Committee adopted Recommendation X.62 for Teletex. Using these standards, the International Standards Organization (ISO) has proposed its own projected standard [80,81].

The task of the session protocol is to support exchange of data

TABLE 4.5.

Service furnished by session protocol

No.	Instruction	Functions executed
1.	Connect	Establishment of session connection and agreement on parameters and type of connection
2.	Disconnect	Normal termination of session, agreed upon during interaction of application processes
3.	Break	Abnormal termination of session
4.	Data	Partitioning (if necessary) and transmission of data blocks
5.	Expedited	Transmission of data blocks out of turn
6.	Deliver	Transmission of indivisible message (disassembly into blocks, transmission, checking, assembly)
7.	Replace	Elimination of received parts of indivisible message because the remaining parts cannot be delivered
8.	Token	Issuing of token to user for use of certain resources
9.	Token-passing	Passing of token for the use of resources by user to another user
10.	Request token	User's request for token
11.	Synchronization	Timing of point in application process
12.	End of dialogue	Completion of transmission of expedited data blocks
13.	Resynchronization	Repeat synchronization after restoration of connection (following an error)

blocks between application-layer entities that are users of sessions. This exchange provides the following:

— reliable and code-independent data transmission;

— organization of data transmission;

— synchronization of the data to be transmitted.

To implement data exchange, the session protocol performs a large number of functions (shown in Table 4.5). Execution of these functions is controlled by transmitting the appropriate instructions. The first ten functions (1-10) provide organization of data transmission. The last three (11-13) are used to synchronize the interaction procedures.

Establishment of a session enables two application processes to conduct a dialogue at the beginning of a session and thus to agree on

161

session parameters that are acceptable to both sides. In the case of *completion of a session*, three cases are possible. The first case is normal completion, agreed to by both partners engaged in the session. Here there is no loss of data blocks circulating between the partners. The second case involves expedited completion of the session, effected by the user. Finally, in the third case, the session layer terminates the session in expedited fashion. The last two cases involve the appearance of unexpected situations, e.g., some malfunction. In both cases, some data blocks may be lost.

Data transmission involves the transit of both ordinary and expedited data. **Expedited data** are needed in performing a number of control procedures. No authorization or agreement is required to transmit such data, and they are sent "out of turn." Identification of the transmitted data blocks is provided (i.e., specification of which blocks belong to which partner). Each partner can refer to preceding steps of the dialogue. There is control of authorization to transmit data; here three modes of operation are possible. In the first mode, both partners can transmit. In the second, or token-passing mode, the user who transmits is the one who is authorized to do so. The partner begins to transmit upon receiving the authorization, or token, from the other party. In the third mode, it is always only one authorized partner who transmits. Data transmission is controlled in such a way as to avoid contention between the various users in requesting the same resources or types of service.

Figure 4.6 shows an example of the dialogue conducted by partners A and B in establishing and terminating a session. Here entity A proposes to entity B that a session be established. Since entity B is not ready to do so, it replies in the negative. Somewhat later, upon being asked again, entity B agrees to establish a connection to conduct a session. Then both partners transmit data to each other. Since entity A has transmitted everything it needs to, it proposes that the session be terminated. However, entity B has not yet transmitted all its data. Therefore it requests that the session not be terminated and transmits the remaining data. Thereupon, after being asked a second time, entity B terminates the session, by sending a disconnect instruction.

An important factor in conducting dialogue is *session synchronization*, i.e., ordering of the interaction of the participants. To provide synchronization, the partners are given the capability of establishing points during the session whose numbers can subsequently be

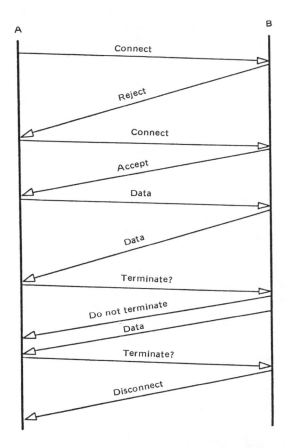

Fig. 4.6. Dialogue in establishing and completing a session.

referred to, and a return to these points can be requested. In addition, upon appearance of an error, these points make it possible to avoid returning to the beginning of the dialogue and starting all over again. As a result, only part of what has been done is lost.

The protocol performs a number of other functions to ensure reliable operation. In particular, it provides transmission of information on the beginning and end of activity, interrupts, and resets. The protocol also provides notification of errors and of the appearance of nonrestorable situations.

The **ECMA-75 standard** defines four classes of service. *Class A* is the simplest subset of functions. It includes functions that establish and identify connections and acknowledge the integrity and error-free nature of data blocks.

Class B supports interactive procedures; it performs the following:

- choice of full-duplex or half-duplex modes during interaction;
- the possibility of transmitting large nondivisible messages sent in the form of a group of data blocks;
- agreement on termination of operation.

This class is intended for interaction with a virtual-termination protocol.

Class C makes extensive use of procedures that support organization of interaction with synchronization. For this it performs the following procedures:

- choice of full-duplex or half-duplex mode;
- transmission of large nondivisible messages;
- possibility of synchronization and resynchronization;
- token control of operation.

Here there is no expedited data flow, since there is no need for one. This class is intended for operating with a virtual-file protocol.

Class D defines a simplified interactive procedure, for which it includes the following:

- control of the *data* token to indicate whose turn it is to transmit;
- execution of normal termination of a session.

This class is intended for application processes that do not require complex operating conditions.

The appropriate class is chosen at the beginning of each session. During their dialogue the application processes agree to conduct the session using class A, B, C, or D. Each of these classes defines a subset of procedures described by the ECMA-75 session protocol.

In preparing its session-protocol standard, the ISO has reduced the number of service classes to three and has changed their names. In ISO nomenclature they are known as mixed, with synchronization and with control of activity. The types of service performed by the classes are given in Table 4.6. Empty cells of the table indicate that there is no corresponding type of service. If the type of service is possible but not obligatory, it is designated by "poss." Types of service which must necessarily be executed in the given class are indicated by "yes."

TABLE 4.6.

Classes of session service

No.	Type of service	Classes		
		Mixed	With synchro-nization	With acti-vity control
1.	Establishment of session	Yes	Yes	Yes
2.	Orderly termination of session	Yes	Yes	Yes
3.	Expedited termination of session by user	Yes	Yes	Yes
4.	Expedited termination of session by session layer	Yes	Yes	Yes
5.	Ordinary data exchange	Yes	Yes	Yes
6.	Expedited data exchange	Poss.		
7.	Indication of data-exchange possibilities prior to commencement of activity			Yes
8.	Authorization control	Poss.	Yes	Yes
9.	Synchronization of session		Yes	Yes
I0.	Activity control			Yes
II.	Error messages	Poss.		Yes
I2.	Transmission of special data	Yes	Yes	Yes

4.5.
DATA TRANSPORT

The **transport protocol** (Fig. 4.7) occupies a central position in the hierarchy of the layer concept of computer networks. This protocol defines the interaction of entities on the transport layer. For the upper layers (application, presentation, and session) the transport protocol furnishes service which is available to them via the access points to the transport service.

To perform its functions, the transport protocol relies on the

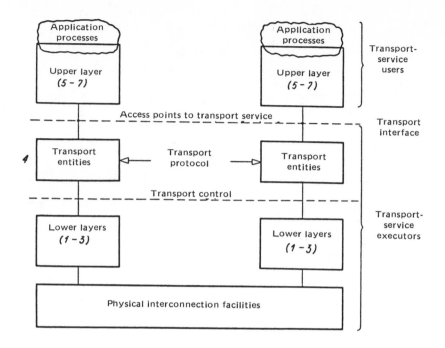

Fig. 4.7. Transport protocol in Basic Reference Model of Open Systems Interconnection.

service furnished to it by the lower layers (network, data-link, and physical). As a result, all the entities defined by the Basic Reference Model of Open Systems Interconnection are divided by transport-service points into users and executors of transport service.

The availability of a **transport service** frees the users from the need to examine all the information switching, routing, and selection functions. Consider an example involving interaction of two subscribers, A and B (Fig. 4.8). Information is transmitted between them via three communications subnetworks: a baseband system, a multiple-node subnetwork, and a ring subnetwork. The interaction is effected via a variety of links, three communications systems, and two network systems. However, the transport-service user is unaware of this.

An international transport protocol satisfies the following four important requirements:

1. It provides *end-to-end transmission*, an essential feature of which is that the characteristics of the transport service are indepen-

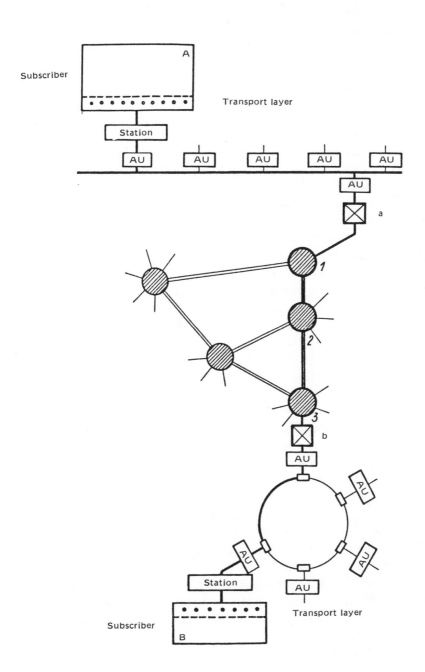

Fig. 4.8. Structure of interaction of two subscribers.

dent of the type of communications subnetwork employed, or of the use of several subnetworks.

2. Transport-service users have the capability of choosing the necessary *quality of service,* including throughput, transit delay, undetected error rate, reliability, etc.

3. The transport service is *transparent,* i.e., it is independent of the formats and codes of the transmitted information.

4. In implementing the transport service, *addressing* is employed that is independent of the addresses used on other layers.

5. Transport entities have unique addresses (i.e., they are not found elsewhere in the network).

The instructions with which the transport-service user operates enables him to perform all necessary functions associated with data transmission through one or more communications subnetworks. The basic functions in question are the following:

— establishment of connections;
— agreement by interacting partners on quality of service;
— transmission of ordinary data;
— transmission of expedited (out-of-turn) data;
— flow control of data blocks;
— abnormal dissolution of connections;
— normal dissolution of connections.

The concept of **quality of service** involves the definition of many characteristics of importance for transmission, namely:

— support of interaction between several transport connections and one network connection (**multiplexing**); or, conversely, between one transport connection and several network connections (**splitting**);
— choice of optimal size of transport data blocks (need for assembly/disassembly of these blocks);
— use of error detection and correction functions;
— agreement on possible error frequency (loss, duplication or distortion of data);
— capability of transport connection to be restored after the appearance of errors, determined by the probability that, for whatever reason, the transport connection will suddenly be broken;
— throughput and establishment time of connections; transport delays.

TABLE 4.7.

Service furnished by transport protocol

Class	Establishment of connection, data transmission, error notification	Multi-plexing	Error elimination and return to original state	Expedited data transmission
0	Yes		Yes	Yes
1	Yes	Yes		
2	Yes	Yes		Yes
3	Yes	Yes	Yes	Yes
4	Yes	Yes	Yes	Yes

The so-called **window mechanism** performs an important function on the transport layer. The essentials of the mechanism are as follows. For reliable transmission, the sender needs to know that his data have transited through the communications subnetwork, have duly reached the recipient, and that no errors have appeared in transmission. For this, the recipient must acknowledge to the sender that he has received the data, and received them error-free. This acknowledgement can be sent after each data block is received. However, this requires that the communications subnetwork be loaded with additional control information. To avoid this, the term **window** has been introduced; this is understood to mean the sender's right to transmit several data blocks (usually up to eight) to the recipient without acknowledgement. Then the recipient acknowledges receipt of the group of data blocks (or notifies that errors have occurred). The "window mechanism" refers to the procedures for executing this function.

In 1981 the ECMA adopted the **ECMA-72 transport protocol** [82]. This protocol contains procedures of four classes: 0, 1, 2, and 3. The ISO has adopted these classes but has also added class 4. The CCITT has also affirmed the distinction of five classes of transport protocol.

Thus, the ISO has proposed a transport protocol with five classes of procedures [20,82]. The types of service performed by these classes are indicated in Table 4.7. The most complex class is the fourth, which furnishes the maximum service, but which naturally requires substantial computer resources. The simplest class, class 0, provides the minimum types of service.

Class 0 was developed jointly by the CCITT (Recommendation S.70) and ECMA (ECMA-72). It is oriented toward the use of very simple subscriber systems, such as Teletex. This class supports transmission control via the communications subnetwork, establishing transport connections and controlling their operation. However, class 0 does not check the transmitted information, does not correct errors, and does not allow multiplexing of connections to be employed.

Class 1 was also developed by the CCITT. It performs all functions implemented by class 0, and is therefore compatible with it. At the same time, class 1 expands the service and provides checking of transmitted information with error corrections.

TABLE 4.8.

Quality of transport-protocol service

No.	Characteristic	Classes of transport protocol				
		0	1	2	3	4
1	Throughput					Yes
2	Transit delay					Poss.
3.	Error rate					Yes
4	Delay in establishing connection		Poss.	Poss.	Poss.	Poss.
5.	Capability for restoration		Yes	Poss.	Yes	Yes

Class 2 performs all functions of class 0 and is compatible with it. In addition, however, class 2 offers the possibility of multiplexing. Errors are partially corrected.

Class 3 is a combination of classes 1 and 2. Therefore it is compatible with all the above classes (0, 1, 2).

Class 4 is the most complex. It supports multiplexing and includes the most complete form of error correction. In addition to the functions of classes 0-3, class 4 checks the received sequence of data blocks and also eliminates distortions that appear in these blocks. Therefore it supports operation, on the network layer, of not only virtual channels (like classes 0-3) but also of datagrams. In contrast to the other classes, class 4 assumes that the communications subnetwork is unreliable. Experimental implementation of class 4 has shown [20] that around 65 kbytes of on-line storage are required for its operation.

Table 4.8 shows the quality of service furnished by the various classes [83]. Here empty cells refer to characteristics not provided by the corresponding class. The abbreviation "poss" indicates that the characteristic in question is possible but not necessary in the

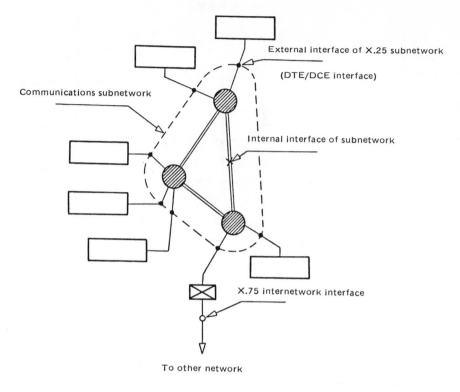

External interface of X.25 subnetwork

(DTE/DCE interface)

Communications subnetwork

Internal interface of subnetwork

X.75 internetwork interface

To other network

Fig. 4:9. Network interface points.

given class. Finally, characteristics that are always provided by functions of a class are indicated by a "yes."

4.6.
PROTOCOLS OF NETWORKS WITH INFORMATION ROUTING

In accordance with their definition (Sec. 2.5), networks with information routing include (Fig. 4.1) a common protocol group of transport-service users (application, presentation, and session) and a special protocol group of transport-service executors (transport, network, data-link, and physical). The first group was considered in Secs. 4.2-4.4. Transport protocols were analyzed in the preceding section. The remaining protocols in the second group, specific to networks with information routing, will be considered below. In the set of these protocols three combinations, intended for different possible pairs of systems, can be distinguished:

TABLE 4.9.

CCITT recommendations used in conjunction with recommendation X.25

Recommen-dation	Purpose
X.1	International classes of user service in public data networks
X.2	International user services and facilities in public data networks
X.3	Packet assembly/disassembly facility in public data networks
X.21	DTE/DCE interface for synchronous transmission in public data networks
X.21bis	Use of DTE intended for interacting with synchronous V-series modems
X.28	DTE/DCE interface for start-stop DTE
X.29	Procedures for exchange of control information and user data between a packet assembly/disassembly facility and a packet-mode DTE
X.75	Call control procedures and data transmission system between packet-switching networks
X.96	Call-process signals in public data networks
X.121	Addressing

Remarks: DTE — Data Terminal Equipment (in computer networks, this refers to subscriber systems and gateways);
DCE — Data Circuit-Terminating Equipment.

— subscriber/communications;
— communications/communications;
— internetwork/internetwork.

The interface between subscriber and communications systems is simultaneously an **external communications-subnetwork interface** (Fig. 4.9). This interface has been standardized by CCITT and is called Recommendation X.25 [84,85]. The **internetwork interface** adopted by the CCITT is called Recommendation X.75. However, there are no international standards for an **internal communications-subnetwork interface.** Here developers employ various standards, frequently a modified version of Recommendation X.75.

In considering Recommendation X.25, it should first be noted that this standard relies on a group of other standards approved by the CCITT. The principal ones are shown in Table 4.9. Because of Recommendation X.25 and the group of standards in the table, all the characteristics of the external communications-subnetwork interface are defined. Therefore, its strict observance ensures the possibility of connecting subscriber systems implemented using any types of modern computers.

Recommendation X.25 defines the interface between **data terminal equipment** (DTE) and data circuit-terminating equipment (DCE) for terminals operating in the packet mode on public data subnetworks. In communications, DTE is understood to mean a communications-subnetwork subscriber, corresponding to a subscriber or gateway system in computer networks. Recommendation X.25 was adopted in 1976 and subsequently refined in 1980 and 1984.

Structurally, Recommendation X.25 defines the network (3), data-link (2), and physical (1) layer protocols at a point of the external communications-subnetwork interface. On the physical layer, **bit sequences** are transmitted over subscriber links. Data blocks transmitted on the data-link layer are called **frames,** while blocks transmitted on the network layer are called **packets.**

On the first layer, described by Recommendations X.21 or X.21bis, the standard defines the mechanical, electrical, functional, and procedural characteristics required to establish (activate), maintain, and dissolve (deactivate) a link (physical connection) between DTE and DCE.

The second (data-link) layer defines the link control procedure for data exchange between DTE and DCE. The third (network) layer of Recommendation X.25 describes packet formats and control procedure for packet transmission between DTE and DCE.

The physical and data-link layers define the characteristics of physical links and the corresponding transmission techniques for frames, which are the containers in which packets are transported. The principal task of the network layer is that of running up to 4095 logical channels in each physical link, thus greatly increasing the economy of utilization of the link. Upon obtaining a logical channel, each pair of users operates with it as if they had only an interconnecting physical link.

Figure 4.11 shows the movement of data blocks on the lower layers of a subscriber system (in accordance with Recommendation

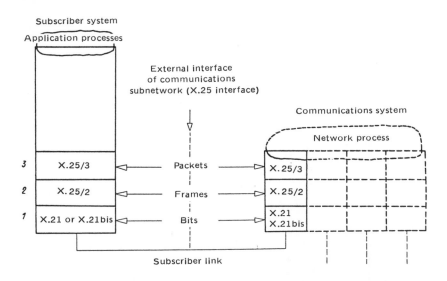

Fig. 4.10. Structure of Recommendation X.25.

X.25). Here the transport control (procedures performed on the transport layer) transmits information in the form of a flow of data blocks, called **fragments.** The fragments must be transmitted through the entire single- or multiple-node communications subnetwork. For this a packet header (Pack. hdr) is added to the fragment on the network layer, converting the fragment to a **packet.** This header determines the movement of the packet through the subnetwork from sender to recipient. On the data-link layer, a frame header (Frame hdr), which is necessary to transmit the packet over the physical link to the system at the other end, is also added. Moreover, a frame trailer (Frame trlr), containing a sequence of bits for checking the frame after transmission, is also added. As a result, the packet becomes a **frame.** On the physical layer, the frame becomes a **bit sequence** transmitted over the physical link.

Similar processes occur in a communications system (Fig. 4.12). The input bit sequence is converted to a frame, then to a packet. After the packet is processed by the network process (which includes determining its onward transmission route), the packet is again converted into a frame and then into a bit sequence. This sequence is transmitted to the next communications system or subscriber system.

175

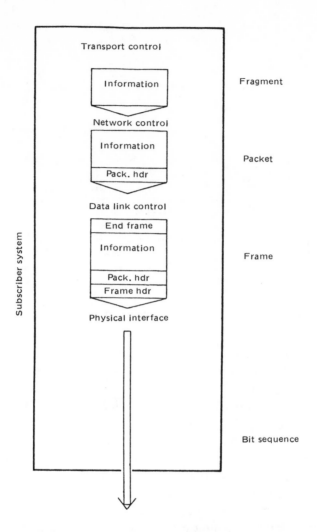

Fig. 4.11. Transmission of data blocks on lower layers of subscriber systems.

Recommendation X.25 makes it possible to set up both temporary and permanent logical channels (which are used to provide virtual-call and permanent virtual circuit service respectively). A temporary channel is provided only for the period of a session, whereas a permanent channel is furnished for any period of time that may be required. Each channel (temporary or permanent) is given a number,

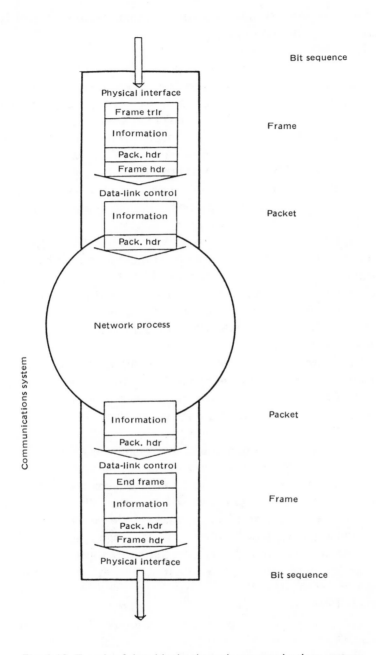

Fig. 4.12. Transit of data blocks through communications system.

by which the channel can be identified among the other channels between the user and the subnet.

The network layer provides procedures associated with transmission of data in packets. These procedures include establishment and disconnection of logical channels, data transmission proper, control of packet flows, interruption of transmission, and restoration of connection after the appearance of error situations.

The second-layer protocol of Recommendation X.25 is a particular case of a broader standard, known as HDLC, which was developed by the ISO [86]. The **HDLC protocol** defines data-link control procedures for synchronous code-independent data transmission. This transmission, in theory, can be conducted in one of three ways: full-duplex, half-duplex, and simplex.

A normal cycle of data transmission between two systems involves the transmission of information-containing frames from sender to recipient. After a frame has arrived at the recipient, the latter must acknowledge that the frame has arrived and that it contains no errors. Until the sender receives this acknowledgement, he stores a copy of the frame and sends it again if errors occurred in it during the preceding transmission.

For purposes of tracking and control, frames are numbered cyclically. Each system in the network performs its own numbering, independently of the other systems. In acknowledging receipt of a frame, the number of the next expected frame is communicated.

HDLC procedures are employed in two modes, unbalanced and balanced. In the first mode one of the systems is the controlling or main system, while in the second mode both systems are of equal status. In the unbalanced mode two or more systems can interact via a multipoint connection. One system is the controlling system, while the others are controlled. The balanced mode employs a point-to-point connection, via which only two systems can operate.

Recommendation X.75 defines the control procedures for an internetwork link. Strictly speaking, it applies to international links connecting communications subnetworks in different countries. However, Recommendation X.75 is widely employed for connecting computer networks of any type (although intended for interconnecting public data networks), regardless of their size and national affiliation. Therefore it is fully applicable to local-area networks as well.

Recommendation X.75 (like Recommendation X.25) defines network, data-link, and physical layers, via which packets, frames,

TABLE 4.10

Main differences between recommendations X.25 and X.75

No.	Characteristic	X.25	X.75
1.	Sphere of application	Between communication and subscriber systems of one network	Between internetwork gateways of different networks
2.	Use of permanent logical channels (virtual circuits)	Yes	No
3.	Use of datagrams	Possible	No
4.	Transmission of network-service messages in establishing a network connection	No	Yes
5.	Actions in establishing improper packet structure	Reset with indication of type of error	Reset with indication of overflow of network
6.	Exiting from contentions for establishing communication	Rejection of communications systems in favor of subscriber systems	Rejection of both internetwork gateways

and bits are transmitted, respectively (as in Fig. 4.10). Both recommendations are very similar, but there are also certain differences. The main differences in the recommendations on the network layer are shown in Table 4.10. They also differ in terms of the structure of the control packets.

In accordance with Recommendation X.75, each internetwork gateway is located at a packet-switching node and is connected to a communications system. The overall structure of the internetwork gateway proposed by Recommendation X.75 is shown in Fig. 4.13. The figure shows only the principal characteristics of this system, associated with packet control and transmission. Several internetwork links, rather than just one, can be run between internetwork gateways. The recommended transmission rate over each of these

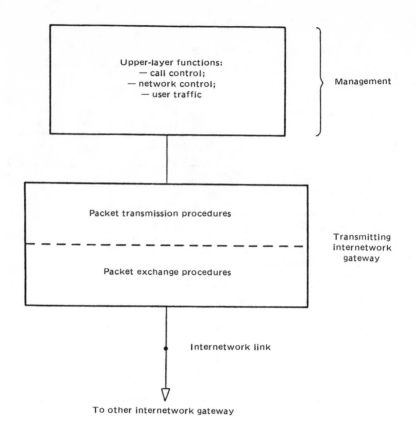

Fig. 4.13. Structure of internetwork gateway.

links is 64 kbit/sec. Other rates can be established, however, by agreement of the network representatives.

Since several links can be run between internetwork gateways, on the data-link layer Recommendation X.75 provides for control of a group of data links, rather than just one (as in the case of X.25). This control provides transmission of a (single) common packet flow over several data links.

The CCITT has also proposed the ISDN standard for **integrated-service digital networks.** The principal feature of this standard is that it supports the integration of digital speech and data transmission in the same communications subnetwork. This standard applies to single- and multiple-node communications subnetworks.

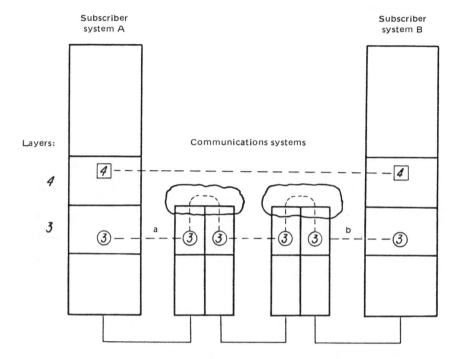

Fig. 4.14. Formation of logical channels in a network
with information routing.

An important characteristic of integrated-service digital networks is the interface at subscriber-system connection points. At
each of these points, the network provides subscriber systems with
channels for data and speech transmission. The combined rate of
these channels is 192 kbit/sec.

In addition, channels operating at 384 kbit/sec are provided for
teleconferencing, image transmission, and for performing the functions of institutional PABX's.

The ISDN protocols are based on the Basic Reference Model of
Open Systems Interconnection of the ISO. The three lowest layers
(network, data-link, and physical) define the interface between the
network and subscriber systems. In addition, the standard stipulated
conditions for furnishing various services for the four upper layers
(application, presentation, session, and transport).

181

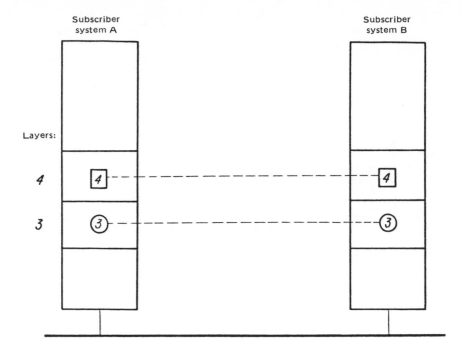

Fig. 4.15. Logical channels in a network with information selection.

4.7.
PROTOCOLS OF NETWORKS WITH INFORMATION SELECTION

In analyzing the protocols of networks with information selection, we should point out that here the significance of the network layer is different from what we find in networks with routing. Let us consider this issue.

In analyzing the protocols of networks with information selection, it should be noted that here the significance of the network layer is different from that found in networks with routing. Let us are two pairs of such systems. Correspondingly, when subscriber systems A and B interact, a sequence is created on the network layer (3), consisting of two logical channels (a and b). The channels are connected by the network processes of the communications systems into a single whole. In contrast, the (single) logical channel on the transport layer (4) is run directly between the entities residing in subscriber systems A and B. Thus, the transport and network layers in a network with routing perform different tasks.

Let us consider the analogous arrangement for a network with selection (Fig. 4.15). Here, as before, the transport-layer (4) entities of subscriber systems A and B are connected by a single logical channel. Here, however, there are no communications systems. Therefore, the network-layer (3) entities of these systems are also connected by a single end-to-end logical channel. It turns out that one of the important groups of network-layer functions duplicates the corresponding transport-layer functions.

This duplication can be eliminated in two ways. The first way involves the fact that the network can employ a simple transport protocol that does not execute functions associated with establishment and elimination of logical channels and does not control transmission over individual logical channels. These functions are entrusted to the network layer. In the second way, the essential feature is that the transport layer establishes, eliminates, and controls logical channels. Then the network layer is not needed to implement intranetwork tasks. It is utilized only to support interaction between two or more communications subnetworks. The second way is more efficient and is employed in current international standards.

Protocols of networks with selection are defined most completely by the standards of the European Computer Manufacturers Association (ECMA). Initially the Association adopted the group of standards shown in Fig. 4.16, comprising a set of protocols of the transport, network, data-link, and physical layers [65,67-69,76].

The **ECMA-TR/14 standard** describes a general approach to organization of the protocols of the four lower layers. The transport layer is described by class 4 of the transport protocols considered in Sec. 4.5. The ECMA architecture supports control of logical channels on the transport layer and therefore does not as yet incorporate a network-layer standard. It has been agreed that such standard will be considered later; it is intended for supporting interaction of several communications subnetworks.

In the ECMA-TR/14 standard, data blocks are addressed on the data-link, network, and transport layers. Access points to the physical interconnection facilities (communications subnetwork) are identified on the data-link layer. Both single-point and multipoint addressing (addressing of frames of one point or a group of points) are em-

183

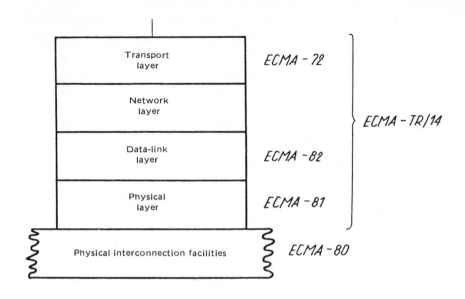

Fig. 4.16. First group of lower-layer protocols adopted by ECMA.

ployed. On the network layer, addressing is related to the internetwork gateways linking the communications subnetwork. Addressing on the transport layer is required because a given subscriber (e.g., a computer) may have several destination points (terminals or application processes). On all layers, addressing generally includes the name of the sender and the name of the recipient. The protocol of any layer may have zero addresses (i.e., it does not perform addressing) if the addresses are adequately defined by one or more lower layers.

Multiplexing is supported on the transport layer, i.e., the simultaneous existence of large numbers of transport connections is organized. Data flow control involves the appropriate organization of transmission of transport blocks by the sending station. Usually, these blocks are transmitted after the receiving station acknowledges that it is ready to receive them. An exception is provided by control blocks, whose transmission does not require agreement of the recipient.

If necessary, on the transport layer it is also possible to transmit data blocks by clocking, without establishing a connection between

184

transport entities. As a result, datagrams can also be transmitted over the communications subnetwork. There is no flow control in datagram transmission. Therefore, the communications subnetwork may overflow; in this case, the datagrams are discarded. Lockouts of the subnetworks are eliminated in this fashion.

The ECMA standards are intended primarily for providing all types of service necessary for the following:

— file transfer;
— transmission of graphics;
— text processing;
— electronic mail;
— access to data bases.

In the group of standards under consideration (Fig. 4.16), the communications network (physical interconnection facilities) is a baseband system. Therefore, the **ECMA-80 standard** establishes the parameters and characteristics of the physical baseband medium [67]. In conformity with the standard, baseband systems employ coaxial cable with **terminators** - resistors that prevent signal reflection from the end of the cable - installed at both ends. The ECMA-80 standard establishes requirements for the following:

— electrical and physical characteristics of cables and terminators;
— configuration rules for the physical medium;
— laying of cables;
— external conditions.

According to the standards, the coaxial cable should be of constant impedance. The length of a cable segment should not exceed 500 m. Permissible attenuation in a segment is not more than 8.5 dB at 10 MHz. The signal propagation velocity through the cable cannot be less than 0.77 of the speed of light in a vacuum.

An important problem which must be dealt with in setting up a physical medium is that of minimizing various kinds of signal reflection, which introduce undesirable distortion. To solve this problem, first of all, it is necessary to employ terminators to provide a cable impedance that is equal in magnitude to the wave impedance. This reduces signal reflection from the end of the cable. Moreover, the cable should be uniform enough over its length so that the amplitude of the reflected signal resulting from any change in impedance at any point does not exceed 7% of the amplitude of the signal itself.

TABLE 4.11.

Types of service which must be performed by data-link layer

No.	Type of service	Description
	A. Instructions transmitted to data-link layer	
1.	Indication of signal distortion	Indication of errors in signal transmitted via physical interconnection facilities, and notification of data-link layer to this effect
2.	Indication of data input	Sending of signal received from physical interconnection facilities to data-link layer
3.	Indication of distortion in transmission	Sending of signal to data-link layer, indicating data transmission or errors that have appeared in physical interconnection facilities
4.	Request for data output	Sending of request to data-link layer for transmission of next successive bit to physical interconnection facilities
	B. Instructions received from data-link layer	
5.	Indication of completion of output	Message by data-link layer, in response to request for data output (from physical layer) to the effect that all data have been transmitted
6.	Response regarding data output	Message by data-link layer, in response to request for data output, to the effect that not all data have yet been transmitted
7.	Request for output	Message from data-link layer to the effect that it wishes to feed data to physical layer

The **ECMA-81 standard** defines the **physical layer protocol** of a system that interacts with a baseband system [68]. In contrast to the case of broadband transmission, the baseband system with which the system interacts is intended for simultaneous transmission of one signal only.

The **physical protocol** defines primarily the electrical characteristics which any system must have at a point of interaction with the baseband system. In addition, it describes the service (Table 4.11) which must be performed on the physical layer. The first three types of this service pertain to generation of indicator signals for various events that occur in the baseband system. For instance, the instruction *indication of distortion in transmission* is related primarily to observation of **frame collision** in the baseband system. Collisions occur when two or more systems attempt to transmit frames simultaneously. This is not allowed, since it leads to distortion of information. Therefore, the physical layer constantly monitors the baseband and notifies the data-link layer, which conducts data transmission, about what has happened. The indication is cancelled after the data-link layer ceases to transmit data.

In addition to the above functions, a check is performed on the frame transmission system. This is necessary to eliminate errors associated with possible appearance of an infinite bit sequence. The physical layer interrupts transmission if it lasts for more than 150 msec. The interruption can be reset manually by the operator, or automatically after the bit stream coming from the data-link layer has disappeared.

The following four types of service (Table 4.11) are associated with transmission of data blocks. Upon sending a bit to the baseband system, the physical layer proposes (4) to the data-link layer that it send the next bit in sequence to it for transmission to the physical interconnection facilities. If there is nothing to transmit, the data-link layer provides notification of this by a *completion of output indication.* If not all information has been transmitted, it sends the baseband system a *data output response.* The last type of service (7) is a request of the data-link layer for data output via the physical layer to the baseband system.

The physical layer must always execute the above types of service. In addition, the ECMA-81 standard provides for the so-called optional types of service. In any network these services may be executed to improve its characteristics, but they may also be absent.

Table 4.12 lists the optional types of service supported by the physical layer. They are related to the need for terminating operation (deactivating) of the data-link layer and disconnecting it from the baseband system. This occurs in the following cases:
— malfunction of some system component, which may lead to erroneous transmission of a bit stream to the baseband system;
— detection of errors in the data stream.

After the physical layer has been deactivated and disconnected from the baseband system, the data-link layer must naturally perform the reverse operations. The types of service under consideration are unnecessary in cases in which the baseband system is protected

TABLE 4.12.

Optional types of service

No.	Type of service	Requirement of data-link layer
1.	Activation of physical layer	Set physical layer in operating state
2.	Deactivation of physical layer	Eliminate the requirement that the physical layer be operational
3.	Establishment of monitoring mode	Disconnect transmitter from physical interconnection facility
4.	Cancellation of monitoring mode	Cancellation of requirement that transmitter be disconnected

from noise at higher layers of the systems. Therefore, the types of service shown in Table 4.12 are optional.

An important function of the physical layer involves coding of data. It is necessary bécause network subscribers operate with binary codes, whereas the baseband system employs a **"ternary code"** (Fig. 4.17). This code allows three symbols to be transmitted: 0, 1, and "no signal." As a result, it is possible not only to transmit data but also to detect breaks in the baseband system, and to send **clocking signals** in addition to information signals. Clocking signals are required to synchronize the operation of interacting transmitters and receivers in the network. As a result, the physical layer converts two distinct and physically separate binary data and synchronization signals into one self-synchronization serial bit stream.

Figure 4.17 shows the logic of conversion of binary signals to a type of code called **Manchester code.** There, the time is divided into intervals called **bit intervals.** The shape of the signal on a bit interval is called a **bit symbol.** In transmitting a 0 or 1, the potential at the center of a bit interval must change from low to high level or vice versa (from high to low). The instant that the potential changes is the **clocking signal** for the network systems.

Two forms of Manchester code can be distinguished, depending on the procedure used to encode 0's and 1's. In **phase Manchester en-**

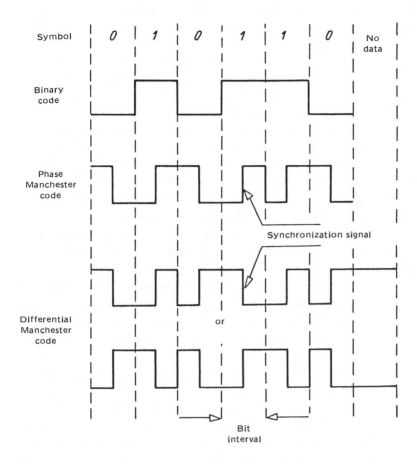

Fig. 4.17. Manchester encoding.

coding a 0 is encoded (Fig. 4.17) by a signal change from high to low at the center of the bit interval. The opposite change, from low to high, indicates a 1. In the example shown in Fig. 4.17, the number 010110 is thus encoded.

A different procedure is employed in the case of **differential Manchester encoding.** Here a 0 is represented by a bit symbol that repeats the shape of the preceding bit symbol. If the shape of the bit symbol in question is the inverse of the preceding one, it represents a 1.

The EMCA-81 standard employs phase Manchester encoding.

Here the data and synchronization signal are mixed in the sending station to a single self-synchronized serial stream to be transmitted over the baseband system. The synchronization rate must be 10 Mbit/sec (±0.01%). To extract the synchronization signal from the serial stream at the receiving end, the receiving system sets up an automatic frequency-control component. The data signals that remain after this are then processed in this system.

The **data-link layer protocol** in a computer network with information selection differs substantially from the corresponding protocol in a network with routing. This stems from the fact that selection is performed in addition to the ordinary link control functions.

The international data-link layer protocol for networks with selection is described by the **ECMA-82 standard** [69]. This standard defines the characteristics and procedures of **multiple access** (to a baseband system) **with carrier sensing and collision detection.** This class of control procedures provides the following:

— access of a set of systems to the baseband system without explicit preliminary coordination of their operation;
— reduction of the possible number of contentions for use of the baseband system (monitoring of contentions and delay of frame transmission);
— elimination of contentions that appear (detection of frame collisions and repeat transmission of frames).

The data-link layer protocol consists of four parts. The first two parts describe the types of service offered to the network layer and the requests for service made to the physical layer. The third part deals with description of the functions which the layer performs. Finally, the fourth part defines the structure and codes of data blocks (frames) transmitted on the data-link layer.

To provide service to the network layer, the data-link layer interacts with it using two instructions related to data transmission: *LDATA request and LDATA indication.* Transmission can be point-to-point or multipoint. *LDATA request* is the request of the network layer to the data-link layer for reception of a data block to be subsequently fed to the baseband system. The instruction *LDATA indication* is transmitted in the opposite direction, from the data-link to the network layer; it notifies that the data block has been received by the data-link layer.

On the data-link layer, systems generate and transmit frames to

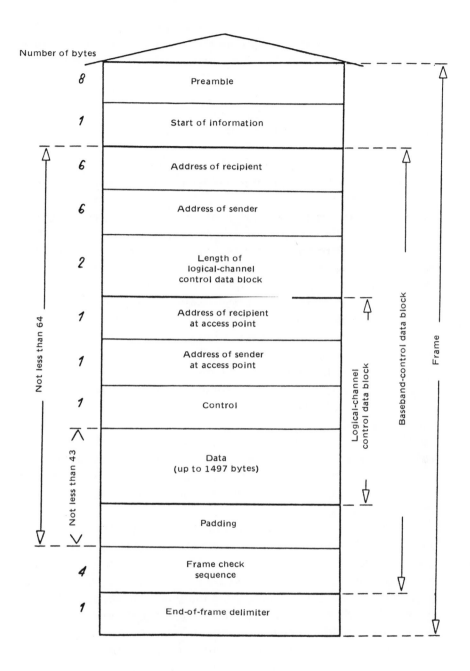

Fig. 4.18. Frame structure

one another using the physical layer and baseband system. Since messages are not created on the data-link layer, there are no control frames here (as, e.g., in Recommendation X.25). Only information frames, whose structure is shown in Fig. 4.18, are transmitted. As is evident from the figure, the frame contains a *baseband control data block*. The latter, in turn, contains a *logical channel control data block*. This is due to the fact that, on the data-link layer, frames are created in stages (by parts).

There is a *Preamble* at the beginning of a frame. The preamble is required so that, when the frame appears, the electrical circuitry of the subscriber system can assume a stable operating state. The same word, 10101010, is transmitted eight times (the sequence 10101011 is transmitted the eighth time). *Start of information* is a field containing a signal that what follows is a baseband-control data block. This signal is transmitted by a one-byte word: 10101011.

The *Address of recipient* field has 6 bytes. This field gives the address of the system to which the frame is being sent. The first bit is reserved for a special message; if there is a 0 in the first bit, what follows is the individual address of the recipient system. If, however, there is a 1 in this bit, the address need not be subsequently analyzed, since the frame. is intended for all subscriber systems of the networks. This is the so-called **common address.** The *Address of sender* field is of the same size as the *Address of recipient* field, namely 6 bytes.

The logical channel control data block (Fig. 4.18) may be of variable length. Therefore, this length must be known in order to determine the point at which it terminates. The length is specified in the *Length of logical channel control data block* field; the size of this field is two bytes.

The logical channel control data block consists of four fields. In a given recipient system, this block may be addressed to different application processes. In addition, it can be sent by different application processes of the sending system. Therefore, the initial part of this block contains the addresses of the sender and recipient at the access point (from the network-layer side) to the data-link layer. Each of these fields is one byte in size.

The *Control* field provides notification that what follows is the data transmitted by the frame. This field, one byte in size, contains the following word: 11000011. It is followed by the *Data* field. This field can contain up to 1497 bytes of information transmitted be-

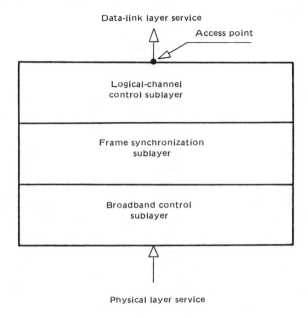

Data-link layer service

Access point

Logical-channel
control sublayer

Frame synchronization
sublayer

Broadband control
sublayer

Physical layer service

Fig. 4.19. Sublayers of data-link layer in ECMA standards.

tween application processes. The number of bytes must always be an integer. Hence a **bit burst** that does not contain an integer number of bytes can be identified as an impermissible bit sequence. Such a burst appears as a result of errors in transmission or collision of frames in the baseband system.

The *Padding* field is used for the following purposes. The requirement is introduced that the frame length should be greater than a certain value. As a result, if the resultant sequence is too small, it is assumed to be erroneous. This requires, however, that when the *Data* field is very small, some additional bit sequence must be added. The standard does not define this sequence. In practice, a group of 0's or 1's is used. These symbols are entered into the *Padding* field.

The *Frame check sequence* field is four bytes in length. It performs a cyclical check on the contents of the frame. This field contains a number that is a function of the contents of all the fields of the baseband control data block. The large size of the field means that the reliability of checking is high.

Frames terminate in a field called the *End-of-frame delimiter.*

The word contained therein informs that frame transmission has been completed.

For convenience in specifying the group of functions executed by the data-link layer, this layer is divided into three sublayers (Fig. 4.19). The *logical channel control sublayer* performs three inter-related functions:

— connection of network-layer access point to data-link service;
— reception of data blocks from network layer and transmission of blocks to network layer;
— conversion of data blocks to a format convenient for the frame-synchronization sublayer, and creation of the logical channel control data block (Fig. 4.18).

The *frame-synchronization sublayer* implements functions that are performed before transmission and after reception of frames. Before transmission, the sublayer generates the baseband control data block (Fig. 4.18). It is taken into account in this process that the length of the block cannot be less than 64 bytes (Fig. 4.18). If, however, the *Data* field contains a small amount of data, bits are added to the *Padding* field so that there are not less than 43 bytes in both fields.

After reception of a frame, the frame-synchronization sublayer first checks to see whether the baseband-control data block is intact, i.e., whether it satisfies the minimum-length requirements. Then it inspects the address field to determine whether the frame is addressed to the given system. If so, the frame is sent to the logical-channel control sublayer; if not, it is eliminated.

The *baseband control sublayer* (Fig. 4.19) is the lowest one in the sublayer hierarchy. Its main task is the final generation of frames. In addition, it transmits frames. Moreover, by means of the physical layer and access unit, this sublayer detects collisions of frames in the baseband system and restores transmission after a collision has been detected.

The procedures for eliminating the effects of collisions are governed by three factors:

— upper limit of monopoly of baseband system (any station can transmit a frame during a limited time interval);
— maximum length of bit burst generated in collisions;
— planned time after which another attempt to transmit the frame can be made.

194

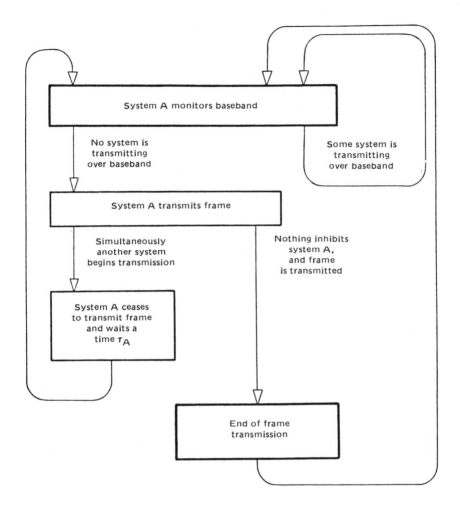

Fig. 4.20. Frame transmission procedure.

Frames are transmitted by the sending system as shown in Fig. 4.20. Via the physical layer, the data-link layer continuously monitors the baseband. As soon as the need arises, frame transmission is initiated after the baseband becomes free. If, at the instant a frame begins to be transmitted, some other system also begins transmission, frame collision occurs. All systems whose frames have collided cease transmission and then resume it after different time intervals.

Corresponding to this frame transmission procedure, two cases are possible. The first case arises when frame transmission (and reception) does not involve any contentions. In the second case, frame collisions occur and are eliminated in the baseband. The sequence of execution of data-link layer functions is different in the two cases. Let us consider these functions.

Transmission by the sending system in the absence of contention occurs as follows:

1. The logical channel control sublayer (Fig. 4.19) generates a logical channel control data block (Fig. 4.18) and notifies the frame-synchronization sublayer that this block must be transmitted; it then transmits the block to it.

2. The physical layer passes the frame on to the baseband-control sublayer. Then the same functions as in the case of transmission are performed, but in reverse order.

3. This block is passed on to the baseband-control sublayer. This sublayer adds the *Preamble* and *Start of information* fields to the blocks, thus generating a frame that is virtually complete. It passes it on to the physical layer.

4. The physical layer adds the *End-of-frame delimiter*, performs phase Manchester encoding of the received bit sequence, and transmits the information to the baseband system bit by bit.

In the absence of contention, the receiving system receives the frame and performs functions in the following order:

1. The physical layer synchronizes the receiving system by means of the eight-byte frame preamble, and decodes the bits (i.e., replaces the ternary phase Manchester code by a binary one).

2. The physical layer passes the frame on to the baseband-control sublayer. Then the same functions as in the case of transmission are performed, but in reverse order.

Contention in frame transmission and reception is by no means an infrequent occurrence. When contention arises, it is first necessary to detect it and to amplify the effect that results from frame collision. For this, if one of the systems detects frame collision during transmission, frame transmission is not immediately terminated. The collision must last long enough to be noticed by all the stations connected to the baseband system. For this, the system that detected the collision generates a *Jam* signal, which must be from 32 to 48 bits long. The contents (or code) of this signal may be arbitrary, i.e., the **jam signal** is any sequence of bits of fixed or variable (within specified limits) length.

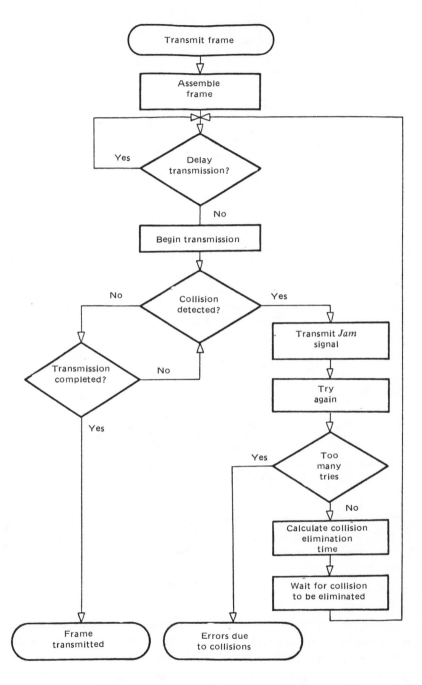

Fig. 4.21. Process of frame transmission.

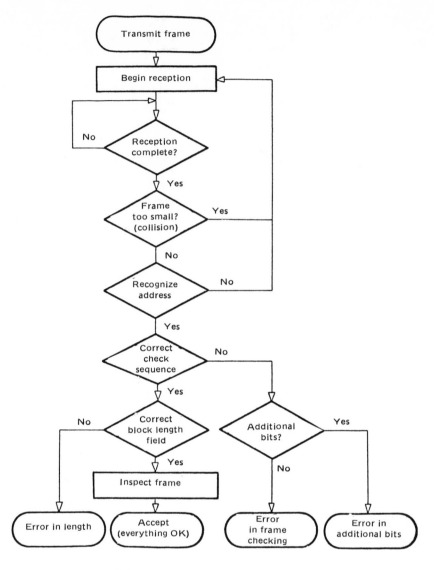

Fig. 4.22. Process of frame reception.

Two important rules must be observed in eliminating collisions and organizing repeat transmissions. The first rule is that the data-link layer must transmit the frames in the sequence in which it obtained the data blocks from the upper layers. Until a given frame in sequence has been delivered to the receiving system, therefore, the

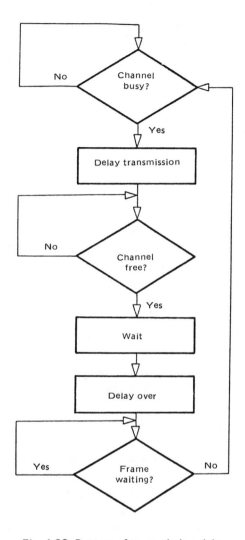

Fig. 4.23. Process of transmission delay.

next frame is not transmitted but waits its turn. Thus the receiving system obtains the frames (and hence the packets) in the sequence in which they were sent. In this respect the transmission process differs from the datagram arrangement, in which the packets may be delivered in arbitrary sequence, which then must be ordered. Thus, when the ECMA-82 standard is employed, there is no need to order the sequence of data blocks.

199

The second important rule defines the sequence of organization of repeat frame transmissions after a collision. Each repeat transmission (there may be as many as 15 of them) is performed some time after the *Jam* signal is sent. This time, known as the delay, is defined as an integer multiple of the **time segment,** i.e., the minimum time unit of repeat transmission. This unit should be greater than the overall delay time of the physical layer and the existence time of the *Jam* signal. The number of time units by which a given system delays repeat transmission is specified by the system arbitrarily (it ranges from 2 to 10).

The ECMA-82 standard introduces a **procedural model** that defines five parallel processes to be executed on the data-link layer. The model represents the different processes and their interaction procedures. They form two cycles. The first cycle deals with frame and bit transmission, the second with frame and bit reception. Frame transmission is initiated by the logical-channel control sublayer. The baseband-control sublayer provides synchronization of operation.

The dynamic processes specified by the procedural model are shown in Figs. 4.21-4.23. The arrangement in Fig. 4.21 describes the procedures associated with frame transmission. Similarly, Fig. 4.22 depicts the frame-reception procedures. Finally, Fig. 4.23 describes the waiting procedures for repeat frame transmission. In the figures, the procedures represent the steps which must be performed in executing the corresponding process.

It should be pointed out that many intersection procedures with the layer immediately above the data-link layer refer to the network layer. As noted, however, the network layer is not defined by the ECMA standards. In this case, therefore, the data-link layer interacts directly with the transport layer. It passes on to the transport layer the service furnished by the data-link and physical layers.

A description of the transport protocol defined by the ECMA-72 standard was given in Sec. 4.5.

Subsequently to the first group of standards shown in Fig. 4.16, ECMA began to issue standards for new types of local-area networks with information selection. These standards expand the capabilities of local data transmission and processing. To ensure architectural uniformity with the IEEE-802 Committee, the new ECMA standards divide the data-link layer into two sublayers, rather than three, as

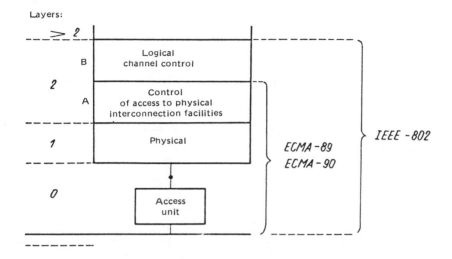

Fig. 4.24. Protocol hierarchy.

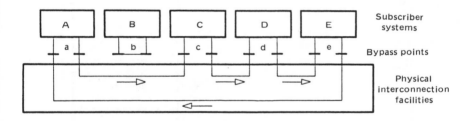

Fig. 4.25. Logical structure of ring.

was formerly the case (Fig. 4.19). These sublayers are shown in Fig. 4.24. Here the logical-channel control sublayer (2B) describes interaction of subscriber systems via physical interconnection facilities. The functions of the sublayer of control of access to physical interconnection facilities (2A) are evident from its name.

The **ECMA-89 standard** (Fig. 4.24) describes the protocols of the lower data-link sublayer (2A) and physical layer, as well as the characteristics of the physical interconnection facilities used to set

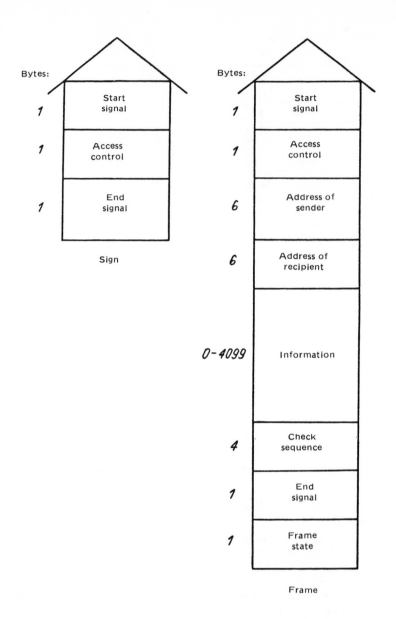

Fig. 4.26. Structure of sign and frame data block.

up a ring subnetwork. The structure of this ring is shown in Fig. 3.23.

Here the physical interconnection facilities form a multipoint ring link (Fig. 4.25), to which the subscriber systems (A-E) are connected. Bypass points are established where the systems are connected to the ring, so that any inactive system (e.g. system B) can be removed from the ring.

Information is transmitted bit by bit around the ring from one subscriber system to another. The sending system feeds frames into the ring and removes them after they have traversed all the systems. The receiving system takes copies of frames intended for it as they pass by this system.

The ECMA-89 standard for ring subnetworks employs access with **token-passing.** The essential feature of this method is that the user-system stations pass the right to use the ring, called the **token**, to one another. A station that receives the token transmits data and then passes the token to another station. If the station with the token has nothing to transmit, it immediately passes the token on to another one.

Two types of data blocks, *Sign* and *Frame,* are transmitted in the ring subnetwork under consideration. *Sign* is used for token-passing. *Sign* circulates continuously around the ring, successively traversing the stations of all the user systems. The structure of *Sign* is shown in Fig. 4.26. It contains three one-byte fields. The first and third fields contain the begin-sign and end-sign signals, respectively. The second field is the main one, since it contains the information that implements the token-passing method.

Frame is used to transmit information from one subscriber system to another. The first two fields of *Frame* are the same as the corresponding fields of *Sign*. These are followed by the *addresses of the recipient and sender*. The addresses are followed by the basic field, in which the system can enter up to 4099 bytes of information (a packet) to be transmitted. In turn, the information is followed by a four-byte field that contains the *frame check sequence.*

At the end of *Frame* there is an ending signal (as in *Sign*) and a field that indicates the *frame state.* The eight-bit *frame state* field contains messages dealing with three states:

1. No such station in the network, or station is not active.

2. Station unable to accept a copy of the frame (e.g., because its buffers have overflowed).

3. Station has accepted a copy of the frame.

The ECMA-89 standard describes the following:

— the format of *Frame,* including addressing and the manner of checking its contents;
— *Frame* timers and counters;
— access procedures to ring subnetwork;
— types of service furnished by the logical-channel control sublayer;
— service performed on the physical layer;
— encoding/decoding procedure for symbols transmitted via physical interconnection facilities;
— synchronization of transmitted symbols;
— interface with physical interconnection facilities.

The *logical-channel control sublayer* describes transmission functions that are independent of the type of communications subnetwork employed (baseband, broadband, ring subnetwork) and of the access method to this subnetwork. In all types of networks with information selection, therefore, this sublayer furnishes the network layer with the same types of service. The *sublayer of control of access to physical interconnection facilities* depends on the type of these facilities and defines the functions that support access to them.

The *physical layer* performs interaction with the physical interconnection facilities, generates the signals transmitted via these facilities, and converts the signals received from them. The physical medium in a ring subnetwork may be provided by twisted pair, coaxial cable, or optical fiber (light guide). Pulses, whose shape is determined by the differential Manchester code (Fig. 4.17), are transmitted through the physical medium. Thus both synchronization and data signals can be transmitted through the same medium.

Two types of delays, artificial and natural, are employed in ring subnetworks. Artificial delays are created (Fig. 3.23) at the points of connection of the access units to the physical medium (in the repeaters). Natural delays are determined by the signal-propagation delay over the physical medium. Each repeater in the ring must have a switch that enables a malfunctioning subscriber system to be disconnected from the ring.

The structure of the *access control* field, which appears in both *Sign* and *Frame* (Fig. 4.26), is shown in Fig. 4.27. This eight-bit field consists of three parts: priority bits (1-3), a token bit (4), and reserve

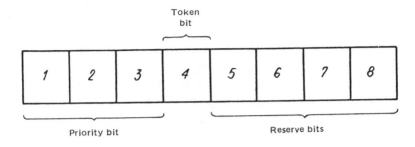

Fig. 4.27. Structure of access-control field.

bits (5-8). The priority bits define the priority of a station authorized to employ the ring subnetwork. The token bit gives authorization for transmission. The reserve bits provide information on the priority of a station that is requesting authorization to transmit.

Token-passing in a ring subnetwork is performed as follows. A *Sign* in which the token bit is 0 circulates around the ring. If the station receiving the *Sign* has nothing to transmit, it forwards this *Sign* around the ring. If, however, the station does have data ready for transmission, it changes the token bit from 0 to 1 and adds fields that convert *Sign* to *Frame* (Fig. 4.26). The *Frame* thus created traverses the entire ring. After this *Frame* arrives, the station generates the new *Sign* in which the token bit is 0, and it forwards it along the ring.

The priority policy for a ring subnetwork is as follows. The *Sign* received by station A has bits that indicate the priority of the stations authorized to transmit (Fig. 4.27). If the priority of station A that wishes to transmit a *Frame* is higher than or equal to the priority in question, it begins to transmit. If, however, the priority of station A is lower, the *Sign* is sent onward around the ring. Before this happens, however, station A indicates its priority in the reserve-bit field. In the course of moving around the ring, it may turn out that station E, whose priority is also lower than the specified one but higher than that of A, is awaiting authorization to transmit. Then station E erases the priority of A in the reserve bits and enters its own priority. The station E forwards the *Sign* around the ring.

This procedure continues until one of two events occurs. The first event is that *Sign* arrives at a station whose priority is high enough that it can accept the token and begin to transmit a *Frame*. If this does not occur, the second event takes place; a station receives a *Sign* in which the priority does not enable it to transmit, but the reserve-bit field contains its own request for transmission with its own priority. In this case the station begins to utilize the ring. When transmission is completed, the station generates a new *Sign*, in which it enters the highest priority in the subnetwork (in the priority bit).

The **ECMA-90 standard** (Fig. 4.24) describes the sublayer of control of access to physical interconnection facilities, the physical layer, and the physical interconnection facilities of a computer network whose core is provided by one of a group of multipoint frequency channels in a broadband system. To create these channels, 7-MHz frequency bands are allotted in the broadband system. Data are transmitted over these channels at a standard rate of 5 Mbit/sec. In addition, other rates can be employed in each particular frequency band (or subband).

The ECMA-90 standard defines the following:
— the electrical and physical characteristics of the physical interconnection facilities;
— the electrical characteristics of the interface between the subscriber system and multipoint frequency channel;
— the physical-layer functions;
— the functions of the sublayer of control of access to the physical interconnection facilities;
— the service that the sublayer of control of access to physical interconnection facilities furnishes to the logical-channel control sublayer.

Access to a multipoint frequency channel is provided by successive token-passing from one station to another in a logical-ring arrangement. The access-control mechanism defines the instant at which the next station in sequence gains access to a shared channel. The right of access occurs after recognition and acceptance of the token sent by the preceding station (in the logical sense). The logical ring network via which the token is passed can be restored after loss of the token.

Figure 4.28 shows the structure of a broadband system defined by the ECMA-90 standard. The central part of the broadband system is provided by a tree coaxial cable. The base of the tree formed by

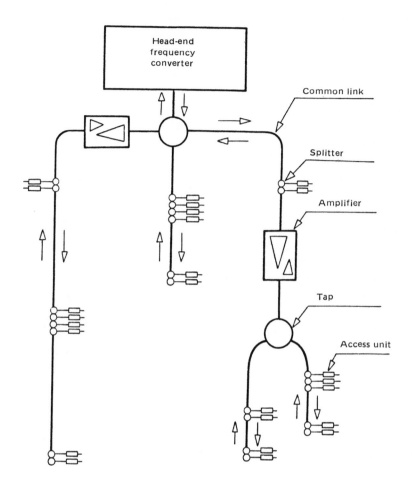

Fig. 4.28. Broadband system.

the cable (front end of the local-area network) is connected to a
head-end frequency converter, referred to here as a **remodulator.** The
cable is divided into two parts in terms of frequency. The first of
these comprises the forward direction of transmission, from the
head-end converter to the subscriber systems of the network. The
second part comprises the reverse direction, from the subscriber systems to the head-end converter. In the frequency-conversion process,
the converter retranslates the information from the reverse to the
forward direction. Thus, information from the sending subscriber

207

system to the receiving subscriber system passes successively to two different multipoint frequency channels, a forward one and a reverse one.

Branches of the tree are formed by insertion of taps at appropriate points. A **tap** is a hardware module that electrically and mechanically interfaces three or more cables, thus making it possible to create a tree topology of a broadband system.

Signal *amplifiers* are installed on long branches of the tree. Each of these **broadband amplifiers** is a device that restores the shape and amplifies all the signals of the high-frequency part of the broadband spectrum that are received in the forward direction and the signals of the low-frequency part of the spectrum received in the reverse direction.

Splitters are installed at the point of connection of the axis units to the coaxial cable. These are modules that electrically and mechanically connect these units to the common link of the broadband system. Each splitter segregates part of the basic signal power transmitted through the common link and directs it to the access unit. Splitters contain only passive electrical elements (resistors, capacitors, inductors). Small broadband systems may avoid taps and amplifiers. In this case their physical medium has only a trunk coaxial cable and splitters.

Five types of symbols are employed for transmission over the physical medium: *Zero, One, Delimiter, Padding,* and *Silence. Zero* and *One* are employed for data transmission. The other three symbols are required to control this transmission. Thus, *Delimiter* is employed to separate frames from one another in the physical medium. *Padding* is transmitted in the inactive state of the medium, while *Silence* is transmitted between frames. All five symbols are encoded by the three digits 0, 2, and 4. For example, *Zero, One,* and *Silence* are represented by 0, 2, and 2204, respectively.

The access method to the pair of multipoint frequency channels formed by the two frequency bands of the broadband system is as follows:

— the token confers the right of access to the channel;

— the token is exchanged by the stations connected to the physical interconnection facilities;

— a logical ring is formed as the token is passed from one station to another;

208

— a station has two phases of operation: data transmission or token-passing;

— the stations collectively initialize the logical ring, restore lost tokens, eliminate duplicate tokens, and add or remove new stations to and from the ring.

It should be borne in mind that the stations are connected to the multipoint frequency channel in parallel. When one station transmits data, the others can interfere with the process. To avoid this, the stations monitor the channel. Appearance of more than one token, or loss of the token, is detected by them. Therefore, the network does not contain any special monitor station to perform the functions of token restoration.

The **IEEE-802 Committee** has been extensively engaged in the preparation of international standards. Prior to 1982, the Committee was engaged in creating a single universal standard oriented toward all types of local-area networks [87-89,126,127]. Then the Committee undertook the development of individual standards. For each of these, the Committee established a working group. The resultant working groups are developing international standards on methods and means of interaction of systems in networks.

The protocols developed by the 802 Committee correspond to the Basic Reference Model of Open Systems Interconnection. At the same time, the model incorporates two supplementary features, shown in Fig. 4.24. The first is that the data-link layer (2) is subdivided into two sublayers. One of them (B) controls the logical channel connecting the subscriber systems of the network. Sublayer B is independent of the physical interconnection facilities that are employed. Sublayer A supports access to particular physical interconnection facilities. The 802 standards provide for three types of physical interconnection facilities: baseband, broadband, and ring subnetworks.

The second supplement to the Basic Reference Model involves the introduction of a zero layer. The Model does not consider physical interconnection facilities. In local-area networks, however, the characteristics of these facilities substantially affect the structure of the lower layers of the model. In addition, physical interconnection facilities must be standardized. Therefore the 802 Committee has introduced a zero layer, which encompasses all the hardware and cables specified by the types of physical interconnection facilities in use.

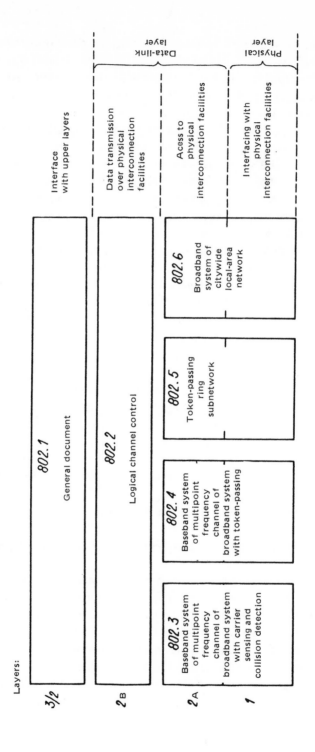

Fig. 4.29. Structure of 802 Committee standard.

210

Figure 4.29 shows the structure of the six standards developed by the 802 Committee. **Standard 802.1** reflects general theoretical problems of setting up local-area networks, as well as practical problems of describing the operation of the network and its components, data transmission control, and interaction of several networks. In addition, the Standard describes the interface between the layers it considers and the upper layers of the network.

Standard 802.2 is general for all types of physical interconnection facilities and is independent of their characteristics. The standard defines the data-exchange procedures (Fig. 4.24) between subscriber sytems on the logical-channel control sublayer (2B). To satisfy the various transmission requirements, two classes of logical-channel control procedures are employed. The first supports data transmission *without establishment of a data-link connection.* This class is very simple, but it can be employed only when the transport protocol layer provides control of end-to-end transmission over the physical interconnection facilities, checking of data, and ordering of block sequences. The second class of logical-channel control defines *establishment of data-link connection,* i.e., it provides sequencing of the delivery of data blocks, as well as block checking and error correction.

Standard 802.3 describes the procedures and characteristics of access to a baseband system or multipoint frequency channel of a broadband system. Like ECMA-82 this standard employs an access method with checking prior to data transmission and monitoring of the system (or channel) during transmission. The transmission ring is 5 or 10 Mbit/sec.

The 802.3 Standard, using a 10-Mbit/sec baseband system, was brought into agreement with the corresponding ECMA standards and was approved in 1983. As a result, many manufacturers have undertaken to create local-area networks meeting this standard; these include Data General, DEC, Hewlett-Packard, Intel, Siemens, 3Com, Xerox, etc.

Two cases are considered when a multipoint frequency channel of a broadband system is employed. In the first case, data is transmitted at 10 Mbit/sec. In a broadband television cable, this requires a bandwidth that is equivalent to at least two television channels. In the second case, the transmission rate is 5 Mbit/sec, so that a bandwidth equal to only one television channel is required.

Like the preceding standard, **Standard 802.4** assumes the use of a baseband system or multipoint frequency channel of a broadband system. Here, however, a different access method is employed, namely token-passing. The token-passing procedure is based on a multilevel protocol hierarchy for using the baseband system or multipoint frequency length. In a broadband system, a loop coaxial cable is employed, one part of which receives data from all subscriber systems (Fig. 3.19b), while the other part transmits data to these systems. Frequency bands forming multipoint channels are allotted in the broadband system; each of these channels can transmit data at 1, 5, or 10 Mbit/sec. The transmission rate over the baseband system is 1, 5, 10, or 20 Mbit/sec.

Standard 802.5 describes a network whose basis is provided by a ring subnetwork. Access to this ring is based on token-passing. The standard defines the use of two types of ring subnetworks. Low-speed rings are based on shielded twisted pairs with a wave impedance of 150 ohms. These rings operate at 1 or 4 Mbit/sec. High-speed rings employ 75-ohm coaxial cable. Here the transmission rate is 10 or 20 Mbit/sec.

Standard 802.6 describes large broadband systems spanning areas up to 25 km in radius. Such systems are intended for citywide local-area networks. They are based on cable-television technology and are used to transmit graphics, speech, and data.

Thus, the 802 standards define two methods of access to physical interconnection facilities: random access and token-passing (Fig. 4.29). The type of random access is the same in this case as in the ECMA-80 standard, namely carrier sensing and collision detection. This method is employed in two types of physical interconnection facilities: baseband and broadband. The token-passing method is employed in three types of interconnection facilities: baseband, broadband, and ring.

4.8.
IMPLEMENTATION OF STANDARDS

The international standards that have been developed define ever-expanding capabilities of, and requirements on, local-area networks. These concern primarily the rapidly expanding set of tasks which can now be feasibly implemented in such networks. In addition, we are witnessing the appearance of more and more new types of communications subnetworks, which offer a variety of ways of delivering data.

Among the earliest tasks entrusted to the networks were distributed job-execution tasks. This made it possible to obtain resources that could not be achieved in a single computer (even a very large one). Then the transmission rates began to increase; dynamic methods of interaction between users and information and computing resources began to appear. Networks began to employ various interactive operations involving interactive software-debugging modes, retrieval in data bases, etc.

The recent rapid increases in transmission rates have made it possible and feasible to execute synchronously related application processes in such networks. This has enabled the networks to handle tasks associated with automation of production and scientific research. The development of network capabilities has resulted in the transmission and processing of speech and graphics in addition to data. Information processing has become more comprehensive. Entirely new information resources have appeared: electronic mail, text processing, graphics, teleconferencing, etc.

The transport capabilities of networks are increasing rapidly. Networks first employed telephone circuits and twisted pairs. Then it became possible and necessary to employ coaxial cables. Local-area networks are starting to use infrared, radio, and video links as well. Lasers and light guides are becoming familiar components in communications subnetworks.

In addition, it should be noted that computer manufacturers want their computer series to be used in the widest possible set of information and computing tasks and to be connected to a wide variety of communications subnetworks. This poses the problem of efficient **protocol implementation**, such that, with a minimum amount of hardware, the maximum possible covering of the rapidly increasing variety of transmission and processing capabilities is achieved.

This problem is dealt with in various ways. The main trend in overcoming the attending difficulties, however, involves the extensive use of microprocessors, programmable logic arrays, large read-only memories, and special VLSI circuitry. Architecturally, the problem is to develop a minimum number of hardware modules from which it would be possible to assemble the maximum number of

Layers:

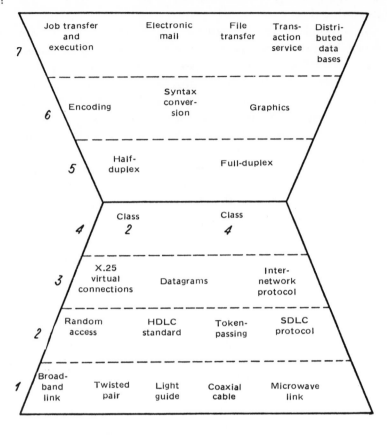

Fig. 4.30. Diagram of set of protocols.

different subscriber-system stations implementing a broad spectrum of tasks associated with information conversion and transmission.

An example of implementation of a variety of protocols is given in Fig. 4.30. The figure shows the list of problems in which the Ungermann-Bass Company is currently engaged [20]. These problems are shown in the form of two trees, whose trunks join between layers 4 and 5. The branches of the first tree comprise the tasks handled by layers 5-7 (upward), while the branches of the second tree represent the capabilities defined by layers 1-4 (downward).

Layer 7 defines the types of application processes for which all the conversions and data transmission are supported. Layer 1

214

shows the types of physical interconnection facilities which can be employed in the network. Layer 2 defines the forms of link control (access methods to these links). Of the international standards, the list cites SDLC. This standard was proposed by IBM, and is still extensively employed in networks; it was the prototype for the HDLC international standard. Ungermann-Bass plans to implement this wide variety of protocols through extensive use of advanced integrated-circuit technology.

CHAPTER 5

NETWORKS WITH INFORMATION ROUTING

Computer networks with information routing represent the oldest and best-established class of local-area networks. In recent years, three factors have provided the impetus for a new stage of development of these networks. The first factor is the manufacture of small and inexpensive microprocessor communications systems. The second factor is that the reliability of these systems and their operating methods are becoming such that the system can be "locked up" and controlled remotely from a network control center. The third factor is that it is now possible to transmit not only data but also speech (in digital form, of course) over the same channels.

5.1.
SINGLE-NODE NETWORKS

Single-node computer networks are characterized by the fact that various types of information are transmitted over them, and jobs are handled in real time. Figure 5.1 shows an example of the structure of such a network. The subscribers of single-node networks may be provided by highly diverse devices; most frequently, however, they are computers, terminals, and telephones.

In a single-node network, data, speech, telemetry, and graphics may be transmitted over the same channels. Therefore such networks are frequently called integrated. The throughput of a single-node network depends on the performance of the communications system, the transmission rate over the channels, and the degree of integration of the functions performed by the network.

An important characteristic of single-node networks is the list of the types of service that they furnish. Naturally, the major form of service is switching and routing. In addition, however, such networks also perform a variety of other functions, including, in particular, the following:
- interface and protocol conversion;
- analog-to-digital and digital-to-analog conversion;
- multiplexing;
- conversion of bit streams into packets and, conversely, packet disassembly;

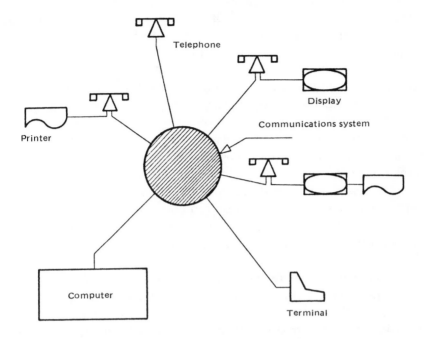

Fig. 5.1. Structure of single-node network.

— information on the network and its resources.

Single-node networks employ both low- and high-speed channels. The former usually operate at 56-64 kbit/sec; high-speed channels have rates of 1.5-2 Mbit/sec.

Single-node networks frequently employ **hybrid switching,** which combines both packet and circuit switching. Hybrid switching provides packet switching for data and circuit switching for speech. The two types of switching can be combined because circuit switching is performed primarily, while packet switching is performed secondarily.

The development of a Recommendation X.25 interface for computers is not an entirely simple task. Therefore, a number of manufacturers of large-scale integrated circuits are attempting to develop sets of circuits that implement the procedures and characteristics specified by Recommendation X.25. For example, Western Digital has packed the X.25 data-link protocol (LAP B) into one very large-scale integrated circuit, designated WD 2511 [130].

As in all local-area networks, there is a progressive tendency to manufacture entire networks, rather than just individual types of hardware. For instance, to manufacture a single-node network, Data General concluded a joint-manufacturing agreement with Northern Telecom [90]. In this network, Eclipse MV/4000 32-bit minicomputers are employed in conjunction with an SL-1 switching node to form a single-node computer network. As a result, users are provided with access to data bases, storage of their own data, text processing, electronic mail, handling of management tasks, and computation. A number of companies in various countries have begun to manufacture "minicomputer/switching node" networks.

Of course, combined transmission of data and speech in the same network requires double speech conversion. Prior to transmission through a switching node, an analog signal is converted to a digital one; after transmission, the digital signal is reconverted to its original analog form.

In single-node networks, the transmission rate for data (and hence speech) is 64 kbit/sec. In most cases, however, there is no need for high-quality speech transmission; an intelligible grade of speech is sufficient. Attempts are under way, therefore, to reduce the speech transmission rate. Researchers at Bolt Beranek and Newman have succeeded in transmitting intelligible speech at a rate of only 150 bit/sec [91].

Under conditions of strong industrial noise, reduction of the transmission rate makes it possible to prolong the time intervals of the 1 and 0 signals, thus substantially enhancing the noise immunity of transmission. It should be pointed out, however, that the slower the speech transmission rate, the more complicated the hardware required to compress it. For instance, compression of speech to 150 bit/sec requires an installation that can perform millions of floating-point operations per second.

Speech transmission in networks requires the solution of a number of specific problems, including the following:
— reduction of the maximum transmission time;
— minimization of the dispersion of network delays;
— resolution of problems associated with loss of packets in the network (in transmission).
The first problem stems from the fact that users talking in a computer network experience greater inconvenience, the more perceptible

TABLE 5.1.

Third-generation PABX's with X.25 interface

No.	Type	Redundancy	Digital tele-phones	Number of wire pairs	Synchronous transmission rates (kbit/sec)	Asynchro-nous trans-mission rate (kbit/sec)	Possibil-ity of protocol conversion
1.	American Bell AIS System 85	No	No	4		19.2	No
2.	Ericsson MD 110	Yes	Yes	2	56	19.2	Yes
3.	Intercom S - 40	Yes	Yes	2	56	19.2	Yes
4.	Rolm CBX Family	Yes	Yes	2	64	19.2	Yes
5.	ZTEL PNX	Yes	Yes	2	56	19.2	Yes

the delay in the partner's response. Thus, the requirements on the dispersion (time spread) of the delay of speech-transmitting packets are fairly stringent. The greater this dispersion, the more the transmitted speech "floats." Therefore, it is desirable to transmit short packets over the network.

Communications subnetworks operate more efficiently, the longer the transmitted frame. Since frames should be short in order to reduce the dispersion, the problem of determining the optimum packet length is encountered. It is assumed that the main part of the packet (the *Data* field) should have around 160 bits.

In connection with the problem of packet loss the following should be noted. Experience shows that speech is not very sensitive to this loss. Frequently, therefore, individual speech-transporting packets that are lost are not requested and not transmitted again.

In considering speech, the virtual and datagram methods of transmitting it should be compared. As shown in [92], virtual transmission of speech packets is characterized by smaller delays over the entire range of communications-network loads. For interative traffic with short sessions and modest amounts of transmitted data, the datagram method is more efficient. As regards file transmission, both methods yield roughly equal results. If a mixture of speech and data is transmitted in the subnetwork, the virtual method proves to be more efficient, regardless of the proportions of this mixture.

As indicated in Sec. 3.2, automatic telephone exchanges have undergone three stages of development. The list of types of communications systems that constitute **third-generation automatic branch exchanges** (PABX-3) is increasing rapidly. Table 5.1 gives a list of only those systems that provide an X.25 interface [93]. A problem of ever-increasing importance in these systems is the problem of redundancy that will ensure uninterrupted network operation. Therefore, most of the systems being manufactured have the requisite degree of redundancy.

A PABX-3 switches digital channels. Frequently, therefore, attachments to telephone sets that provide analog-to-digital conversion are furnished together with the PABX-3. Thus digital speech-transmission telephones are created in the network. However, a number of manufacturers prefer to perform analog-to-digital conversion in the PABX itself.

As for the number of wire pairs in the channels, there are two

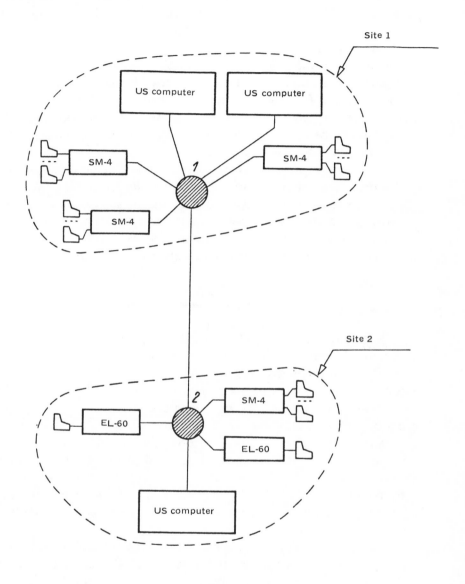

Fig. 5.2. Two-node network.

different versions. In earlier PABX's, one pair of wires was connected to each telephone. In general, therefore, PABX-3's also employ two-wire circuits. For convenience in supporting full-duplex transmission, however, four-wire circuits are frequently required.

Subscribers having different protocol hierarchies are frequently connected to a single node. These can be executed in the necessary standards or can be converted to the network standards in the subscriber systems. Frequently, however, a PABX-3 includes microprocessor hardware that provides the necessary conversion itself. In these cases, subscribers can connect to the PABX-3 operating in accordance with their own protocols.

More and more frequently, particularly in large organizations and enterprises, groups of local-area networks are coming into use. Each of these networks performs a particular set of tasks: process control, distributed data bases, management, etc. Their interconnection and connection to large computer networks can be conveniently effected on the basis of a single-node network.

5.2.
MULTIPLE-NODE NETWORKS

Naturally, multiple-node computer networks are more complicated than single-node ones. In an organization or enterprise, however, they can be used to create much more extensive resources, furnished to wide groups of users. Multiple-node local-area networks are particularly convenient for organizations located in different parts of a given city. An example is shown in Fig. 5.2. Here the organization occupies two sites. Accordingly, the network has two communications systems (1 and 2). Each of these connects the computers at one site, and is connected to the other system. An important feature of multiple-node networks is that hundreds or even thousands of computers, terminals, and hardware can be connected to them.

An example of a multiple-node local-area network is furnished by the **Experimental Computer Network** (ECN) created by the Institute of Electronics and Computer Technology of the Academy of Sciences of the Latvian SSR. Figure 5.3 shows its overall structure. The network is intended for handling two tasks. First of all, it provides an experimental base for research in computer networks. In addition, the network resources are furnished to scientific users in various fields, including network analysis and synthesis.

222

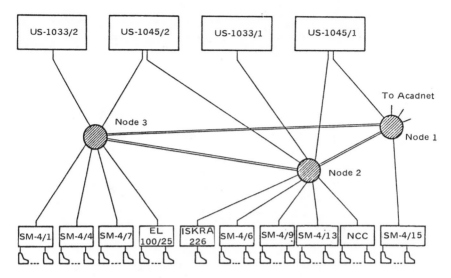

Fig. 5.3. Experimental Computer Network (ECN) of the
Academy of Sciences of the Latvian SSR.

ECN encompasses the computers and terminals of an "academic community" including five institutes of the Academy of Sciences of the Latvian SSR. The distance between the most remote subscriber systems is around 1.5 km. Three communications systems (packet-switching nodes) provide the necessary data transmission. In addition, the network can be divided into subnetworks that handle different tasks: network experiments, user service, support of access to Acadnet.

Acadnet* is a large computer network that includes computers in scientific institutes of the Academies of Science of the USSR and of the Union Republics. The network is divided into regions (subnetworks) encompassing computers of different scientific centers. Acadnet subscribers are computers, computer installations, and local-area networks. The resources of Acadnet cover a wide variety of data-processing problems related to scientific research. The architecture of Acadnet conforms to the Basic Reference Model of the ISO. The interconnection functions performed by the subscriber systems of Acadnet are divided into seven layers. Each layer is defined by an Acadnet protocol that conforms to international standards or recommendations.

---

*The Russian name is *Akademset'* [translator's note].

223

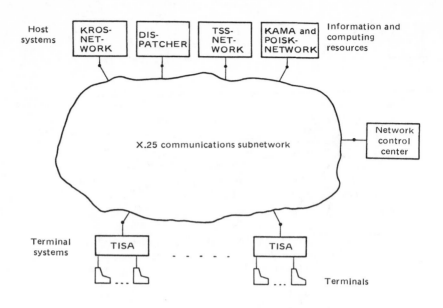

Fig. 5.4. Logical structure of ECN.

In the ECN local-area network (Fig. 5.3), four large Unified System computers perform the functions of host systems. They furnish users with the basic information and computing resources. SM-4 and Elektronika 100/25 minicomputers and ISKRA-226 microcomputers are terminal units and support user communication with the network. The core of each communications system is provided by an SM-4. In addition, the communications system has a microprocessor network adapter for each channel.

ECN is an open network, and it implements all seven protocol layers defined by the Basic Reference Model. The logical structure of this network is shown in Fig. 5.4. The core of ECN is a three-node communications subnetwork. Its boundaries (interface points with subscriber systems) conform to an X.25 standard. Data, voicegrams, and graphics are transmitted in packets over the subnetwork. The information and computer resources of ECN are based on three standard services of Unified System computers (KROS, TSS, and KAMA/POISK), as well as a new service called DISPATCHER. The functions performed by the services are shown in Table 5.2.

The **KROS service** resides in each computer that performs computations in the network. The number of these computers can vary in response to the job flow.

TABLE 5.2.

Services of Experimental Computer Network (ECN)

No.	Name of service	Functions performed by service
1.	KROS	— optimal job sequencing
		— automaton of a number of operator functions
2.	DISPATCHER	— job allocation among any number of US computers engaged in remote job execution
		— intermediate external storage of jobs and results of job execution
		— immediate or delayed transmission of results to terminal-system users
		— disk storage of user files and file transfer upon user request
		— gathering of statistics on KROS services in network
3.	TSS	— access to network resources using instruction language
		— input, editing, and retrieval of data
		— debugging and execution of user programs in interactive mode
		— dynamic control of service resources
4.	KAMA and POISK	— creation of new data bases
		— addition and removal of documents to and from data bases
		— merging and separation of data bases
		— document retrieval in data bases

The **DISPATCHER service** is an application process that handles optimization of computational job allocation for the set of Unified System computers operating under the control of KROS. DISPATCHER resides in one of the machines where KROS resides, or in a separate Unified System computer.

DISPATCHER and the n KROS services form a distributed **network job-execution system.** Users can interact with this system from any terminal system in the network. Moreover, users can transfer a job in one system, obtain information on its execution from another system, and obtain the results at a third system. Local job input to any computer that performs the DISPATCHER or KROS functions is also possible.

DISPATCHER monitors the status of operation in the KROS services. For this it obtains the following information from all computers under the control of KROS:

- a list of jobs currently being executed by each computer;
- a list of jobs in queue at these computers;
- names of the disk packs mounted on the disk drives;
- allocation of on-line storage of all computers.

In addition, all these computers provide information on changes in them associated with the following:

- appearance of a new job in queue for execution and its parameters;
- running of next job in sequence;
- completion of job execution;
- output of results;
- reallocation of on-line storage.

Thus, on the basis of its information on the dynamics of the KROS services in the n computers, DISPATCHER automatically plans and controls the job flow. In addition, DISPATCHER maintains statistics on the operation of the entire network job-execution system and prepares logs and reports on the operation of the computers in the system.

The **TSS-NETWORK service** is an expansion of the standard operating system of Unified System computers, which provides dynamic resource allocation among large numbers of users. In this manner, TSS permits efficient interaction execution of three types of operations: creating and debugging of new programs, job setup for already-existing programs, and job execution. In addition to interactive modes of operation, TSS supports background job execution (sometimes still called batch processing).

The **KAMA/POISK-NETWORK service** is used for creating data bases in which documents are stored. The number of bases may vary as a result of addition of new ones, elimination of unnecessary ones, and merging of existing ones. The service provides for simple addition of newly appearing documents whose storage is no longer needed. A convenient language provides rapid retrieval and selection of necessary documents.

The task of terminal systems is that of supporting **user interfaces**, i.e., convenient forms of interaction between users and information and computing resources. This task is handled by the **TISA package** (Terminal Information System) of software. This package covers a large number of functions which determine the information-processing functions furnished to users.

In particular, these functions include automatic-programming functions employing local and remote resources. This group of functions includes the following:

- set of program setup and editing facilities (symbol and page editor, programmable editor, etc.);
- local libraries, debuggers, translators, and editors (for PASCAL, FORTRAN, PL/1, C);
- interactive job setup and editing for Unified System computers;
- access to remote resources furnished by the TSS-NETWORK, KROS-NETWORK, KAMA/POISK-NETWORK and DISPATCHER services.

In addition, the TISA system supports local interaction with hardware, control of this hardware, and interaction between the hardware and network resources. The hardware in question includes video and audio systems that support access to the network, transmission, and output from the network of sound and graphics. TISA also enables scientific experiments to communicate with application programs in various computers of the network.

The additional functions performed by TISA include the following:

- interactive instruction of users;
- testing of computer peripherals and adapters;
- preparation of network documentation in accordance with the USSR All-Union State Standards;
- file exchange and dialogue between terminal systems.

The TISA system operates in the standard computer operating-system environment. Since each terminal system has extensive external storage, a considerable part of the functions defined by TISA are executed in the terminal system. The basic functions are implemented through interaction between TISA and the services residing in the Unified System computers.

ECN is controlled from a Network Control Center (NCC). The

Center employs the standard SM-4 minicomputer. Architecturally, the Center is an ordinary subscriber system, and it has the same protocol hierarchy. The Center differs from subscriber systems only in terms of the application processes, which perform local-area network control functions.

As already noted, ECN implements the seven-layer protocol hierarchy of open systems interconnection. The upper layers (application and presentation layers) of the subscriber systems are defined by the standards employed in Unified System computers, as well as in the KROS, DISPATCHER, TSS, and KAMA/POISK services. The session layer is described by the SESSION-1 protocol, which conforms to the recommendations of the ISO [94,95].

The SESSION-1 protocol supports execution of the following types of service:

— establishment of interactive sessions with application processes in simplex, half-duplex, and full-duplex modes;
— normal dissolution of sessions at the request of application processes and users;
— expedited (abnormal) dissolution of sessions when continuation is impossible;
— simultaneous control of independent sessions between one application process and different partners;
— delimitation of data into different types (simple, indivisible, interactive, etc., data elements);
— guaranteed delivery of data to partner in the same sequence as they were sent;
— notification of application processes of error situations that cannot be corrected on the session layer.

Simple data elements are data arrays that are transmitted during one interaction between partners. A data array needed for processing can also be transmitted by performing several interactions. *Indivisible data elements* are employed in this case. As for *interactive data elements,* they are required in dialogue mode, when the direction of transmission is changed after each transmission.

The transport layer of ECN is defined by the TRANSPORT-1 protocol, which conforms to the ECMA-72 standard [65]. The protocol performs four groups of functions: data flow control, data transmission, flow synchronization, and purging of the transport channel. TRANSPORT-1 furnishes the following types of services to the session layer:

- up to 64,000 transport channels;
- message transmission with integrity and sequencing maintained;
- message flow control;
- acknowledgement of message receipt;
- purging of transport channels (elimination of messages or parts of messages remaining in the transport channel).

The protocol also disassembles long messages into blocks and subsequently assembles blocks into messages after transmission. Block transmission is time-controlled. Flow control is effected by a window mechanism. The window mechanism provides **credit,** i.e., authorization to transmit up to N blocks. The following functions are performed in transmission and reception:
- message assembly/disassembly into data blocks;
- checking of block sequence numbers;
- checking of acknowledgement of receipt;
- checking of "last block" marker of messages.

The operation of the three lowest layers of ECN conforms to Recommendation X.25. For this the following functions are performed on the network layer (X.25/3):
- packet transmission with control of sequence numbers;
- flow control;
- control of packet transmission sequence;
- multiplexing and combining of network channels;
- reset of network channels;
- reset of interface with communications networks.

Standard LAP B procedures are performed on the data-link layer (X.25/2). On the physical layer (X.25/1), physical interconnections are established, maintained, and dissolved in accordance with Recommendation X.21bis.

On the basis of the adopted protocol hierarchy, the logical structure of an ECN **host system** has the form shown in Fig. 5.5. The protocols of the five lower layers define a set of software that is called the Network Access Method.

The **Network Access Method** makes it possible to establish logical connections between application processes (users or user programs) in one or more than one subscriber systems of the network. After a session is established, application processes can exchange data blocks; when exchange is completed, they can dissolve the session.

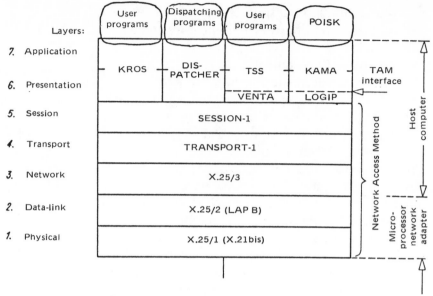

Fig. 5.5. Logical structure of host system.

The number of sessions that can be furnished simultaneously by the Network Access Method is limited only by the resources of the subscriber systems.

In establishing sessions, application processes can specify necessary characteristics of the Network Access Method, in particular the types of data blocks and their mode of transition. Sessions are established when the interacting partners propose mutually acceptable characteristics. The Network Access Method makes it possible to transmit data in three modes: full-duplex, half-duplex, and simplex. In the first case, both partners transmit data simultaneously. In the second case, the partners transmit in alternation. Finally, in the third case, only one partner transmits data during sessions.

Large data arrays may be transmitted in parts by the Network Access Method. In this case the Method specifies the beginning and end of each large array. To perform functions associated with exchange of data blocks, the Method furnishes application processes with the requisite set of instructions.

An application process connected to the Network Access Method must declare its inclusion in the network and must request the necessary number of ports (i.e., logical points of interaction with other application processes). The procedure of connecting an application process to the Method is executed using the instruction OPENPT.

Via any port, an application process can itself establish a session with any partner (or process) or can propose establishment of a session to a partner. An application process that desires to establish a session issues a request in the form of a CONNECT instruction, specifying the address of its port, the name of the partner, and the desired session characteristics. An application process indicates its agreement in establishing a session by using the instruction RESERVE. The address of the partner's port and the necessary session characteristics are communicated.

Data transmission and reception are effected by the instructions SEND and RECEIVE, respectively. In this case the necessary name of the destination (reception) port, output (input) buffer number, and buffer length are communicated. If an application process transmitting a large data array finds it necessary to interrupt transmission, it can do so without dissolving the session by issuing the instruction DELETEQ to the partner. The direction of data transmission is changed by using the instruction RIGHT.

An application process can terminate a session in two ways. When the process in question has no further need of interacting with the chosen partner, it sends the instruction DISC, thus effecting normal dissolution of the session. If conditions that prevent normal operation arise (errors, malfunctions, etc.), the instruction DISCE is used for expedited dissolution of the session. In contrast to normal dissolution, however, expedited dissolution may involve loss of data blocks still in the network.

An application process that desires to cease operation with the Network Access Method (i.e., to leave the network) or to close part of its ports does so using the instruction CLOSEPT. Closing of ports via which data continue to be transmitted may involve loss of data blocks.

The Network Access Method checks the correctness of each request issued by application processes. If an application process issues an erroneous request or performs an erroneous action, the Network Access Method informs the process to this effect.

In the standard remote network processing of Unified System computers, the TSS and KAMA interact with telecommunications

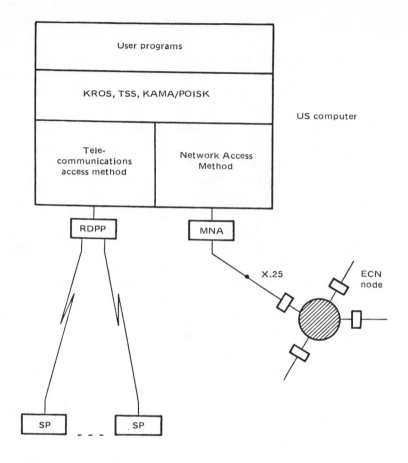

Fig. 5.6. Structure of incorporation of Unified System computer into ECN.

access methods (TMD), whose interface does not correspond to that of the Network Access Method. Therefore, operation with these services is via logical converters called VENTA and LOGIP (Fig. 5.5).

The lower layers (data-link and physical layers) are implemented in a microprocessor network adapter. The five upper layers, in contrast, are implemented in a Unified System computer. If it is of adequate size, this computer can operate simultaneously with several access methods. Use of telecommunications access methods also enables the Unified System computer to operate (Fig. 5.6) via a remote

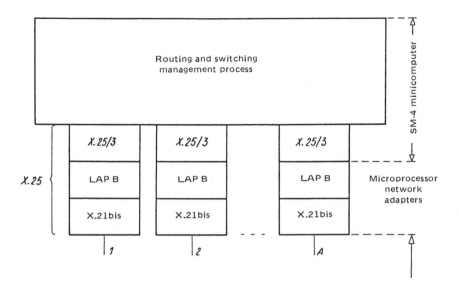

Fig. 5.7. Logical structure of communications system.

data processing processor (RDPP) with subscriber points (SP) that are standard for Unified System computers. The Network Access Method supports inclusion of this computer in ECN.

The logical structure of the ECN **communications system** is shown in Fig. 5.7. The functions of the network, data-link, and physical layers, defined by Recommendation X.25, are repeated here A times (corresponding to the number of channels entering the system). Above these levels there is a Management Control Process that is common to the entire system. It has a routing table and supports the execution of packet switching and routing functions. The data-link and physical layers are implemented in A microprocessor adapters. The remaining functions are performed by the processor of the SM-4 minicomputer.

Figure 5.8 shows the physical structure of the communications system. Here the SM-4 processor and on-line storage, and A microprocessor network adapters, are connected to a common bus. In addition, the operator console of the communications system, which consists of a display and a printer, is connected to the bus. The disks in the system are not involved in executing the main system functions. The disks are used to load programs for all A + 1 processors

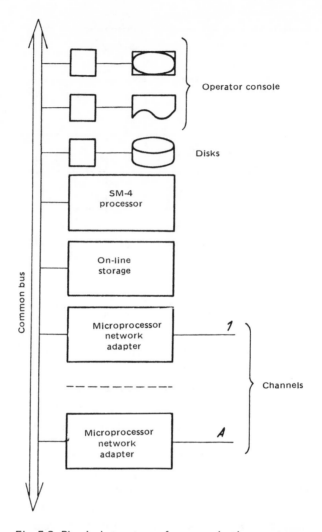

Fig. 5.8. Physical structure of communications system.

and also to gather statistics on the operation of the communications system.

Figure 5.9 shows the logical structure of the ECN **terminal system.** It is easy to see that it is very similar to the logical structure of a host system (Fig. 5.5). The terminal system has a network access method represented by a set of software that describes the five lower protocol layers. Here the network access method is the same as the

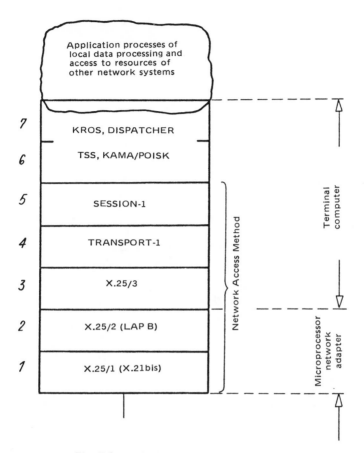

Fig. 5.9. Logical structure of terminal system.

one described previously (Fig. 5.5) for host systems. The application and presentation layers lie above the network access method (Fig. 5.9). Above them there is an application process which supports the following:

— local information processing in the terminal system;
— access to the KROS-NETWORK, DISPATCHER, TSS-NET-WORK and KAMA/POISK-NETWORK services residing in the host systems;
— interaction with other terminal systems of the network.

Figure 5.10 shows the physical structure of a terminal system. The data-link and physical layers are implemented (Fig. 5.9) in a microprocessor network adapter (MNA). The remaining part of the system

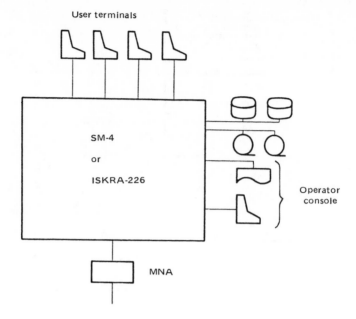

Fig. 5.10. Physical structure of terminal system.

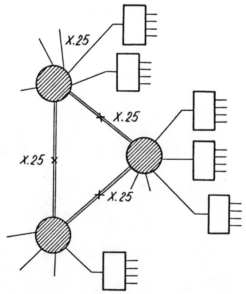

Fig. 5.11. Structure of multiple-node network.

236

resides in a terminal computer: SM-4 (Elektronika 100/5) or ISKRA-226.

Multiple-node local-area networks are manufactured by a number of companies in different countries. Figure 5.11 shows an example of such a network, whose hardware is manufactured by GTE Telenet Communications [11]. It consists of nine TP 4000 systems. Each of them can function as a communications system (circles) or terminal system (rectangles). The terminals of the terminal system are installed next to the computers or are connected via links. The network computers are connected directly to the communications systems.

The TP 4000 system supports control of up to 2400 channels, operating at up to 64 kbit/sec (not all channels can operate at this rate). The communications systems offer an X.25 interface, while the terminal systems support connections of terminals of IBM 2741 or IBM 2780/3780 type. Accordingly, the TP 4000 system performs a large number of functions, including the following in particular:
- packet routing and switching;
- multiplexing of channels;
- message assembly/disassembly;
- fault detection and diagnostics;
- network diagnostics.

5.3.
COMBINED NETWORKS

The advantages and shortcomings of different classics of communications subnetworks have led to the development of computer networks based on several communications subnetworks of different classes (see Sec. 2.5). Such networks have at least one communications subnetwork that provides routing and one that provides selection.

Figure 5.12 shows an example of a network containing three communications subnetworks of two different classes. Here the ability of node A in the network to provide routing over a large number of channels is combined with the high data-exchange rates in baseband systems B and C. Intersubnet gateways are employed to interconnect the communications subnetworks.

The above ideas are employed in **C & C Net,** a development of the Japanese firm NEC [128,137]. This network is designed for

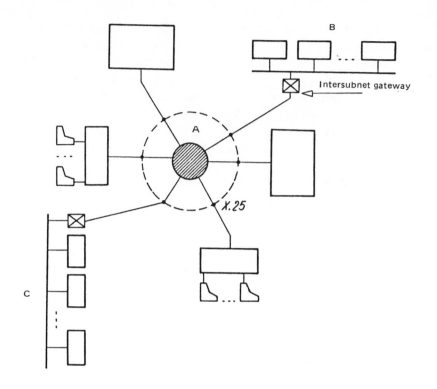

Fig. 5.12. Combined network.

transmission of data, speech, and video information in organizations and enterprises. It is set up in such a way that four types of communications subsystems can be employed to transmit data in any combination (Fig. 5.13). Three of these systems (baseband, ring, broadband) employ selection, while one (single-node subsystem) employs routing. These subnetworks can use different physical media (open "air" glass fiber, copper). The subnetworks are interconnected by intersubnet gateways that perform the necessary protocol and address conversions.

The baseband system of C & C Net provides transmission at 10 Mbit/sec. Multiple access with carrier sensing and collision detection is employed. The baseband can have either a trunk or a tree structure. The physical medium is provided by coaxial or optical cable.

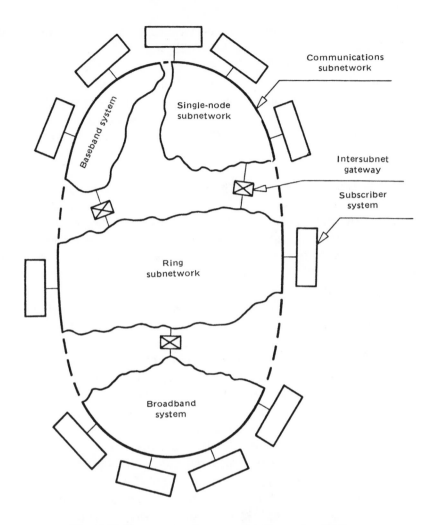

Fig. 5.13. Four types of communications subsystems.

The broadband system is used for simultaneous transmission of data, speech, and graphics. As usual, the architecture of the broad-band system is based on cable-television techniques. The frequency channel employed for television transmission has a working band-width of 6 MHz. The other frequency channels provide packet switching and dedicated point-to-point and multipoint links. A 10-Mbit/sec channel supports multiple access with carrier sensing and collision detection. A 1-Mbit/sec channel has multiple access with carrier sensing only.

The NEC single-node subnetwork supports a wide variety of CCITT interfaces, including V.24, V.35, X.2, X.3, X.20, X.21, X.25, X.28, X.29, and X.75. The Star 2600 communications system that is employed can service up to 1,000 64-kbit/sec channels. The system throughput is 1,500 packets/sec. The communications system makes it possible to span a large geographical area in connecting subscriber systems. Twisted pairs provide the physical medium. In addition to packet switching, the single-node subnetwork also supports circuit switching.

The NEC ring subnetwork is a connecting link that combines other types of subnetworks into a single unified communications subnetwork (Fig. 5.13). Access to the ring is based on token-passing between subscriber systems. Five types of ring subnetworks, differing in terms of rate (from 1.2 to 32 Mbit/sec), number of connected subscriber systems (32 to 126), and distance between systems (2 to 20 km), have been developed.

Subscriber systems in networks with communications subnetworks of different classes can have two types of structures. In the first case the hardware and software of the subscriber system are intended for connection of the system to only one of the types of communications subnetworks. In the second case, the subscriber system is designed in such a way that it can operate in all the available types of subnetworks. For this the system must have different types of stations that support the requisite connection.

Figure 5.14 shows an example of the structure of such a universal subscriber system. The figure represents the logical structure of the system developed by DEC for the DECNET network [37]. The system supports execution of a large number of information and computing tasks. It employs different stations for connection with different types of communications subnetworks. One of these (X.25) offers the capability of connection to a single-node or multiple-node communications subnetwork. The other (Ethernet) permits connection to a baseband system. As a result, this system can be connected to any communications subnetwork of the network shown in Fig. 5.12.

Plexus Corporation has also developed network software [143]. An important aspect of this development is that the software operates in the environment of the UNIX operating system. This operating system is employed (see Sec. 2.3) in computers of various manufacturers (Unified System and SM computers, IBM, DEC, Intel,

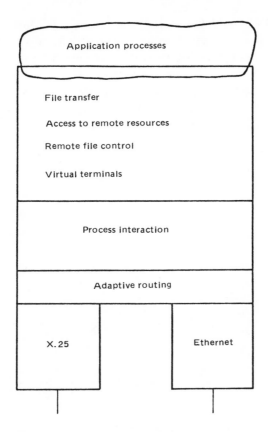

Fig. 5.14. Structure of universal subscriber system.

etc.). As a result, the Plexus software can be employed in all the computers in the network.

The structure of the software encompasses all seven layers of the open systems interconnection environment, from the physical layer through the application layer. On the application layer, two types of interaction processes are supported: file control and virtual terminal. Operation is in a multiuser mode with parallel access to network resources. Rapid response of the software to requests is provided.

The network data-transmission facilities reside on the presentation layer. Their task is to isolate application-layer programs from the particular data-transmission facilities that are employed. As a result, the application-layer programs are simple and are independent of the rest of the network.

The session layer contains the servicing programs for virtual circuits (i.e., creation, maintenance, and elimination of such circuits). The network resources for providing reliable control of data flow transmission reside on the transport layer. The data-link and physical layers have programs that support operation in two classes of communications subnetworks: one- or multiple-node X.25 subnetworks and Ethernet baseband systems.

CHAPTER 6

NETWORKS WITH INFORMATION SELECTION

Computer networks with information selection constitute a new class of networks that have appeared in the last several years. The possibility of using simple and inexpensive communications subnetworks that provide highly reliable high-speed delivery of information makes this class of networks particularly attractive. Despite their novelty, therefore, networks with selection have already gained widespread acceptance.

6.1.
CHARACTERISTICS OF NETWORKS

As was shown in Chapter 3, through the execution of packet-routing procedures, single- or multiple-node communications subnetworks can deliver information to any specified addresses. Thus, in both the single-node and multiple-node communications subnetworks shown in Fig. 6.1, information can be transmitted from a sending subscriber system (point a) to any recipient subscriber system (point b).

In contrast, the communications subnetwork of a network with selection transmits information from the sending subscriber system to all recipient subscriber systems that operate in the network. Then each station (ST) must inspect the addresses of all frames transmitted by the subnetworks. A system accepts the frame addressed to it and eliminates the others. Only then does the subscriber system obtain the information addressed to it.

It follows from the above that in a network with selection, not only the communications subnetwork (baseband, broadband, ring subnetwork) but also the stations are involved in transmitting frames from the sending subscriber system (a) to the recipient system. This has led to the development and manufacture of subnetworks such that each subnetwork incorporates both a communications subnetwork and a set of stations. Depending on how many protocol layers of the subscriber system these stations implement, they will be refered to as transport or data-link subnetworks. For example, Fig. 6.2 shows the logical structure of a **transport subnetwork**. It consists of a communications subnetwork and N stations. Each of the stations

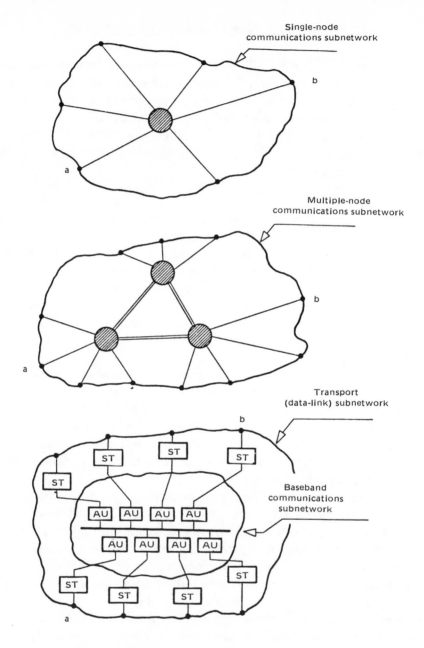

Single-node
communications subnetwork

b

a

Multiple-node
communications subnetwork

b

a

Transport
(data-link) subnetwork

b

Baseband
communications
subnetwork

ST ST ST

ST

AU AU AU AU

AU AU AU AU

ST

ST ST

ST

a

Fig. 6.1. Subnetworks providing delivery of information
to specified addressees.

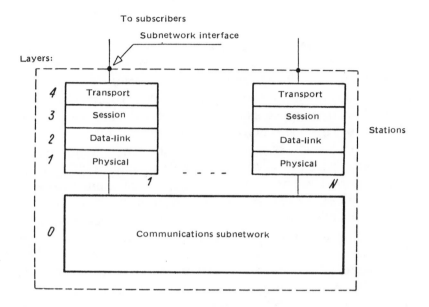

Fig. 6.2. Logical structure of transport subnetworks.

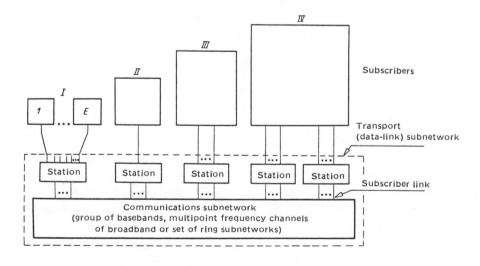

Fig. 6.3. Multicomputer network.

performs the functions of four protocol layers of the subscriber system. Network subscribers are connected to the stations. If the stations implement only two protocol layers, namely the data-link and physical layers, the logical structure in Fig. 6.2 becomes a **data-link subnetwork.**

Thus, the overall structure of a network with selection is as shown in Fig. 6.3. Here the communications subnetworks are represented by q, q $\geqslant$ 1, baseband systems, multipoint frequency channels of a broadband system or ring subnetworks. Together with the stations, these q subnetworks form a transport or data-link subnetwork. The network users are connected to this subnetwork.

Networks with selection are characterized by a wide assortment of subscribers. Subscribers may include computers, processors with on-line storage, stand-alone processors, on-line storage units, disks, tapes, printers, terminals, etc. Various types of networks are obtained depending on the set of these users. The most frequent types of networks are multicomputer, multiprocessor, and single-computer networks.

Figure 6.3 shows the structure of a **multicomputer network** with selection. In the general case, the network has q communications subnetworks that operate in parallel, and each subscriber system is connected to 1 + q access units to these subnetworks. The number of communications subnetworks employed by a subscriber system is determined by the data-transmission arrangement that is adopted in the network. For instance, it may be that it is necessary to provide all subscriber systems with the capability of transmitting over any of the q communications subnetworks. In this case, the systems are connected to all q subnetworks. If, however, not all subscriber systems have the right to employ all q subnetworks, then some systems are connected to q subnetworks, others to some fraction of them (in the limit, one of them).

Four versions of interaction between stations and subscribers are possible. If the E subscribers operate at low rates and the traffic of each of them is modest, they can all be connected to one station (version I in Fig. 6.3). This is the procedure when the subscribers are low-speed devices such as displays, printers, copiers, etc. As a rule, each medium-performance computer has its own station (version II), to which it is connected by one channel. Frequently, medium-size or large computers are connected to their stations by several channels

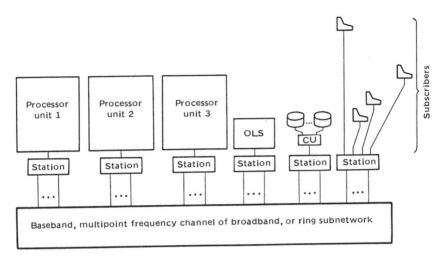

Fig. 6.4. Structure of multiprocessor network with
distributed peripherals.

(version III) in order to enhance reliability or performance. Finally,
cases are possible in which a large computer operates via several stations in order to further enhance the data-transmission reliability and
performance (version IV).

Figure 6.4 shows the structure of a **multiprocessor network**
with selection. Here, in contrast to Fig. 6.3, the subscribers are computer components and terminals, rather than computers themselves.
Each processor unit consists of a processor and an on-line storage
(OLS). In addition, a network subscriber may be a common OLS to
which the remaining subscribers of the network gain access. The network also has a common external storage consisting of a control unit
(CU) and a group of disk or tape drives. Terminals connected to the
network can interact with any of the processors.

When the network in Fig. 6.4 employs one processor unit,
rather than several, it becomes a **single-computer network.** In such a
network the processor interacts only with its peripherals and terminals. In this case, the network is essentially a computer whose components are at considerable distances from one another (up to 2-5 km).

The protocols of the four lowest layers (transport, network,
data-link, and physical) are independent of the set and types of subscribers connected to the network. Therefore, all the networks con-

sidered can be set up on the basis of any types of communications subnetworks: baseband systems, multipoint frequency channels or ring subnetworks. As for the higher-layer protocols (application, presentation, and session), they are determined by the sets of subscribers involved. For instance, multicomputer networks (Fig. 6.3) are generally open and have balanced forms of subscriber interaction. In contrast, subscribers of multiprocessor and single-computer networks are not of equal status. Here the processors are the principal subscribers, while the peripherals and terminals are subordinate subscribers. Therefore, the forms of interaction of the processors and these devices should be unbalanced and should correspond to the procedures and parameters adopted in the computer.

In networks with selection, large numbers of subscriber systems may be connected to the same communications subnetwork. However, only one system can transmit at a time over this subnetwork. Thus, the problem of developing access methods to communications subnetworks that ensure efficient use in alternation by the set of subscriber systems arises.

The choice of access method for a particular local-area subnetwork is a complicated issue. It can be stated definitively that there is no universal access method that is effective in all cases. A given method that gives a good account of itself under certain conditions may turn out to be poor in others.

There are a large number of **access methods.** All of them, however, can be categorized in four groups: time-sharing, token-passing, random access, and combined.

The essential feature of the **time-sharing method** is that the network contains a device that performs dispatching functions. Its task is to plan the allocation time for shared physical interconnection facilities. Subscriber priorities and necessary interaction times may be taken into account in this planning. In planning, the operating time of the network is divided into equal or unequal intervals that are furnished to subscribers. During each interval, in accordance with the adopted algorithm, only one of the subscribers can transmit data over the physical interconnection facilities. In this way, with allowance for the priorities, the dispatcher successively furnishes the interconnection facilities to different subscribers.

Time-sharing of physical interconnection facilities among subscriber systems is the simplest and longest-known method; it has a number of advantages, which are listed in Table 6.1. It is also evident

TABLE 6.1.

Time-sharing method

Advantages	Shortcomings
— Possibility of high-quality synchronization of application processes	— Unreliability of link operation as a result of dispatcher
— Simplicity of access to multipoint link	— Poor utilization of throughput
— Ease of execution of priority discipline	

TABLE 6.2.

Token-passing method

Advantages	Shortcomings
— Real-time control of synchronous application processes	— Need for matching of subscriber system in data transmission
— Fairly complete utilization of throughput of physical interconnection facilities	— Loss of token
— Relative diagnostic simplicity of physical interconnection facilities	— Duplication of token
— Possibility of providing access priorities	
— Guaranteed frame delivery time	

from the table, however, that the method also has major shortcomings, which limits its sphere of use. The chief shortcoming is that the entire network ceases to operate when the dispatcher malfunctions. Poor utilization of the interconnection facilities stems from the fact that some systems do not utilize their alotted time intervals because they have nothing to transmit at the moment. Other systems, in contrast, are not able to transmit everything they need to in the alotted time.

As indicated previously, the **token-passing method** involves the use of an algorithm in which the systems pass the authorization to use the physical interconnection facilities, or token, to one another. Upon receiving the token, a system passes an alotted number of frames to the subnetwork and then forwards the token to another system. If the system that receives the token has nothing to transmit, it immediately sends the token onward.

This method has the advantages listed in Table 6.2. It supports real-time operation and thus enables the throughput of the physical interconnection facilities to be utilized most fully. In normal network operation, frame collisions in the interconnection facilities are impossible, and therefore the diagnostics of these facilities become simpler. Nor are there any problems involved in executing priority disciplines. Token-passing does not require a dispatcher that allocates the operating times for the connections. Therefore, the operating reliability of the communications subnetwork is substantially enhanced.

At the same time, token-passing requires coordination of the operation of the subscriber systems associated with use of the physical interconnection facilities. This coordination is greatly complicated by the fact that the token exchanged by the systems can be lost, and therefore a process of recovering it is necessary. Moreover, the token may be erroneously duplicated. Then, more than one token will circulate in the network. Elimination of this error also calls for certain procedures to be executed.

Loss of tokens and the appearance of double tokens are dealt with in various ways. For example, in Prime Computer's **Ringnet ring subnetwork,** the procedure is as follows [96]. Upon completing a given transmission over the subnetwork, a subscriber system starts a timer. If after a specified amount of time it is still not authorized to transmit, it assumes that the token has been lost. Then the system

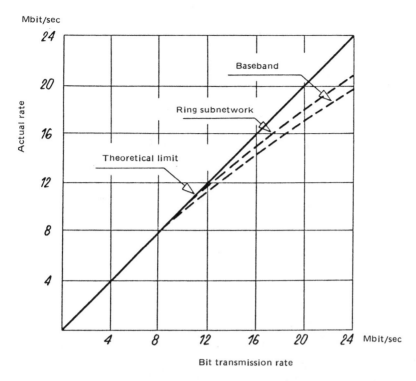

Fig. 6.5. Behavior of actual data-transmission rate
in token-passing.

transmits data to the subnetwork, generates a new token, and forwards it to the next system on the list (or algorithm). To avoid having several systems initiate a new token simultaneously, each system
waits a different amount of time. In addition, a special control is set
up in the network. If several tokens appear simultaneously, all but
one are eliminated in this manner.

The rate characteristics of networks that employ token-passing
methods are shown in Fig. 6.5 [89]. The figure gives the results of
experiments conducted with ring subnetworks and baseband systems.
The abscissa axis shows the physical transmission rate over the physical medium of the baseband, while the ordinate axis gives the actual
rate, taking account of pauses between frames that result from the
access method. In all the experiments, the same number of active
stations (100) were connected to the physical facilities, while the size
of the packet passed to the data-link layer was 2000 bits.

TABLE 6.3.

Random-access method

Advantages	Shortcomings
— Independent operation of subscriber system	— Indeterminate frame-delivery time
— Particularly high reliability of network operation	— Incomplete utilization of throughput of physical connection facilities
— Incorporation of new subscriber systems without halting network operation	— Reduced throughput when distance between systems and load increases
	— No access priorities

The theoretical limit of the actual transmission rate over a baseband or ring subnetwork is given by the diagonal line in Fig. 6.5. The line indicates that, ideally, the actual rate is equal to the rate adopted in the physical interconnection facilities. At moderate rates, up to 8-10 Mbit/sec, this is in fact the case. As the rate increases further, however, the losses due to interruption and token-passing increase. Therefore, the actual transmission rates in the baseband and ring subnetwork depart more and more from the theoretical limit.

Comparison of the curves in Fig. 6.5 indicates that the actual operating rates of ring subnetworks and baseband systems in the case of token-passing are virtually the same.

In the **random-access method**, systems send data to the physical interconnection facilities without making any explicit agreement with the other systems. There are many varieties of this method. The one most frequently encountered, however, is the carrier sensing and collision detection method. It was described in Sec. 4.7.

The random-access method has considerable advantages, as well as a number of shortcomings (Table 6.3). With random access there is no need for a dispatcher. The systems operate virtually independently of one another. Therefore, this method is the simplest and most reliable. However, under heavy traffic, the number of frame

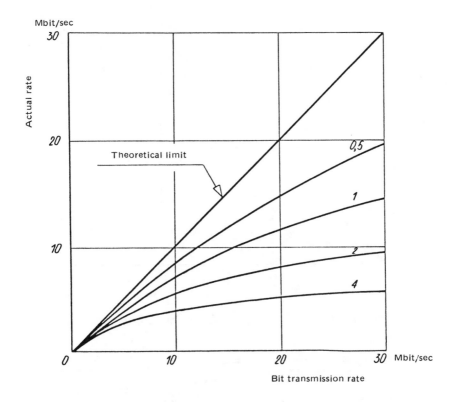

Fig. 6.6. Actual transmission rates in the case of random
access to baseband.

collisions in the communications subnetwork increases, and this
causes the guaranteed frame delivery time to become indeterminate.
This in turn gives rise to difficulties in maintaining synchronous interaction of several application processes. It becomes difficult to organize priority access, although it is frequently desirable to expedite
the transmission of short messages and to make the transmission of
long ones a secondary priority.

Both developers and users of networks employing random access are interested in the way in which the transmission rate and
throughput depend on the parameters of the communications subnetworks. A good deal of research is being conducted to determine
the characteristics of the subnetworks. For instance Fig. 6.6 shows

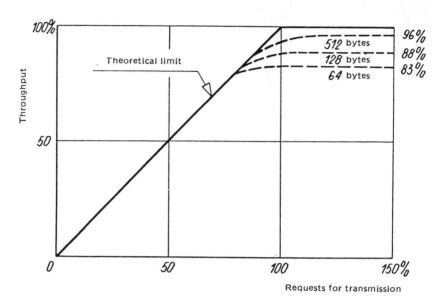

Fig. 6.7. Baseband throughput under various degrees of loading.

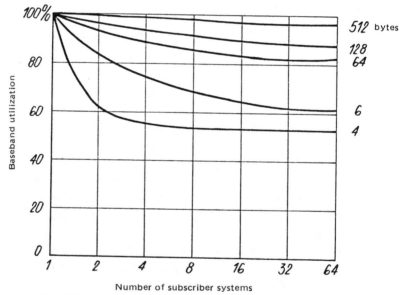

Fig. 6.8. Degree of baseband utilization as the number of subscriber systems varies.

254

the theoretical limit of the transmission rate over a baseband system and the actual departures from this limit [152]. The numbers were determined using an access method with carrier sensing and collision detection. The curves characterizing the actual transmission rate are shown for four more cases. Each of them is defined by the ratio of the length of the baseband system (km) to the length of the transmitted frame (kbit). Four such ratios are represented: 0, 5, 1.2, and 4. The curves indicate that the actual rate is determined to a considerable extent by the bit transmission rate over the baseband that is adopted in the communications subnetwork. The shorter the length of the baseband, and the longer the frames transmitted over it, the higher the actual rate and the closer it is to the theoretical limit.

Figures 6.7 and 6.8 show the throughput [153] and degree of utilization of the baseband system when an access method with carrier sensing and collision detection is employed. Here, the transmission rate over the baseband is assumed to be 10 Mbit/sec. In the experiments described in Fig. 6.7, a load (requests for transmission) was created that fluctuated over very wide limits - from 0 to 150%. The figure indicates that for the case of 512-byte frames the throughput of the baseband remains high even under considerable traffic and is equal to 96% of the theoretical limit. As the frame length decreases (to 128 or 64 kbytes) so does the throughput. In the experiments described in Fig. 6.8, each subscriber system had a large queue of frames and attempted to generate a baseband load corresponding to 100% of its throughput. As can be seen from the figure, the degree of utilization of the baseband decreases as subscriber systems are connected (beginning with one system). This is more pronounced, the shorter the frame length (512-4 bytes). This occurs because, the shorter the frame, the greater the time lost in frame collisions and elimination of their consequences for 512-byte frames. It turned out that the baseband utilization decreased by only 3% for the case of 64 simultaneously operating subscriber systems (as compared to the case of just one system).

It is maintained [135,136] that the random-access method to a baseband system is particularly efficient when the signal propagation time over the physical medium amounts to only 2-5% of the frame transmission time. This limits the length of the baseband but enhances its operating efficiency when long frames are transmitted. As compared to other methods, the random method provides the least

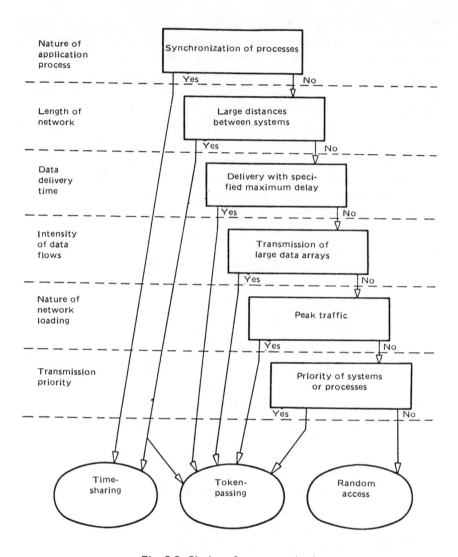

Fig. 6.9. Choice of access method.

delay in frame transmission when the load on the physical medium is small. However, the situation changes under heavy traffic.

In the **combined access method,** the operating time of the network used is divided into alternating intervals. On some of these intervals the token-passing method is employed to reduce the peak loads; on others the random method is employed. The combined method provides the most complete utilization of the throughput of physical interconnection facilities. However, it is the most complicated method, and its use requires certain network resources.

Analysis of established local-area networks with selection [53, 97] permits an approximate comparison of access methods. This comparison is shown in Fig. 6.9. Here the choice of access method depends on six characteristics, indicated on the left side of the diagram. Synchronization of application processes is necessary when two or more of these processes interact in real time. Such situations arise most frequently in executing production application processes, i.e., when several systems control an automated production line. If process synchronization is required or the distances between the most remote network systems are great, the time-sharing method is frequently favored.

A frequent situation is one in which the delivery of information from one system to another (transmission delay time) cannot be greater than a specified limit or in which the transmission of large data arrays is frequently required in the network. The token-passing method is the most preferable one in these cases (Fig. 6.9).

Finally, it is frequently true in networks that there is virtually no peak traffic, and hence it is unnecessary to assign transmission priorities to systems or processes. In such networks it is advisable to employ the random-access method.

The choice of optimum access method can be related to some extent to the sphere of application of the local-area network. One such attempt is shown in Table 6.4 [53]. The table delineates five spheres of network application and offers brief characteristics of each. The access methods that are preferable in most cases are recommended for each of the five spheres.

Of course, there are other criteria besides those given in Fig. 6.9 and Table 6.4. These include, in particular, the following: cost of hardware, reliability of transmission, simplicity of network control, and so forth. Therefore, only the complete accounting of all the features of specific local-area networks can yield a definitive choice of the most efficient access method.

6.2.
BASEBAND NETWORKS WITH DETERMINISTIC ACCESS

Deterministic access to a baseband system encompasses two

TABLE 6.4.

Access method in relation to type of application

No.	Characteristics of local-area network	Area of use					
		Scientific and technical	Business	Automation of organizations	Real-time process control	Plant automation
1.	Type of application process	Asynchronous	Asynchronous	Asynchronous	Synchronous	Mixed
2.	Permissible transmission delay	Limited	Arbitrary	Unlimited	Relatively limited	Limited
3.	Type of operating mode	Mixed: Uniform and nonuniform	Generally nonuniform	Nonuniform	Mixed	Mixed
4.	Best access method	Token-passing	Random access or token-passing	Random access	Time-sharing	Token-passing

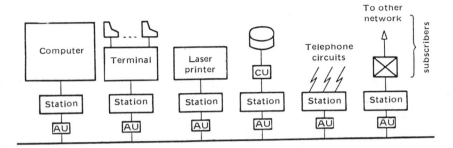

Fig. 6.10. ARC-net.

methods: *time-sharing* of the baseband and *token-passing* in the base-band. Networks with deterministic access are used primarily when the frame delivery time must be rigorously defined by a permissible limit. In particular, this is necessary in the case of real-time interaction of subscriber systems. In data transmission and processing two areas can be distinguished in particular. The first includes networks in which both data and speech are to be transmitted. The second includes networks that control production systems or scientific experiments.

ARC-net, a network created by the Datapoint Corporation, is an example of a baseband network intended for combined transmission and processing of data and speech [99,100]. Access to its baseband is provided by token-passing procedures between subscriber systems.

The structure of ARC-net is shown in Fig. 6.10. In this network the length of a baseband system does not exceed 600 m, while the maximum distance between stations is not greater tham 6.5 km. The transmission rate over the baseband is 2.5 Mbit/sec. Various types of subscribers are connected to stations: computers, terminals, laser printers, disks, and tapes. Connection to remote subscribers via telephone circuits and interaction with other local-area networks is also supported.

ARC-net users can perform four types of operations: word processing, electronic mail, control of speech transmission, and graphics. Word processing includes preparation of texts, creation and management of text libraries, and retrieval in these libraries. Electronic mail

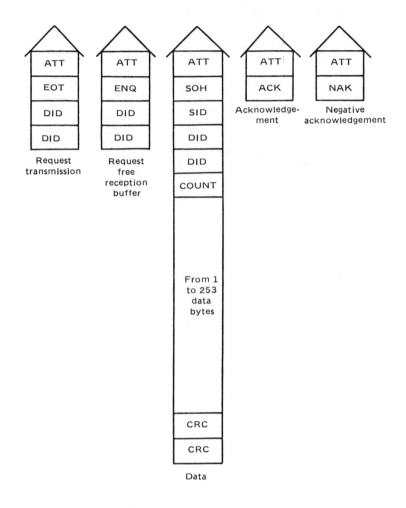

Fig. 6.11. Frame structure.

provides delivery of messages to any address. Speech transmission control provides for organization of remote user calls, allocation of these calls in time, organization of billing, and maintenance of an automatic telephone directory. Graphics control furnishes the capability of using black-and-white and color graphics (diagrams, drawings, figures, photographs, etc.). Users can print out these graphics and can also employ colored slides.

Five types of frames are transmitted in ARC-net; their structure is shown in Fig. 6.11. One of the frames (*Data*) is intended for data transmission. The remaining four frames are control frames. The frame structure includes the following fields:

ATT — attention

EOT — end of transmission

DID — identifier (address) destination; if DID = 000, the frame
    is transmitted to all stations simultaneously.

SID — identifier (address) of sender

ENQ — inquiry

SOH — start of header

COUNT — number of bytes in frame

CRC — cyclical redundancy check

ACK — (positive) acknowledgement

NAK — negative acknowledgement

Any data transmission in the network requires obligatory acknowledgement. If no errors appeared in transmission, the receiving station sends the sending station an *Acknowledgement* frame; otherwise it sends a *Negative acknowledgement* frame.

Token-passing is supported by executing a complex set of interrelated procedures. Only **active stations,** engaged in data transmission, are involved in executing these procedures (Fig. 6.10); **passive stations** (i.e., those that are logically disconnected from the network) and malfunctioning stations are not involved. This reduces the inevitable time losses in token-passing.

The access strategy to the baseband is such that after each data transmission by one of the stations, it is necessary to poll the stations and to offer the token to the next station in sequence. The station that receives the token becomes the primary station in the network and is entrusted with control of the entire network.

Let us consider the cycle of procedures involved in specifying the primary station. All the stations are numbered in accordance with their priorities and monitor the baseband during operation. If the baseband becomes free after a given data transmission, the active stations wait for a signal to propagate over the entire baseband and to reach the most remote stations. After this waiting period, each station enters the symbols ID in its register, and the timing begins:

$$T_i = \tau(255 - i) \ \mu\text{sec}$$

where τ is the interval between the instants at which the station can

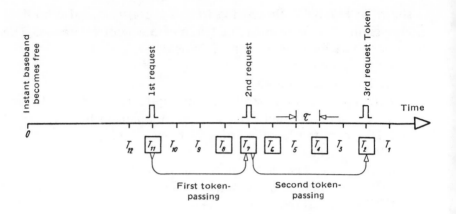

Fig. 6.12. Token-passing arrangement.

send a *Request transmission* frame; 255 is the maximum number of stations in a network; i is the number of the station. According to the formula, T_i is smallest for station K with the largest number. Station K sends a *Request transmission* frame to the baseband and monitors it. If after an interval τ the baseband is empty, station K declares itself to be the primary station, inserts the letter N in front of its identifier DID and waits for the end of the polling cycle of all the remaining active stations. If bytes appear in the baseband during the polling cycle, then station K does not assume the role of the primary station. This procedure continues until the baseband is empty after a given *Request transmission* and completion of the polling cycle. As a result, the station with the *lowest number* (in the set of active stations) obtains the token for the baseband and it becomes the primary station in the network.

The above is illustrated by the token-passing arrangement shown in Fig. 6.12. Assume that 12 stations are connected to the baseband. The timing instants T_i for all these stations, beginning with 0, are denoted on the time axis by $T_{12} - T_1$. Assume that, on the time interval under consideration, the active stations are those for which the T_i are enclosed in boxes. Stations 12, 10, 9, 5, 3, and 1 are passive or malfunctioning and are not involved in the given polling and token-passing cycle. Let us assume also that only stations 11, 7, and 2 wish to transmit data during the cycle. The remaining stations have nothing to transmit in this period.

In accordance with the above formula, station 11 is the first to complete the timing process (at T_{11}). Since it needs to transmit data, it sends a *Request transmission* frame to the baseband and monitors it. In Fig. 6.12 the sending of the frame is denoted by the pulse labeled "1-st request." Station 8 completes the timing process at T_8. However, it has nothing to transmit, and therefore it does not send a *Request transmission* frame.

At T_7, the timing process is completed by station 7, which has data to transmit. The station issues a second request (in this cycle) for the baseband. For this it sends a *Request transmission* frame and monitors the baseband. This frame is picked up by station 11, which has also sent a *Request transmission* frame. Since a second *Request transmission* has appeared, station 11 passes the token to station 7.

Similarly, at T_2 station 2, which has data to transmit, issues a *Request transmission* (the third request in the cycle). Upon receiving this request, station 7 passes the token to station 2. Station 1 is passive and not involved in token-passing. Therefore the token-passing cycle terminates at this point. Station 2 becomes the primary one, occupies the baseband, and transmits the allotted number of frames.

Subsequently, at the instant that station 2 frees up the baseband, a new token-passing cycle begins. At this point the list of both active stations and of stations that need to transmit data may have changed. The process of determining the primary station in the new cycle begins. The time spent in this process depends on the number of stations involved in the cycle, and may be as much as 61 msec.

Data transmission by the station that has obtained the token begins by sending the receiving station a request to furnish the necessary memory (buffer storage). For this the sending station sends a *Request free receiving buffer* frame (Fig. 6.11) and waits 74 μsec (the signal propagation time over the baseband). If the sending station receives an *Acknowledgement* frame from the receiving station during this time, it then sends a *Data* frame containing the information to be transmitted. Otherwise the sending station frees up the baseband and waits for its next turn.

Each station that is newly connected to the network must initiate a rearrangement of control of access to the baseband. For this, after being physically connected, the station distorts a frame being sent to some other station via the baseband. The resultant frame is of nonstandard length, and this is noted by the receiving station.

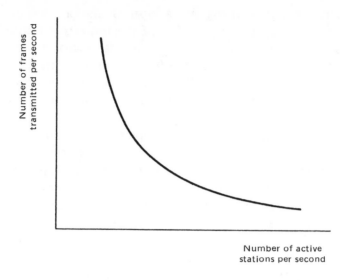

Fig. 6.13. Transmission rate as a function of the number of stations.

This event constitutes the "reconfiguration" signal and the primary station is deprived of its status. If, however, a station is physically disconnected from the network, no rearrangement of access control is necessary.

A number of networks of the ARC-net type have been created and are currently in operation. More than 4,000 subscriber systems are involved in them. The largest such network is that of the original designers; 175 stations are connected to it. The transmission rate in ARC-net depends on the number of stations and is defined by the curve shown in Fig. 6.13. Analysis of this curve shows that the rate drops off particularly rapidly when there is an initial increase in the number of stations.

Now let us consider **small baseband networks,** intended for real-time data transmission and processing. An example is provided by the **Philips networks** [101]. These networks are intended for automating the control of electronic instruments, technological equipment, and domestic electronic devices. These networks are intended primarily for laboratories, organizations, and educational settings. The subscribers of Philips networks may be microcomputers, automobile equipment, measurement instruments, control devices, robots, and domestic electronic equipment and components.

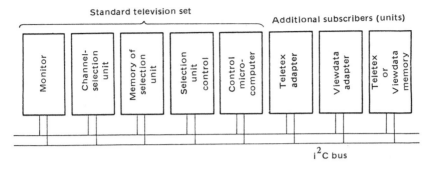

Fig. 6.14. Baseband network of electronic devices.

The cost and complexity of the subscribers are modest as compared to that of medium- and high-performance computers. In developing the network architecture, therefore, much attention was paid to simplification and cost reduction. This was done by introducing a high degree of specialization, so that the networks support only interaction between electronic instruments and devices.

To simplify the networks, the stations and access units are combined and built directly into the instruments or devices to be connected to the network. What remains external, therefore, is only the physical medium of the baseband system, called a bus. Philips networks employ two types of buses, I^2C or D^2B. The I^2C bus is intended primarily for connection of components of instruments and devices. Its length, therefore, does not exceed 10 m. The transmission rate over the I^2C bus is 7.5 kbit/sec for an average frame size of 2.5 bytes or 10.8 kbit/sec for a frame size of 64 bytes.

Figure 6.14 shows an example of an I^2C-based Philips network. As the figure indicates, the bus has two single-wire circuits. The first is intended for transmission and reduction of control signals (start and stop bits). Data are transmitted over the second bus. There is no common source of synchronization pulses for synchronizing network operation; interacting subscribers themselves mutually align their synchronization pulses.

Figure 6.14 depicts a television set constructed in the form of a baseband network. As a minimum, it includes five electronic units which deal with reception, conversion, and output of television images and sound. In addition, the network (television set) may incor-

265

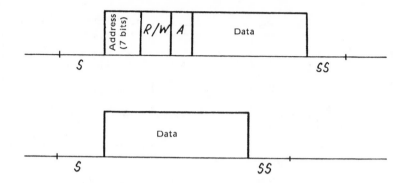

Fig. 6.15. Frames transmitted via I^2C bus.

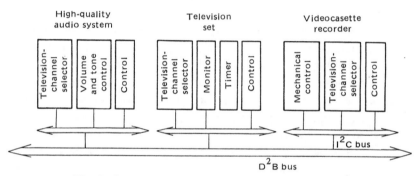

Fig. 6.16. Baseband network of electronic equipment.

porate electronic units which receive, store, and retrieve information transmitted over television channels. Since television companies employ different transmission standards, the network may employ either a Teletex or a Viewdata unit. Addition of one of these units converts the television set into a data-bank terminal.

Figure 6.15 shows the structure of frames transmitted in an I^2C network. Here R/W is a *bit flag,* which indicates what the recipient should do after receiving the frame (receive or transmit data). The presence of the **bit flag** enables the initiating subscriber (or unit) to be the primary one and the receiving subscriber (or unit) to execute subordinate functions. Bit A notifies that the receiving subscriber (unit) has received the data. A start bit (S) is transmitted over the

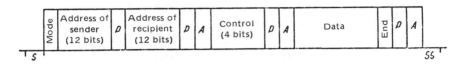

Fig. 6.17. Frames transmitted via D^2B bus.

bus before each frame, while a stop bit (SS) is sent after the frame has been transmitted.

The **D^2B bus** in Philips networks is a larger bus. It may be as long as 150 m and up to 50 devices can be connected to it. Figure 6.16 shows an example of a D^2B-based Philips network. Here three interacting systems (or devices) are connected to the bus.

The systems exchange frames whose structure is shown in Fig. 6.17. Three different modes of operation of the D^2B bus are provided. Therefore, the initial part of the frame specifies which mode is employed. The *parity bit* p performs a simple check on the transmitted data. As in the I^2C bus, bit A acknowledges receipt of the frame. Control synchronization signals and data are transmitted over the same bus in this case; the necessary time multiplexing is employed for this purpose.

The access method to the baseband is extremely simple; it utilizes the circumstance that the bus is short, and hence the signal propagation time is small. Each subscriber is assigned a certain priority for using the baseband.

Any subscriber can initiate frame transmission when the bus is free. Before doing so, however, the subscriber sends the bus a request to monopolize it. This request has the form of a *start bit*. If several start bits are sent by different subscribers, the subscriber with the highest priority is given the right to transmit.

6.3.
BASEBAND NETWORKS WITH RANDOM ACCESS

The physical and logical structure of baseband networks with random access is the same as in the case of networks with deterministic access. All these networks have the same protocol hierarchy of the open systems interconnection environment, and they can have the same protocols on all layers except the data-link layer. On the data-link layer, the protocols of random-access networks differ markedly from the corresponding protocols of deterministic-access networks.

ALOHA was the first network to employ a baseband with random access [98]. It was developed by the University of Hawaii to support interconnection of subscriber systems in the Hawaiian Islands. ALOHA employs a radio link and a satellite-based retranslator. This network provided the impetus for the creation of local-area networks with random access. Naturally, the random-access method itself was further developed and is currently employed in a quite different and much more sophisticated form.

The most widespread network of this type is the **Ethernet Data-Link Subnetwork,** developed by Xerox, DEC, and Intel. The Ethernet standards subsequently came to be employed by more than 40 other organizations [48]. Because of its positive features, Ethernet became the basis for the ECMA-80, ECMA-81, and ECMA-82 international standards. In these standards, the random-access method with carrier sensing and collision detection was further developed, encompassing four protocol levels rather than just two (as in the case of Ethernet). At the same time, the new standards were developed in such a way that Ethernet hardware, already being manufactured by many companies worldwide, could be utilized.

Ethernet is a data-link subnetwork with a bus structure. The baseband employs coaxial cable and supports transmission at 10 Mbit/sec. The length of a cable segment without repeaters (intermediate amplifiers) is 500 m; when repeaters are used, the maximum end-to-end cable distance can be increased to 2500 m.

Ethernet is described by two layers of the Basic Reference Model of the ISO. Its physical layer specifies the electrical and physical characteristics of the interface with the coaxial-cable baseband. The data-link layer of Ethernet describes the method of access to the baseband, frame format, addressing, and error-detection procedures.

In using Ethernet, various organizations and companies have unfortunately set up networks with different upper-layer (3-7) protocols: DECNET (DEC), iLNA (Intel), Uninet (3Com), Altos-Net (Altos Computer Systems), etc. However, a tendency toward unification of these protocols on the basis of international standards can currently be discerned. A first step in this direction is the use of a common transport-layer protocol.

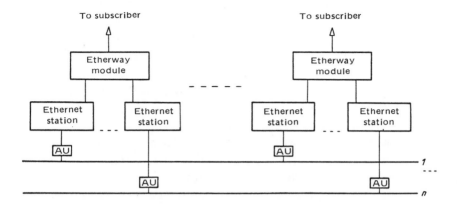

To subscriber

To subscriber

Fig. 6.18. Etherway data-link subnetwork.

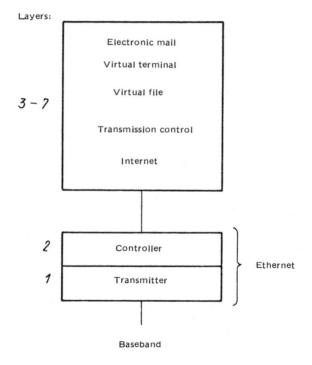

Layers:

3 – 7

Electronic mail

Virtual terminal

Virtual file

Transmission control

Internet

2   Controller

1   Transmitter

Ethernet

Baseband

Fig. 6.19. Logical structure of Uninet.

To increase the throughput of **data-link subnetworks,** arrangements have appeared in which several Ethernet data-link subnetworks, rather than just one, are employed. Figure 6.18 shows the structure of the **Etherway data-link subnetwork** [131], proposed by Technical Concepts Corporation and manufactured by Interlan. This subnetwork employs several (n) ordinary Ethernet data-link subnetworks. For this, Etherway units, which provide subscribers with transmission and reception over n Ethernet subnetworks, are installed on top of the Ethernet stations.

The **Uninet** network, a product of 3Com [11,103], is defined by a seven-layer protocol hierarchy (Fig. 6.19). Here layers 1-2 are described by the Ethernet standards. The session and transport layers of Uninet are the protocols adopted as standard by the Department of Defense of the USA. The network protocol, called Internet, performs a wide assortment of functions, including the following:

- establishment of logical channels (virtual circuits) linking application processes of subscriber systems;
- data transmission over virtual circuits;
- elimination of virtual circuits;
- generation of packets from blocks received from the transport layer.

The Internet protocol provides for simultaneous creation of up to 64 logical channels. It also supports interaction of several communications subnetworks. Operation of the network layer is controlled by simple instructions: OPEN (logical channel), TRANSMIT (data), RECEIVE (data), INTERRUPT (transmission), CLOSE (logical channel).

The transport protocol, called *Transmission control,* performs the following functions:

- control of the window mechanism which specifies the amount of data that can be transmitted without acknowledgement;
- error control;
- repeat transmission of data blocks received with errors;
- multiplexing for creating and controlling a set of simultaneous logical channels.

Initially, Uninet included DEC PDP-11 computers, and DEC and Intel microcomputers. Subsequent developments provided for incorporation of IBM, DEC, and Apple personal computers [104].

Altos-Net, created by Altos Computer Systems [132], repro-

270

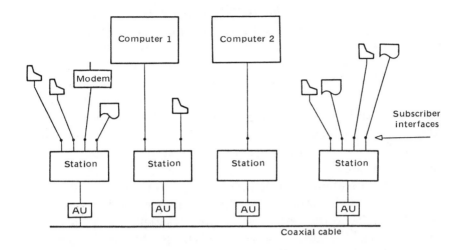

Fig. 6.20. Net/One network.

duces the entire seven-layer protocol hierarchy of Uninet. Its basic hardware, however, is different. System 586's are manufactured for an Intel 8086 microprocessor-based network; these systems are employed as subscribers with displays and other peripherals or as stations for larger computers. Layers 1-2 are implemented by a station controller, while the higher layers are implemented in software, supporting services for file transfer, electronic mail, and virtual terminals.

Each System 586 can have up to six users. The system is a two-processor system. User ports have RS-232C interfaces. The system is controlled by the Xenix operating system, a development of the well-known UNIX operating system developed by Bell Laboratories.

The **Net/One** network is a well-known Ungermann-Bass product [11,105-109] based on the Ethernet subnetwork. Important characteristics of Net/One include the following:

— a wide variety of types of network service, supporting both virtual circuits and datagrams;
— compatibility of different subscribers (including computers) by means of programmable interface ports;
— modular design principles so that the network is simple to use and to expand.

The structure of Net/One is the customary one for baseband

networks; it is shown in Fig. 6.20. The network subscribers are various types of computers, terminals, and other devices. Up to 100 stations can be connected to each coaxial-cable segment. The **non-destructive method** is used to connect access units to the cable.

Two types of stations have been developed for connecting subscribers. Model 1 stations consist of a Z-80 microprocessor, an I/O controller, and a set of interface boards. Model 2 stations differ from Model 1 in that they have up to four microprocessors, interconnected by a high-speed bus. Stations have a common on-line storage of up to 6 Mbytes.

Model 1 stations operate at 0.9 Mbit/sec, while Model 2 stations operate four times faster. The stations furnish subscribers with up to 4 or up to 24 ports, respectively, with a variety of physical interfaces. These interfaces include RS-232C, RS-449, and RS-448, as well as 8- or 32-bit interfaces for connecting computers. The end-to-end transmission rate may be up to 19.2 kbit/sec.

Names are assigned to each subscriber and subscriber application process. They are employed in establishing connections and in transmitting data blocks. Names may contain any symbols, including letters and numbers, e.g., UNIXPORT. Also, one name can be assigned to a group of devices. In this case, connections are established and data blocks are transmitted to any of a group of free devices having the same name. This assignment of names is employed when the network contains equivalent resources or services.

Stations can be programmed in such a way that various computers, terminals, disks, and printers can be connected to them. For this purpose, the stations convert protocols and appropriately generate the frame to be transmitted over the baseband. In addition, the stations perform other functions:
  — virtual-circuit and datagram control;
  — instruction processing;
  — support of full-duplex transmission;
  — recognition of addresses;
  — error detection and correction;
  — remote loading of programs and diagnostics;
  — monitoring of station performance;
  — accounting of station operation.

The **virtual connection service** of the network performs all tasks associated with data transmission over logical channels connecting application processes. In particular, this service performs the following:

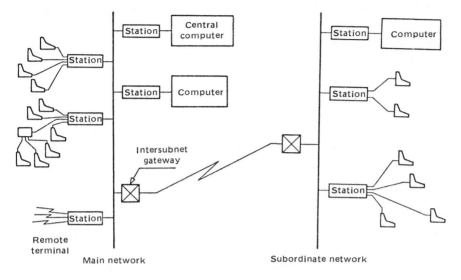

Fig. 6.21. Interconnection of Net/One network.

- regulation of the transmission rate between ports operating at different speeds (e.g., between a large computer and a slow terminal);
- monitoring to ensure that frames are not lost in transmission;
- frame flow control.

This last function enables the recipient, when necessary, to inform the sender that he must temporarily cease frame reception. When the recipient's buffer is freed up, he notifies the sender that he is ready to continue to receive.

The **datagram service** supports execution of procedures associated with transmission of individual and mutually independent frames between stations. This transmission does not require running of logical channels on the data-link layer. Here, however, there is no guarantee of frame delivery, and frames are lost in the event of collisions in the baseband, appearance of errors of buffer overflow. The sequence of frame transmission is also scrambled. When using the datagram service, the subscribers must themselves organize the execution of functions that create logical channels. For this the subscribers request repeat transmission of lost frames, restore the correct sequencing of transmitted frames, and control frame flows.

When necessary, data-link subnetworks of Ethernet type can be

273

combined into general "associations." An example of one such association is shown in Fig. 6.21. Here the association is made up of two Ethernet subnetworks, connected by a pair of intersubnet gateways and a long channel. The result is a Net/One network, based on two Ethernet-type subnetworks.

It is of great importance to be able to connect Ethernet-based networks to local, wide-area, and global single- and multinode communications subnetworks. **Internetwork subgateways** have been developed by various organizations for this purpose. Among these, in particular, subgatteways that make it possible to connect baseband computer networks to networks with information routing shoud be mentioned.

An example of this type of internetwork subgateway is the XNS communications processor developed by Bridge Communications [110]. The basis of this subgateway is provided by a Motorola 68000 microprocessor with a Multibus (IEEE-796 standard). The on-line storage of the subgateway is 256 kbytes, while the end-to-end operating rate of the intersubnet gateway is 1 Mbit/sec.

The XNS subgateway implements the protocols of the Ethernet subnetwork, implements Recommendation X.25, and incorporates all the upper-layer protocols of single-node, multiple-node, and baseband networks that are needed to support interaction of subscriber systems. At present, XNS executes five layers, enabling virtual sessions to be supported. It is planned to add a sixth layer to implement a virtual-terminal protocol. This will enable terminal systems to interact with the resources of host systems residing in the connected networks.

Work is under way to utilize **fiber optics** in Ethernet subnetworks. For example, Codenoll Technology Corporation has developed a baseband employing light guides, called Codenet [111]. This baseband, which operates at 10 Mbit/sec, is star-shaped and employs a light distribution unit (Fig. 3.18). Whereas the coaxial baseband of Ethernet can cover an area of roughly 0.5 km^2, the optical baseband of Codenet can span an area of 5 km^2. Frame collision in Codenet is detected by optical means. The error rate is equal to 10^{-15} bit.

In any complex problem, whenever a "decent" solution exists, attempts are made to find an even better one. This is also true of random-access data-link subnetworks. Attempts to increase transmission efficiency have led to developments along three lines:

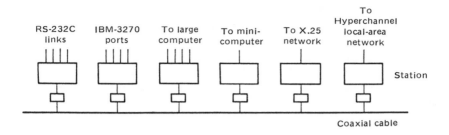

Fig. 6.22. Hyperbus subnetwork.

1. Creation of alternative data-link subnetworks in relation to Ethernet.

2. Reduction of the operating rate of Ethernet for subnetworks that connect microcomputers.

3. Development of special very large-scale integrated circuitry.

Let us consider these trends.

In 1982 Network Systems proposed a data-link subnetwork to compete with Ethernet [11,112]. This subnetwork, known as the **Hyperbus data-link subnetwork,** has roughly the same structure as Ethernet (Fig. 6.22). In this case, however, the transmission rate over the baseband is reduced to 6.312 Mbit/sec.

Hyperbus can incorporate up to 256 stations, and each station can have up to 256 ports. The interfaces of these ports are highly diverse. They include the interface of IBM 3270 serial terminals. Large computers can be incorporated into Hyperbus via RS-366 parallel links, while minicomputers can be incorporated via RS-232C serial links. In addition, provision is made for incorporating Hyperbus into an X.25 packet-switching subnetwork and for connection to Hyperchannel, a large data-link local-area subnetwork developed earlier by Network Systems.

The second trend in simplification of Ethernet involves sharply reducing the transmission rate over the baseband and lowering the cost of the physical medium. An example is provided by the **Omninet transport subnetwork,** a development of Corvus Systems [11, 48]. The structure of this subnetwork is shown in Fig. 6.23. To make the subnetwork simpler and cheaper, stations and access units

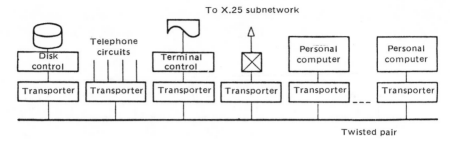

Fig. 6.23. Omninet subnetwork.

are combined into single devices called *transporters*. Instead of relatively expensive coaxial cable, the baseband employs twisted pairs with an RS-422 interface. The transmission rate is 1 Mbit/sec.

Twisted pairs without repeaters are up to 300 m long; with repeaters they can be up to 1200 m long. Up to 64 transporters can be connected to the baseband. The transporters are connected to personal computers, disks, and printers. Connection of remote subscribers via telephone circuits, as well as interconnection to other networks via an X.25 interface, is also provided.

A **personal computer network** can be set up on the basis of Omninet. Such a network is used for data transmission between personal computers and, for utilization of common disk storages and printers. Omninet defines only four layers of the Basic Reference Model, thus supporting only end-to-end transmission of data blocks in a personal-computer network.

Transporters implement the data-link and physical layers and are built into the personal computers or other network subscribers. Transporter operation is controlled by a Motorola MC-6801 microprocessor. This microprocessor is fabricated in one integrated-circuit unit. Stations have a 128-byte on-line storage and a 2-kbyte ROM. Personal computers such as the Apple II, Onyx C800, and LSI-II can be connected to transporters. Disks with 5 to 20 Mbytes of storage are provided for shared use of personal computers. The maximum amount of disk storage in the network is 80 Mbytes. Disk control devices together with their transporters implement the four lower layers of the network protocols. In addition, the control device supports user access to common disk storage.

A similar arrangement, known as the **Cluster/One subnetwork**, has been developed by Nestar Systems. The structure of this subnet-

276

work is similar to that of Omninet as shown in Fig. 6.23. The network is also intended for electronic mail, providing information transmission between personal computers, common external storage devices, and printers. The maximum number of subscribers is also equal to 64. They are connected to a baseband system whose length with and without repeaters is equal to 900 and 300 m, respectively.

To further reduce the cost of transmission, the baseband in Cluster/One employs inexpensive 16-pair flat ribbon cable or 16 twisted pairs. This increased complexity of the physical medium, as compared to Omninet, permits maximum simplification of the structure of the *transporters* (here known as *servers*). These devices do not convert the parallel form of data representation of the microprocessors to the serial signal of the baseband and vice versa; rather, data from the 16-bit registers of one microcomputer are fed directly to the 16-bit registers of another. To reduce the cost even further, the transmission rate is decreased to 0.24 Mbit/sec.

As yet, Cluster/One can accommodate only Apple II and Apple III personal computers. However, these computers can have different operating systems: Apple DOS, Apple Pascal, CP/M. Two 33-Mbyte hard disks and two 8-inch tapes can be connected to the disk server. It is also possible to employ compact cassettes and floppy disks.

The third trend toward simplification and cost reduction of Ethernet involves the development of very large-scale integrated (VLSI) circuitry and correspondingly the development of stations that are both small and schematically simple. For example, Motorola has begun to manufacture special integrated circuits for connecting 68000 microprocessors to Ethernet [114]. Using a 27-mm^2 chip, Xerox has created an integrated circuit that controls the baseband, generates the frame preamble, and checks for errors in the frame [115].

An interesting development, due to Seeq Technology, Silicon Computers, and 3Com [102,116], is a VLSI circuit that executes the data-link layer functions of Ethernet. This single-chip integrated circuit, known as 8001, is mounted on a 225-mm^2 plate and replaces around 60 LSI microcircuits used to implement Ethernet.

The 8001 circuit performs the following functions:
— support of access to the baseband;
— frame reception and transmission;
— detection of frame collisions in the baseband;

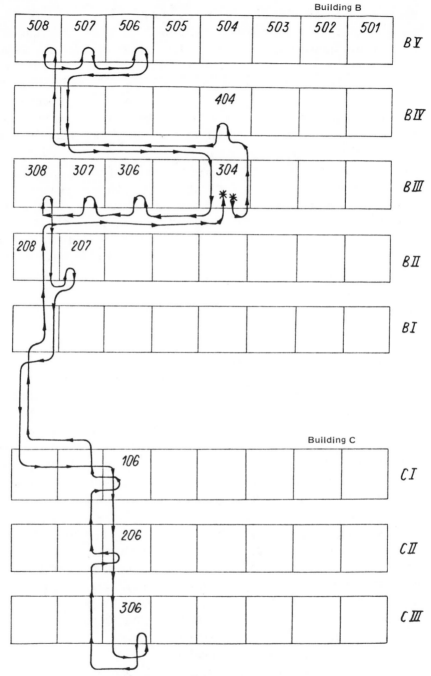

Fig. 6.24. Topology of baseband system.

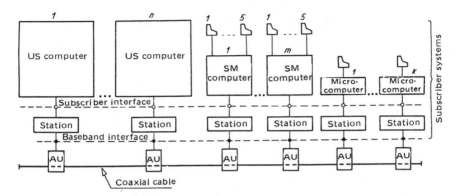

Fig. 6.25. Overall structure of ATRA network.

— repeat access to baseband;
— interaction with network subscribers.

The remaining Ethernet functions are executed by adding external logic. These include: data encoder/decoder, receiver, and buffer. The total number of additional integrated circuits does not exceed twelve.

One of the first baseband local-area networks developed entirely in accordance with the ECMA international standards is the **ATRA network**. (ATRA means "fast" in Lettish). This network was developed by the Institute of Electronics and Computer Technology of the Academy of Sciences of the Latvian SSR in Riga. The network includes laboratories located in two adjacent buildings. The topology of the baseband route in these buildings is shown in Fig. 6.24. The baseband is of bus type. For the convenience of researchers, however, it is run in such a way that the starting point and endpoint of the bus are in the same room. This room also contains a point located roughly in the middle of the bus. The physical medium of the baseband is coaxial cable.

Figure 6.25 shows the overall structure of ATRA. The subscribers of the network consist of large and small computers and microcomputers. Unified System computers provide the main network resources. SM minicomputers and microcomputers utilize these resources.

Subscribers in ATRA execute application processes and also implement protocols of the three upper layers (application, presen-

279

tation, and session). **Stations** execute the four lower-layer protocols (transport, network, data-link, and physical). **Access units** constitute the external part of the baseband and are used to interface stations to the physical medium.

Like the ECN network described in Sec. 5.2, ATRA furnishes users with four types of information and computing resources:
- the KROS.2-NETWORK computing service;
- the TSS-NETWORK interactive time-sharing service;
- the KAMA/POISK-NETWORK data-base service;
- the DISPATCHER service for planning computation.

For convenience of installation, access units in ATRA incorporate a mechanism for nondestructive connection to the central conductor of the coaxial cable. All the components of the access unit are located on one board. This board is connected on one side to the connector of the subscriber link, and on the other, to the needle of the connection mechanism to the coaxial cable. The access unit is installed in a sealed metal box and is generally placed, together with the coaxial cable, under the floor.

Access units are connected to stations via a **subscriber link** consisting of a cable with five twisted-pair circuits. A supply voltage is delivered from the station via one of these pairs. Two pairs are used for serial data transmission from the station to the access unit and from the unit to the station. The remaining two pairs are needed to send the control instructions for the access unit in both directions. The five circuits (or wire pairs) are called for by the ECMA and IEEE 802 standards. At the same time, these circuits are also compatible with the Ethernet standards. In Ethernet there is no circuit for an access-unit control signal; the remaining four twisted pairs, however, have the same function.

Power for access units is supplied from the station. This allows subscriber systems, upon switching to the passive state or disconnecting from the network, to also place the access unit in a passive state. To do so, the unit is simply de-energized.

Access units support execution of the following functions:
- transmission of signals to the coaxial cable;
- reception of signals from the cable and signal correction (after transmission);
- detection of frame collisions in the cable;
- exchange of control signals with the station;
- transmission and reception of data to and from the station;

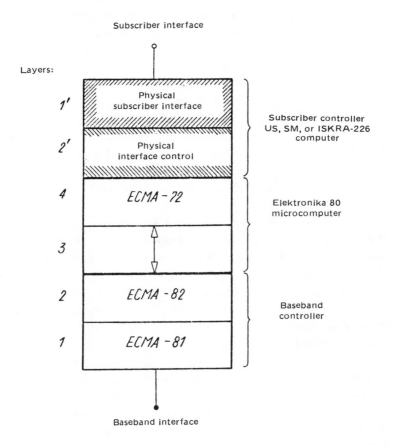

Subscriber interface

Layers:

1' Physical subscriber interface

2' Physical interface control

} Subscriber controller US, SM, or ISKRA-226 computer

4 ECMA - 72

3

} Elektronika 80 microcomputer

2 ECMA - 82

1 ECMA - 81

} Baseband controller

Baseband interface

Fig. 6.26. Logical structure of station.

— isolation of the baseband and station;
— testing of the physical medium (coaxial cable) and self-testing;
— disconnection of the data transmission from the cable and reconnection to the cable at the request of the station;
— monitoring of the cable and determination of whether it is busy.

The logical structure of a station is shown in Fig. 6.26. A **station** consists of three main parts: subscriber controller, Elektronika 80 microcomputer, and baseband controller. Four types of computers are employed in ATRA: Unified System, SM, Elektronika 100/25, and ISKRA-226 microcomputers. Correspondingly, there are three different types of subscriber controllers (SM and Elektronika 100/25 computers have the same type of controller).

The task of the subscriber controller is to support interaction between the transport protocol executed in the microcomputer and the session protocol implemented by the subscriber. For this, the controller is connected to the channel or bus of the subscriber (US, SM, Elektronika 100/25 or ISKRA-226 computer) at the subscriber's physical interface. To support this connection, the subscriber controller implements the data-link layer (2') and physical layer (1') protocols. Interfacing with the subscriber's channel or bus is supported on the physical layer, while control of this interface is effected on the data-link layer.

The Elektronika 80 microcomputer is intended for implementing the transport-layer (4) and network-layer (3) protocols. The microcomputer-implemented transport protocol conforms to the ECMA-72 international standard. The network layer for networks for selection has yet to be defined by international standards. In the first stage, therefore, the network layer performs a transfer function, furnishing the transport layer with data-link layer service.

The baseband controller performs functions defined by the data-link layer (2) and physical layer (1) protocols. These protocols are defined by the ECMA-82 and ECMA-81 standards, respectively.

Unified System computers perform the functions of **host systems,** furnishing resources to ATRA users. Host systems consist of a subscriber (US computer) and an associated station, based on an Elektronika 80 microcomputer. The logical structure of a host-system subscriber is shown in Fig. 6.27.

Subscribers execute application processes described by sets of network-user programs, and functions defined by the application, presentation, and session layers of ATRA. In addition, subscribers implement the data-link and physical layer protocols that support interaction between subscribers (US computers) and stations (Elektronika 80).

The session protocol in ATRA is taken to be the same as in the ECN network described in Sec. 5.2. Similarly, the systems programs that furnish network information and computing resources are the same as in ECN: KROS.2-NETWORK, TSS-NETWORK, KAMA/POISK-NETWORK, and DISPATCHER. In this way, complete compatibility between ECN and ATRA on the upper protocol layers is

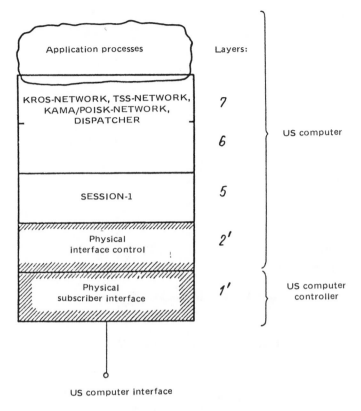

Fig. 6.27. Logical structure of host-system subscriber.

ensured. In other words, subscribers of one network can also be subscribers of the other.

Terminal systems in ATRA consist of a subscriber (SM-4, Elektronika 100/25, or ISKRA-226) and a station (Elektronika 80). The
logical structure of a terminal-system subscriber is roughly the same
as that of the host-system subscriber shown in Fig. 6.27. It is represented in Fig. 6.28. In a terminal system, the application processes
are primarily sets of programs that support interaction between network users and systems programs running in Unified System computers: KROS.2-NETWORK, TSS-NETWORK, KAMA/POISK-NET-
WORK, and DISPATCHER. To support this interaction, terminal
systems furnish the requisite application and presentation service.
The session protocol is the same as in the host systems. The physical
layer (1') is defined by the subscriber's physical interface, while the

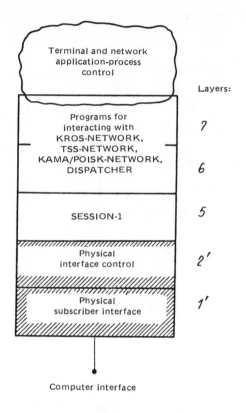

Fig. 6.28. Logical structure of terminal-system subscriber.

data-link layer (2') is described by the control protocol for this interface.

6.4.
BASEBAND NETWORKS WITH COMBINED ACCESS

The advantages and shortcomings of both deterministic and random methods of access to basebands provided the impetus for the development of **combined access methods.** The essential feature of these methods is that the operating time of the network is partitioned into repeating access cycles. In turn, each cycle is divided into intervals, during which the time-sharing method and the random method are employed in alternation.

Naturally, the advantages of combined access methods are achieved at the expense of considerable additional complexity. Except for the data-link protocol, the architecture and all the protocols of networks with combined access are in no way different from those of deterministic-access or random-access networks. The data-link protocol, however, becomes much more complicated.

An example of a network that employs a combination of the time-sharing and random-access methods is the **UniLAN Network.** This network was developed by the Applitek Corporation [147]. Here the operating cycle is divided into time intervals, during which one frame can be transmitted. Subscribers with low traffic on their allotted time intervals compete with other similar users for the right to transmit. In constrast, each "heavy" user obtains one or more intervals of monopolistic use.

The stations that provide this combined access method are based on Motorola 68000 microprocessors. The stations are 10-15% more expensive than those which execute only deterministic access methods. The transmission rate over the baseband is 10 Mbit/sec.

Another combined access method is employed in a baseband network known as **NETEX,** developed by the Network Systems Corporation [11,41,112,117,118]. This method derives from the operation of the core of the network, namely the HYPERchannel data-link subnetwork.

The **HYPERchannel data-link subnetwork** is a transport facility that transmits frames between different subscribers. It consists of 1-4 baseband systems and the requisite number of stations.

The physical medium of the basebands is provided by coaxial cable. Data are transmitted over each cable at 50 Mbit/sec. HYPERchannel subscribers consist of large computers of various manufacture, large disk and tape storages, and a variety of high-speed printers (Fig. 6.29). Satellite, optical, and telephone circuits can also be connected to HYPERchannel via interlink gateways.

HYPERchannel implements the data-link and physical layers of the network and provides subscriber systems with physical interconnection facilities. Its chief purpose is to interconnect up to 6-9 large computers located in one building or in a few adjacent ones. Therefore, the length of the baseband does not exceed 600 m. The principal characteristics of HYPERchannel are the following:

— data transmission at the same rates at which data is exchanged between on-line storage and disk storage in large computers;

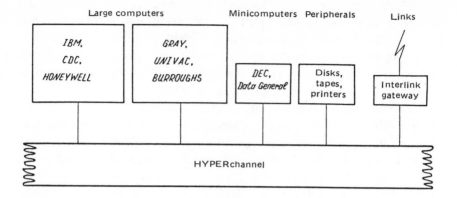

Fig. 6.29. Structure of NETEX network.

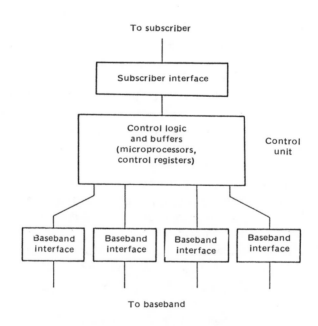

Fig. 6.30. Diagram of station.

- no need for assembly/disassembly of the data blocks with which the systems operate on the upper layers, since frames of up to 4 kbytes can be transmitted.

The logical structure of a HYPERchannel station is shown in Fig. 6.30. It has large buffers (up to 8 kbytes), contains a microprocessor, and executes the following functions:
- control of access to the baseband;
- matching of the subscriber operating rates to the transmission rate over the baseband;
- control of transmission priorities;
- frame flow control.

In accordance with these functions, stations consist of three main parts: a subscriber interface, a central unit, and baseband interfaces. Depending on the subscriber requirements, the number of baseband interfaces ranges from 1 to 4.

The access method to the baseband is based on the fact that all stations have time counters that specify the delay with which the station accesses the baseband. Each station has a different delay. The higher the priority of a station for using the baseband, the less its delay. This is the way in which HYPERchannel ensures the necessary priority policy. Priorities can be allocated not only to stations but also to jobs. For example, first priority may be assigned to transmission of short messages in flows of long messages.

The operating time of HYPERchannel is divided into cycles, each of which has four successive phases (I-IV in Fig. 6.31). The first phase (I) begins at the instant at which the baseband becomes free after a given transmission cycle. The counters of all stations are activated at this instant. During the first phase (τ) no station transmits data, thus enabling a station that received data in the preceding cycle to acknowledge its receipt. The duration of the first phase is given by the formula

$$\tau = 2vl$$

where v is the signal propagation velocity over the baseband (usually 6 nsec per meter); l is the maximum distance between sessions.

After time τ has elapsed, the second phase (II) begins, during which each station receives a time interval for data transmission in accordance with its priority. The start of the interval for the i-th station is given by the formula

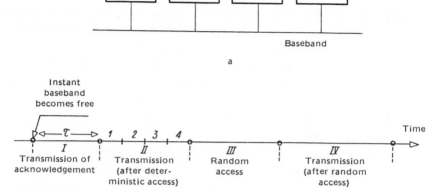

Fig. 6.31. Phases of access to baseband.

$$T_i = i\tau$$

where i is the station number, equal to its priority. Thus, Fig. 6.31a shows an example of a network with four stations (1-4). The numbers of the stations define their priority. Thus station 1 first obtains the right to transmit, then station 2, and then stations 3 and 4, respectively.

Then there follows a free-for-all phase, during which a random-access method is employed. All stations have the same priority in this phase. As a result of contention, one station monopolizes the baseband. This is followed by the last phase in the cycle.

At the beginning of the fourth phase (IV), the counters of all stations are reset to 0. All stations except the one that monopolized the baseband are locked out. The monopolizing station transmits data. HYPERchannel's operating cycle is completed at this point.

Above HYPERchannel, in the subscriber systems, there is a software package that describes the upper-layer protocols of the NETEX network (Flg. 6.29). This package is employed by subscribers who have the IBM/MVS, IBM/VM, DEC/VMS, DEC/RSX-11M, and UNIVAC/OC-1100 operating systems. File and message transfer are performed in the network. Combined utilization of NETEX and

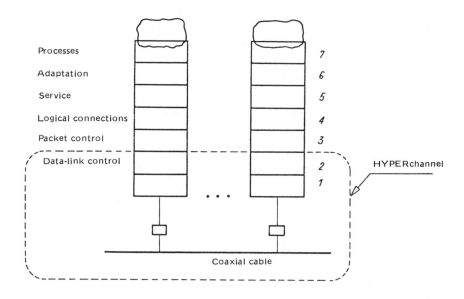

Fig. 6.32. Structure of BLN.

HYPERchannel makes it possible to set up large computer centers based on network architecture.

A second HYPERchannel-based network is the **BLN network** developed by Bell Laboratories [11]. Although this network employs the same data-link sublayer, the software for the upper layers is different from that employed in NETEX. BLN supports file transfer between computers, output of results to peripherals of any computer, and dialogue between users and the network operator. The network subscribers can be computers with UNIX, IBM/MVS, and IBM/TSS operating systems. The software of BLN is written in C.

Figure 6.32 shows the architecture of BLN. All the functions are distributed over seven layers. Although these layers perform tasks corresponding to the Basic Reference Model of Open Systems Interconnection, they have different names. The *Processes* layer is the basic component that supports interaction between network application processes and network service. A large number of application processes can be executed in parallel in BLN. Various protocols and interfaces are employed for their operation on the *Processes* layer.

The *Adaptation* layer converts formats and codes to BLN standards. The *Service* layer performs various types of network service: support of access to files, transfer of data arrays, etc. The task of the *Logical connections* layer is to furnish reliable noise-immune full-duplex logical connections between application processes. The *Packet control* layer, which knows the network topology (in contrast to the upper layers) transmits packets in accordance with their addresses.

The lower layers of BLN employ the HYPERchannel protocols. Their tasks include transmission of packets, packed into frames, over the physical interconnection facilities. In addition to HYPERchannel, the upper layers in BLN can employ communications subnetworks that perform information routing (either multiple-node or single-node).

6.5.
BROADBAND NETWORKS

Broadband networks are based on the attempt to utilize the highly developed techniques of standard **cable television**, including the various types of hardware that have been developed for this purpose: coaxial cables, converters, repeaters, splitters, etc. Cable-television channels have a high throughput and good noise immunity and are capable of high speeds. Therefore, large local-area networks (e.g., municipal networks) can be established on this basis.

However, cable-television signals are intended for handling analog, not digital, signals. Therefore, their use in computer networks requires a double conversion process. First, before being passed onto the channel, the digital signals must be converted to analog form; then, after transmission, the analog signals must be reconverted to digital.

As stated in Sec. 3.5, to utilize the channel throughput more completely, **frequency bands** intended for different purposes are allotted within it. For example, one band, making up a multipoint frequency channel, may be employed for interaction of a large number of computers; another may be employed for television transmission; and so forth. In turn, bands are divided into **subbands,** in which point-to-point frequency channels are created. In this manner, hundreds of frequency channels, connecting computers, terminals, peripherals, and various devices, can be created in the broadband system.

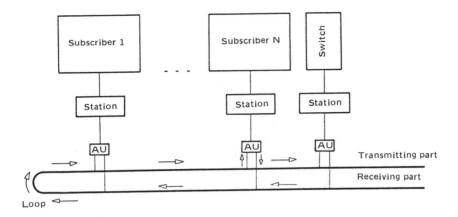

Fig. 6.33. Overall network structure in Wangnet association.

Thus, one broadband system can be used to set up a number of different computer networks. On the logical level, these networks operate independently of one another. As a result of this independence, the computer network can employ different sets of protocols and interfaces. Of course, when necessary, part of the networks can be interconnected in the customary fashion.

As an example of a group of networks utilizing a cable-television system, let us consider the system known as Wangnet, developed by the Wang Corporation [11,119,120].

The Wangnet broadband system is employed for transfer of files, messages, text, electronic mail, and video signals. Thus, Wangnet provides information storage, preparation of documents and reports, and file control. Both Wang computers and computers of other manufacturers can be incorporated into the Wangnet system. When necessary, Wangnet can be connected to other networks.

Figure 6.33 shows the overall structure of a **Wangnet system.** Its core is a broadband arrangement that makes a loop in the middle and runs by each subscriber system twice. Transmitting and receiving parts of the broadband system are created in this manner. The receiving part receives information from the system, while the transmitting part delivers the information to the systems. In the general case, the broadband has a tree structure that incorporates two trees. One of the trees forms the receiving part, while the other, which is a mirror image of the first, forms the transmitting part. The trees are interconnected at their bases.

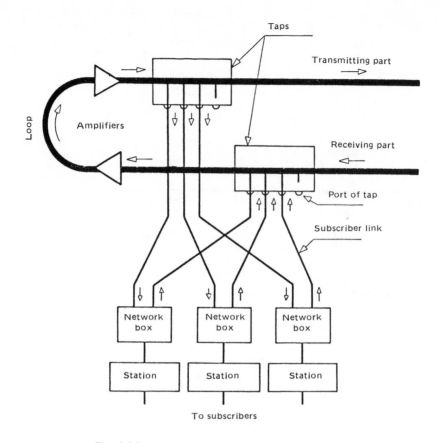

Fig. 6.34. Connection of stations to coaxial cable.

The maximum overall length of the transmitting and receiving parts of the common link of the coaxial cable is 32000 m. The overall passband of the cable is 340 MHz (from 10 to 350 MHz). At present, however, only 35% of this passband is utilized. The rest is held in reserve for future use.

Wangnet employs a **channel switch** (Fig. 6.33), which furnishes the switch channels required by interacting subscriber systems of one or more networks. The switch polls the stations that employ switch channels, gathering requests for connections. If a called station is not busy and is operational, the switch connects the sending station to the receiving station and informs them to this effect. Then data can be exchanged between the stations.

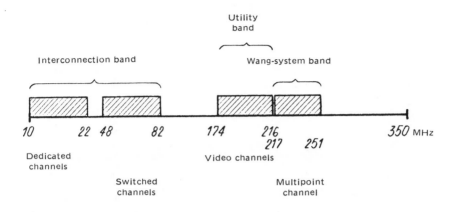

Fig. 6.35. Frequency bands in broadband system.

Figure 6.34 shows the connection of subscriber systems to the common coaxial-cable link of the broadband system. Here subscriber links are connected to the receiving and transmitting parts of the common link by connectors, each of which has four ports. Network boxes are connected to three ports; the fourth port is a spare. Network boxes are generally installed in the wall.

Stations in Wangnet are based on Zilog Z80 microprocessors and have 128 kbytes of on-line storage. For interfacing with the broadband system, the station has a controller to which the coaxial cable from the network box is connected (Fig. 6.34). The station controller, in the direction toward the subscriber, has one of two standard interfaces, RS-232C or RS-449. Stations implement layers 1-5 of the Basic Reference Model; accordingly, they perform the following functions:

— packet assembly/disassembly;
— flow control and data buffering;
— access to broadband;
— control of interaction with subscribers.

Three frequency ranges, shown in Fig. 6.35, are assigned in the broadband system. Corresponding to these three ranges, there are three bands: an interconnect band, a utility band, and a Wang-system band. Point-to-point or multipoint frequency channels are located in the bands. Data is transmitted over them at rates up to 12 Mbit/sec.

The interconnect band (Fig. 6.36) is divided into three sub-

293

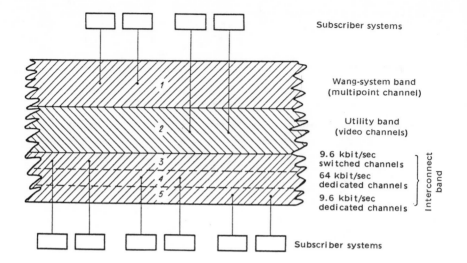

Subscriber systems

Wang-system band
(multipoint channel)

Utility band
(video channels)

9.6 kbit/sec
switched channels

64 kbit/sec
dedicated channels

9.6 kbit/sec
dedicated channels

Interconnect band

Subscriber systems

Fig. 6.36. Five types of communications subnetworks.

bands, forming the following groups: a group of 9.6 kbit/sec switched frequency channels, a group of 64 kbit/sec dedicated frequency channels, and a group of 9.6 kbit/sec dedicated frequency channels.*

As a result, five groups of physical media for setting up communications subsystems are created in the broadband system. These groups, shown in Fig. 6.36, include the following:

1. multipoint frequency channel for Wang systems;
2. group of video frequency channels;
3. group of 9.6 kbit/sec switched frequency channels;
4. group of 64 kbit/sec dedicated frequency channels;
5. group of 9.6 kbit/sec dedicated frequency channels.

The above groups of physical media can be used to create a large number of different communications subsystems. For instance, a multipoint frequency channel is set up in the Wang-systems band. The utility band permits the creation of several video-transmission subnetworks. As for the interconnect band, its point-to-point frequency channels can provide the basis for a group of communications subnetworks that provide dedicated and switched channels. Each of the communications subnetworks under consideration is the

---

*A more recent implementation of the interconnect band employs four subbands.

294

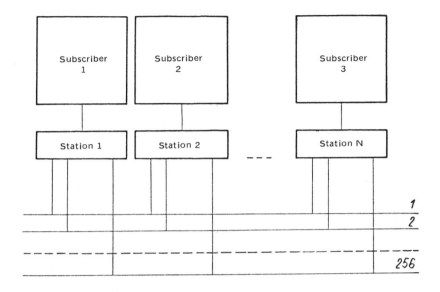

Fig. 6.37. Interaction of stations with switched links.

core of a computer network. These networks can have different architectures, protocols, and interfaces, and can operate at different speeds.

As Fig. 6.36 indicates, dedicated or switched frequency channels are created in the *Interconnect band.* Dedicated channels are used to establish point-to-point or multipoint connections. Sixteen of these channels operate at up to 64 kbit/sec and employ the RS-449 interface. In addition, there are another 32 dedicated channels that operate at up to 9600 bit/sec and have an RS-232C interface. Switched channels (there are 256 of them) are employed only for point-to-point connections. These channels operate at up to 9600 bit/sec and employ an RS-232C interface.

The *Interconnect band* is used to support interaction between computers and terminals of any type. Therefore, it provides interfaces that conform to the most widespread industry standards. In operating with switched channels of the *Interconnect band,* a station must have frequency-tuning capabilities. This is necessary to support operations with different frequency channels furnished by the switch shown in Fig. 6.33.

The stations under consideration can be connected to all 256 switched frequency channels (Fig. 6.37). Since the channels are logi-

295

cal and differ only in terms of frequency, stations have only one physical cable that connects them to the broadband system. The channel switch provides a certain frequency channel to each pair of interacting machines. Then the pair of stations operates at a frequency specified by the switch. The address of the destination station is set up either manually or automatically. Malfunctioning of the channel switch can lead to cessation of operation of all 256 channels. Therefore, several channel switches may be installed in the network to ensure reliable operation.

The *utility band* (Fig. 6.36) furnishes seven dedicated standard cable-television channels, each of which operates at a frequency of 7 MHz. Color or black-and-white pictures and an audio signal can be transmitted over any of these channels. Thus any types of images or television can be transmitted over the channel.

The *Wang band* (Fig. 6.36) supports interaction of up to 65,537 (theoretically, in terms of accessing) Wang-type systems. The Wang band is a multipoint frequency channel that transmits data at 12 Mbit/sec. Stations connected to this channel employ the ordinary random-access method, monopolize the channel, and send frames over it.

A large network system has been set up by MITRE Corporation for the US Patent Office. The main part of this system is a 3000-Gbyte patent-data base. The base combines information on 4.5 million US patents and 9 million patents of other countries. It is planned to enter all this data into an optical-disk-based storage unit. The capacity of each disk ranges from 1600 to 4000 Mbytes.

Figure 6.38 shows the overall structure of the system. As the figure indicates, the core of the system is a high-speed broadband arrangement to which the computers and devices of the patent-data base are connected via stations (ST). The system forms the automated data storage and retrieval service of the US Patent and Trademark Office. This service encompasses five basic types of subscriber:

1. *Text- and graphics-input subscribers.* These subscribers have optical symbol-reading devices for the input data and hardware for converting graphics into arrays of digital symbols. Thus individuals who request patents can submit their requests on paper, disk packs, or tapes, or transmit them over communications channels.

2. *Word- and graphics-processing subscribers.* These subscribers retrieve information against indexes, and perform preliminary analy-

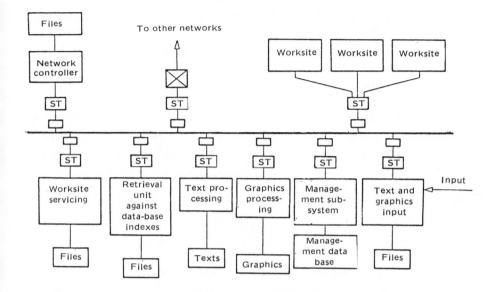

Fig. 6.38. Network of Patent Office.

sis of requests. After analysis, the requests are distributed to the various components of the service.

3. *Worksite subscribers.* These involve users who interact with the resources of the service. The worksites have displays and various types of printers.

4. *Worksite servicing subscribers.* This is part of the network that controls the operation of around 3200 worksites. Part of the worksites are connected directly to the broadband; remote sites are connected via communications channels.

5. *Management subscribers.* These subscribers handle tasks associated with organization of user dialogue, data-base updating, and information processing and computation.

An important positive feature of all the broadband systems is that they can operate with television information. This capability is utilized to transmit and process images of moving objects. Such situations include, in particular, the following:

— monitoring of the situation in, e.g., operating rooms;

— building security;

— remote instruction and teleconferencing;

— presentation of images in scientific experiments;

— observation of critically ill patients.

Another positive feature of the broadband system is that it can be used to set up number of communications subnetworks, providing transmission of any type of data in organizations or enterprises. It should be borne in mind, however, that a group of baseband systems displays exactly the same positive features. In this respect, broadband systems differ from a group of basebands only in terms of the physical medium and its method of use.

It should also be borne in mind that the cost of connecting a subscriber system to a broadband system is higher than in a baseband system. The final choice between baseband and broadband in a particular network is dictated by economic considerations and the reliability of data transmission.

6.6.
RING NETWORKS

Ring networks are characterized by a straightforward procedure of access to the communications subnetworks. This makes it possible to simplify the hardware and software that implement the data-link and physical protocols. As for access control to a ring subnetwork, designers express various opinions. Some regard centralized access control as more efficient; others prefer distributed control.

The **Cambridge Ring network** is the most widespread network with centralized control. It was developed at Cambridge University (England) and is manufactured by Racal (Planet), Logica (Polynet), SEEL (Transring), Toltec (Dataring), Aron, GEC, Racal Data, and Paul Linotype. The network has a variety of different names; they are given in parentheses for some of the manufacturers.

Figure 6.39 shows the structure of the Cambridge Ring [11,96, 122,123]. The network consists of a ring link and access units, to which the subscriber systems and a monitor are connected. The ring link comprises a cable that incorporates two twisted pairs. These pairs are used to transmit data and synchronization signals, to power the repeaters, and to send power on/off signals. Data and synchronization signals are encoded as follows:

— a change in potential on one pair indicates transmission of a 0 and a synchronization point;

— a simultaneous change in potential on both pairs indicates transmission of a 1 and a synchronization point;

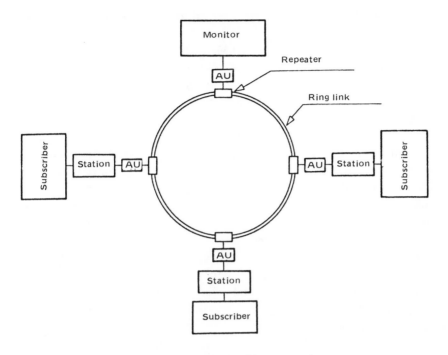

Fig. 6.39. Cambridge Ring network.

— no change in the potentials in both pairs over the synchronization period indicates an error or a break in the wires.
Frames are transmitted over parts of the ring link (between repeaters) at 10 Mbit/sec.

The monitor provides centralized control of data transmission.
For this it performs the following functions:
— initialization of the ring subnetwork in the initial phase of
operation of the network.
— repeat initialization after errors or malfunctions;
— synchronization of the movement of frames about the ring.

In a ring subnetwork made up of a ring link and access units, an
important part is played by natural and artificial delays. The entire
operating strategy of the ring is based on them. The cablet itself creates a signal-transmission delay of roughly 45 nsec per meter of
length. At a transmission rate of 10 Mbit/sec, therefore, the propagation delay over a 10-m cable can be treated as a dynamic storage with
a capacity of 4.5 bits. In this sense, the cable acts as a *dynamic shift*

register. Artificial delays can be inserted into the cable to expand this register.

The network operates at 10 MHz. The frequency must be maintained exactly upon initiation, so that an integer number of bits circulates in the ring. The cable is divided logically into slots. A *slot* is a time span covering a part of the cable that dynamically holds a 40-bit frame.

Within certain limits, ring links can be of arbitrary length. Thus dynamic registers of different sizes can be imitated. However, the number of slots, and hence the number of frames, must be an integer. To meet this requirement, a matching *interval* is created in the link; this interval consists of one or more bits whose value is always equal to zero.

Thus, several *slots* and one *interval* circulate continuously in the ring. During operation of the network, new repeaters with subscriber systems may be connected to it. This changes the length of the ring, and hence the number of frames that circulate. Then the *monitor* (Fig. 6.39) automatically adjusts the interval length so that the number of *slots* remains an integer.

There can be up to 256 addresses in the Cambridge Ring. Stations can have addresses from 1 to 254. Address 255 is used for frames that are intended for all stations in the network. If a station assumes the number 0, it is logically disconnected from the network and does not receive frames from the ring.

The ring subnetwork is of maximum size. This size is due to the fact that the natural cable delay plays an important part in the network. Therefore the minimum configuration should have a monitor, three access units, and a ring cable not more than 100 m long. The maximum distance between repeaters is almost equal to 100 m.

Figure 6.40 shows the structure of the frame and of the minipacket inserted into it. The start bit of the frame must always be a 1. Since frames must terminate in three 0's, the appearance of the 1 signals that what follows is the contents of the frame.

A frame that passes a subscriber system may be either empty or full. Therefore, the second bit of the frame is used to notify the station as follows: the bit is a 1 if the frame is full, and 0 if the frame is empty. Stations can stuff their own minipackets into empty frames.

The *Monitor* bit is required to prevent endless circulation of frames around the ring in the event that some error occurs. The monitor enters a 1 in this bit as soon as a full frame begins to pass by it.

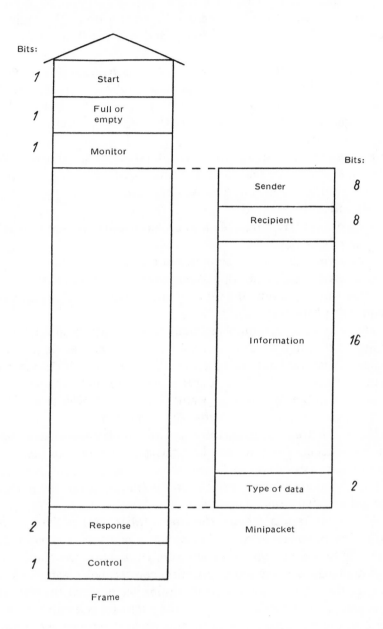

Fig. 6.40. Frame and packet structure.

If a full frame that already has a 1 then passes by the monitor, this means that the frame has come around a second time. The monitor discards the minipacket in this frame and enters a 0 in the *Full* or *Empty* bit.

The 8-bit addresses of the sending and receiving stations are entered in the minipacket. The addresses are followed by 16 bits (2 bytes) of transmitted data in the *Information* field. The last two bits of the minipacket (*Type of data*) are furnished to the user for identification of his data.

Frames are closed by two fields. First there are the two *Response* bits of the receiving station. After receiving a minipacket, a station transmits one of four messages in them:

— minipacket received;
— receiving station rejected minipacket because station is unable to receive it;
— receiving station busy and cannot receive minipacket;
— receiving station not operating or absent from network.

The last bit of the frame, the *Control* bit, provides a parity check on the contents of the frame.

When a sending station has data to transmit, it continuously "monitors" the ring. As soon as an empty frame arrives via the ring, it indicates that the frame will thenceforth be full (i.e., it changes the second bit from 0 to 1). Then it enters the addresses of the recipient and sender and the data into the frame. The frame travels around the ring in this form until it reaches the receiving station.

When the frame reaches the recipient, the latter makes a copy of the minipacket. Then the recipient places one of the four messages to the sending station in the *Response* field: accepted, rejected, station busy, station not operating. Then the frame with its minipacket continues to move around the ring.

The frame moves around the ring until it reaches the sending station. The number of frames (both empty and full) that circulate around the ring is known to the stations. By tallying the number of frames that pass by, therefore, a station can recognize a frame sent by it that has come full circle. The station specifies that the frame is now empty, and checks for errors in the addresses and data. If there are errors, the minipacket is transmitted again. However, the station cannot insert it into the same frame, so it inserts it into the next empty one. Thus, a subscriber-system station executes the set of procedures indicated in Table 6.5. It should be pointed out that in the

TABLE 6.5.

Procedures executed by subscriber system

No.	Type of frame passing subscriber system	Procedures executed by subscriber system
1.	Empty frame (does not contain minipacket)	Places minipacket in frame (if necessary)
2.	Frame contains minipacket not intended for system	Does not respond
3.	Frame contains minipacket intended for system	Makes copy of minipacket (i.e., receives it) and notifies that reception has occurred
4.	Frame contains minipacket sent by system, that has made a complete circuit around the ring	Checks for errors in minipacket after traveling around the ring; if none, it erases (eliminates) the minipacket; if errors have occurred, it transmits the minipacket again

Cambridge Ring it is not possible to transmit broadcast information intended for all users, despite the fact that each frame travels past all subscriber systems. This happens because, in altering the bits of the response field, the receiving station provides notification of what happened to the minipacket, i.e., whether it was accepted at the destination. But only *one* station can provide this notification. Therefore only one station can be the recipient of a frame.

The network known as **Primenet**, developed by Prime Computer Corporation [11,124], is similar in many respects to the Cambridge Ring. It has almost the same structure (Fig. 6.39). To enhance reliability, however, the Primenet does not employ centralized control, and therefore there is no monitor. Naturally, this is achieved at the expense of some added station complexity.

A characteristic feature of Primenet is that its core can be provided not only by a ring subnetwork but also by an X.25 packet-switching communications subnetwork. Correspondingly, the struc-

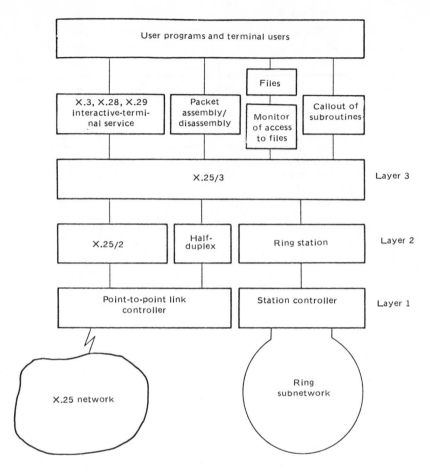

Fig. 6.41. Architecture of Primenet.

ture of Primenet is as shown in Fig. 6.41. As the figure indicates, the upper layers of the network are set up in such a way as to use a ring or X.25 subnetwork. Primenet supports interactive terminal operation, access to files, and interaction of application processes. Virtual circuits, conforming to Recommendation X.25, are established between subscriber systems. Frame structure is described by a somewhat modified HDLC standard. The size of transmitted frames range from 4 (header only) to 2048 bytes. The hardware and software that have been developed enable Prime, CBC, Honeywell, IBM, and Univac computers to be incorporated into Primenet.

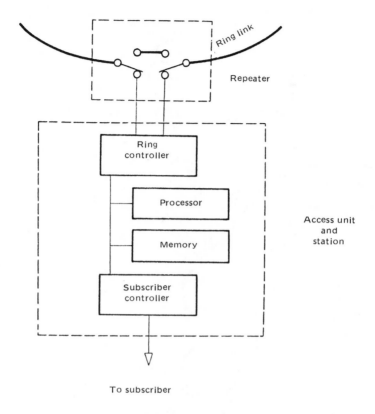

Fig. 6.42. Connection of subscriber to ring link.

The transmission rate around the ring subnetwork is 8 Mbit/sec. The transit time for a frame around the entire ring is 1 sec. Distances between stations may be as much as 230 m. Stations are combined with access units (Fig. 6.42) and have microprocessors. The repeater box contains an electronic relay that removes a malfunctioning station from the ring. Up to 255 stations may be incorporated into the ring subnetwork.

Access to the ring is provided by circulation of a group of token-containing bits around the ring. At any point in time, naturally, only the station that has the token can engage in frame transmission. The frame moves around the ring and picked off by the receiving station. Each repeater delays the frame by 0.35 μsec. This delay is needed by the station to check the addresses of passing frames

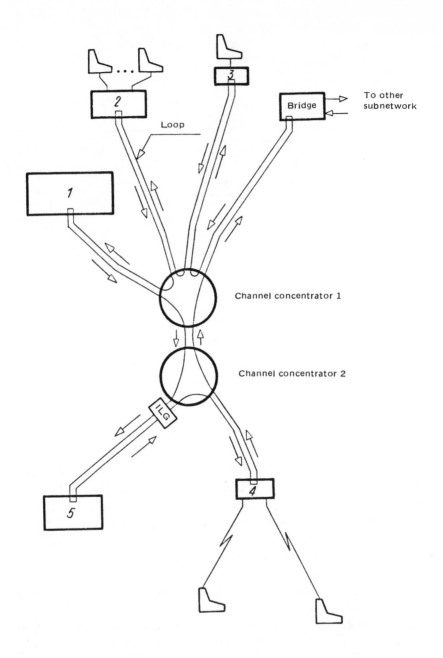

Fig. 6.43. Structure of ring subnetwork.

and to remove frames addressed to it. All stations monitor for loss of the token and appearance of double tokens in the network.

IBM is extensively involved in the field of ring networks. It has developed networks based on the Series/1 and 8100 computers. A characteristic feature of IBM's architecture [134,149] is the use of data-link (or wire) centers (Fig. 3.28) which centralize the electronic switches that disconnect malfunctioning parts of the network.

Figure 6.43 shows the structure of an **IBM ring subnetwork** with data-link centers, called **data-link concentrators.** Here, the ring consists of a group of loops that run from the concentrators in a star configuration. The concentrators are interconnected. As a result, the network is externally similar to a star network. There is a subscriber system or gateway at the end of each ray of the star (loop). Thus, in Fig. 6.43 the ring network includes five subscriber systems (1-5) and one gateway. The latter is called a bridge, and serves to interconnect two ring subnetworks.

The star topology of a ring network has a number of advantages, the principal ones being:

— simple disconnection of malfunctioning or unused loops from the network;
— incorporation at any time of new loops with associated subscriber systems;
— ease of transferring subscriber systems from one location to another.

To perform these functions, each concentrator contains a group of electronic switches. A loop can be disconnected from or connected to the network in two ways. The simplest way involves reconfiguration of the network by a human operator. The other way is automatic switching upon appearance of malfunctions in network components.

Each loop is connected to the network only when the associated system is active and operational in the network. In the passive state, when the system is idle or is undergoing repair, the loop together with this system is disconnected from the network, and information moving along the ring bypasses this system.

IBM's architecture provides for the creation of multiring communications subnetworks. Figure 6.44 shows an example of such a group of subnetworks. Here four ring subnetworks (1-4) are interconnected. In addition, there is a **connecting ring.** The subnetworks operate independently of one another and interact via bridges.

307

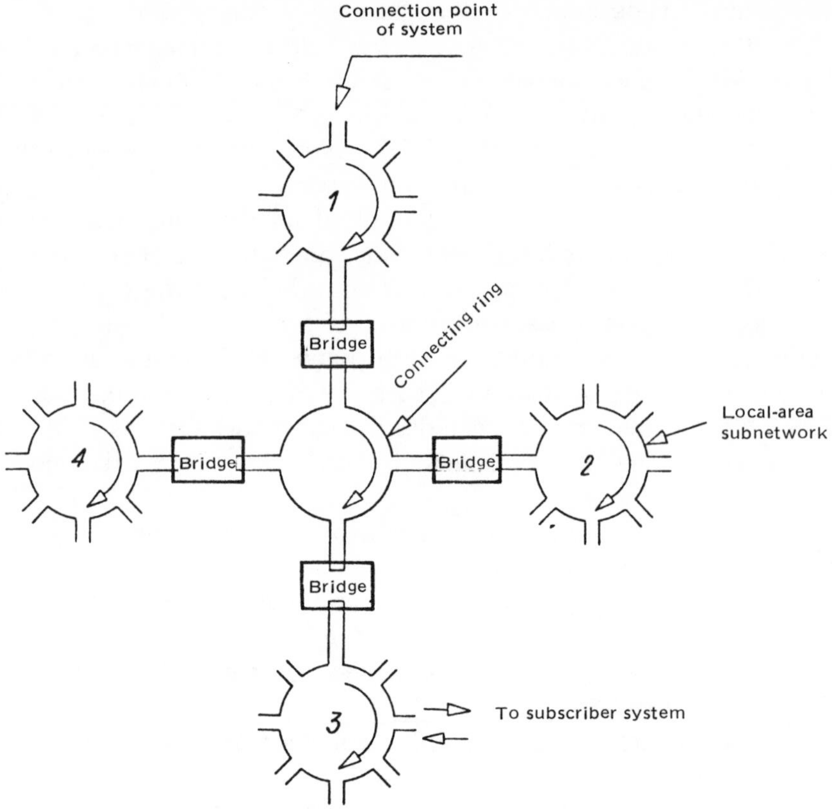

Fig. 6.44. Group of ring subnetworks

Each of the ring subnetworks can be divided into segments that are connected to one another by interlink gateways. This makes it possible to employ different types of physical media in different parts of the ring. For example, subscriber system 5 (Fig. 6.43) can be connected to the interlink gateway (ILG) by a twisted pair, while the ILG can be connected to link concentrator 2 by a pair of light guides. This partitioning into segments facilitates reconstruction and extension of the network.

As is true of IBM's other communications subnetworks, the protocols of IBM's ring network will be defined by the **Systems Network Architecture,** or SNA, currently under development by the company (see Fig. 6.45).

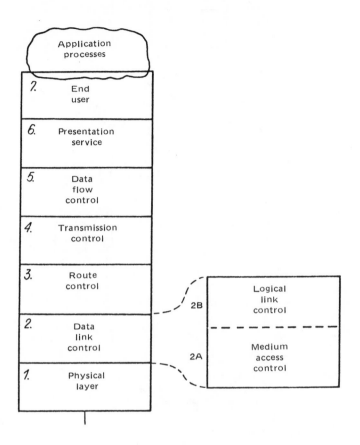

Fig. 6.45. Network protocols.

The *Logical Link Control sublayer* provides running of logical channels that interconnect subscriber systems. Its characteristics are independent of the type of physical medium and of the method of access to this medium. The *Medium Access Control sublayer* supports execution of token-utilization functions. For this the sublayer performs the following:

— transmits frames and tokens;
— executes transmission priorities;
— recognizes addresses;
— determines the start and end of frames (i.e., segregates frames from the bit stream);
— generates check sequences and checks the contents of frames;
— controls token-passing.

309

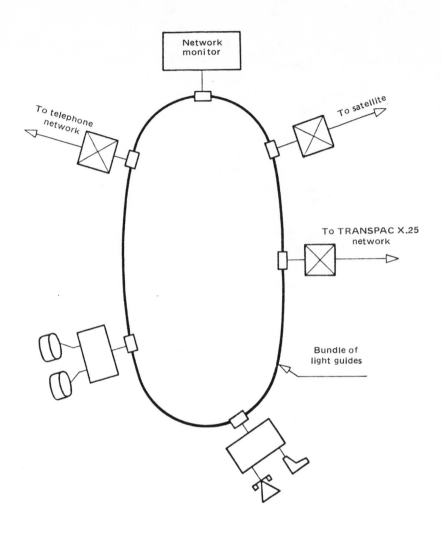

Fig. 6.46. CARTHAGE network.

The token-passing procedures between subscriber systems and the organization of priority access procedures to the frame subnetwork are similar to those specified by the ECMA-89 standards (Sec. 4.7).

The task of the physical layer is to feed signals to the ring subnetwork. For this purpose it generates and receives signals, synchronizes the operating phases of the ring, and executes differential Manchester encoding.

All the subscriber systems in the network monitor for malfunctions in the ring. A system that detects a break in the ring transmits a special signal frame to the remaining systems. The signal frame gives the addresses of two subscriber systems: the system transmitting the signal and the last system in the ring from which data were received. When a break occurs, the corresponding link concentrator (Fig. 6.43) disconnects the loop in which the break was detected.

IBM's ring network includes a management system. It is entrusted with the following functions:

— control of network operation;
— monitoring of the network;
— reconfiguring of the network;
— gathering of error statistics;
— accounting procedures for active subscriber systems.

Ring networks based on light guides and fiber-optic media have begun to appear. An example is the CARTHAGE network [125], whose overall structure is shown in Fig. 6.46. The figure indicates the types of subscribers connected to the ring, including terminals, phones, disk storages, and systems that connect the local-area network to TRANSPAC (the French nationwide network) and a communications satellite. The network was developed by the French Research Center for Broadcasting and Telecommunications, and is intended for data, speech, and graphics transmission.

An interesting feature of CARTHAGE is that it is based on a group of parallel ring subnetworks made up of a bundle of light guides. One of the light guides is used for transmitting speech and data, while the others are employed for video communications. Thus, CARTHAGE is based on a group of ring links, and therefore, can compete with the transmission facilities provided by broadband systems.

Frames are transmitted over the rings at a rate of 8 Mbit/sec. Incorporation of the new station into the ring increases the frame transmission time by 2 μsec.

Data encoding is supported on the physical layer, while detection of transmission errors is supported on the data-link layer. The network layer provides three types of service:

— virtual connection;
— datagram transmission;
— broadcast transmission.

The transport layer ensures that the upper layers are independent of the communications facilities and selects the information and computer resources required by the users.

CONCLUDING REMARKS

Local-area networks provide a universal base for the present-day data-processing industry at organizations, enterprises, and scientific institutes. These networks are characterized by great diversity of methods of processing, storing, and transmitting graphics, speech, data, television, and telemetry and remote-control signals.

As a result, local-area networks can handle virtually all information tasks associated with management and control of production, planning, and accounting; scientific research; design of new tecnology; and automation of production. Local-area networks can incorporate all types of computers, from large computing installations to small personal computers and microcomputers.

Local-area networks are characterized by a high degree of reliability, and their throughput currently runs as high as 300 Mbit/sec. They are also characterized by simple forms of interaction between users and the entire range of information and computing resources.

Development of a variety of types of local-area networks will make it possible to satisfy a wide range of requirements on network size and on the types of entities in them. For example, the following types of networks have appeared:
- mininetworks, including only 4-5 small electronic devices;
- network installations incorporating several mininetworks;
- production-line networks, uniting a group of robots or machine tools;
- classroom networks for students;
- documentation networks, that can handle mail and prepare, edit, store, and locate all types of documents;
- automated design-office networks;
- networks for controlling complex experiments;
- networks for industrial combines;
- municipal-services networks, etc.

This list is rapidly increasing as local-area networks advance into new areas of application.

The diversity of local-area network architectures makes it possible to create highly efficient network hierarchies and highly economical forms of organization of multilevel information-processing structures. In turn, these hierarchies (like individual local-area networks) can be shared users of large wide-area and global networks, handling all the information tasks of contemporary society.

312

REFERENCES

1. V. M. Glushkov, Fundamentals of Soft-Copy Information [in Russian], Nauka, 1982.
2. V. Kvasnitskii, A. Shchers, I. Vinner, et al., Shared-Use Computer Centers [in Russian], V. Myasnikov and F. Peregudov (Editors), Finansy i statistika, 1982.
3. G. Zakharov, Methods of Investigating Data Networks [in Russian], Radio i svyaz, 1982.
4. G. Emel'yanov and V. Shvartsman, Digital Data Transmission [in Russian], Radio i svyaz, 1982.
5. A. Shestopalov, V. Klepikov, and K. Zhevlyuk, Message Switching Centers [in Russian], Radio i svyaz, 1982.
6. Problems in the Theory of Computer Networks: Problems of Cybernetics [in Russian], Nauchnyi sovet po kompleksnoi probleme "Kibernetika," 1983.
7. A. Lazarev and Yu. Lazarev, Dynamic Control of Information Flows in Communications Networks [in Russian], Radio i svyaz, 1983.
8. I. Prangishvili, V. Podlazov, and G. Stetsyura, Local-Area Microprocessor Networks [in Russian], Nauka, 1984.
9. E. Yakubaitis, Computer Networks [in Russian], Finansy i statistika, 1984.
10. K. Boyanov, S. Markov, T. Kunchev, G. Khadzhidimitriev, N. Vetsev, and S. Voinov, Design of Networks of Small Computers [in Bulgarian], Izd. Tekhnika, Sofia, 1983.
11. The Localnetter Designer's Handbook, 1982 Edition, Architecture Technology Corporation, 1-224, 1982.
12. E. Yakubaitis, Network Architecture for Distributed Computing, Allerton Press, 1-416, 1983.
13. B. Davies, Distributed Systems, Springer Verlag, 1-512, 1983.
14. E. Morris, Digital Services and Electronic Mail Pace Network Advances, Communications News, 66-72, May 1981.
15. "Telephone capsule with direct digital signal decoding," Eletronika, no. 27, 7-8, 1980.
16. J. Boyd, Integrated Communications Network: Key to Future Advances in Information Industry, Communications News, 50-51, March 1982.
17. B. Wood, "Open systems interconnection - basic concepts and current status," ICCC-82, 775-780, London.

18. "Information processing systems — open systems interconnection — basic reference model," Draft International Standard, ISO/DIS 7498, 1-78, 1982.

19. Schematic Model, ISO/TC 97/SC I6, 1-14, March 1979.

20. E. Mier, "High-level protocols, standards, and the OSI reference model," Data Communication, 71-101, July 1982.

21. T. Mannel, "Japanese map computer domination," Electronics, no. 24, 83-84, 1981.

22. "DARPA to develop techniques for computer 'intelligence'," Aviation Week and Space Technology, no. 2, 14-16, 1983.

23. "Europeans will join forces in fifth-generation research program," Mini-Micro Systems, no. 8, 81-82, 1983.

24. C. Coher, "Personal computer: Japan's next plum?," Electronics, no. 16, 85-86, 1980.

25. "The microcomputer with big system software," Datamation, 241, May 1980.

26. Computer Weekly, no. 725, 1, I980.

27. R. Johnson, "Z9000 microprocessor intended for operation with virtual storage," Eletronika, no. 23, 3-4, 1980.

28. B. Lebosier, "16-Bit processor with minicomputer set of instructions and 4-Gbyte virtual storage," Elektronika, no. 4, 11-13, 1980.

29. J. Rattner and W. Lattin, "Ada determines architecture of 32-bit microprocessor," Electronics, no. 4, 119-126, 1981.

30. D. Gosh, "Philips grows stronger in the small-computer market," Elektronika, no. 10, 1979, 1980.

31. "Double-precision superminicomputers," Elektronika, no. 26, 112, 1980.

32. Y. Egava and T. Wada, "A I-Mbit full-wafer MOS RAM," IEEE J. Solid-State Circuits, no. 4, 677-686, 1980.

33. "Videodisc systems come of age. Electro-Optical systems design," no. 12, 31-37, 1980.

34. M. Marshal, "Optical discs excite industry," Electronics, no. 9, 97-102, 1981.

35. "Videodiscs," Business Week, no. 2644, 72-81, 1980.

36. W. Iverson, "Optical disk storages," Elektronika, no. 4, 4-5, 1983.

37. Introduction to Local Area Networks, Digital Equipment Corporation, 1-159, 1982.

38. T. Manuel, "Specialized processor of organization of connections with local-area networks," Elektronika, no. 2, 3-5, 1983.

39. "Excelan Products. Special report," Localnetter Newsletter, Architecture Technology Corporation, no. 10, 1-12, October 1983.

40. D. Potter and J. Amand, "Connecting minis to local nets with discrete modules," Data Communications, 161-164, June 1983.

41. K. Coates, D. Dvorak, and R. Watts, "An overview of BLN: a Bell Laboratories computing network," IEEE CH 1694-9, 224-229, 1981.

42. W. Iverson, "Portable computer with two-way radio communication with a data base," Elektronika, no. 7, 3-4, 1983.

43. K. Guttag and J. Hagn, "Video display processor simulates three dimensions," Electronics, no. 25, 123-126, 1980.

44. L. Low, "Terminal system that creates user-convenient keyboards on the screen," Elektronika, no. 13, 3-4, 1980.

45. M. Edwards, "Office automation developments show communications' key role," Communications News, 42-46, July 1980.

46. "Special report: Bridge communications Ethernet system product line," The Localnetter, 1-12, Architecture Technology Corporation, 1983.

47. R. Sherman and M. Garbe, "Considerations in interconnecting diverse local nets," Data Communications, 145-154, June 1983.

48. G. Kotelly, "Personal-computer networks," EDN, no. 5, 83-100, 1983.

49. "Data base for UNIX users," Elektronika, no. 2, 84-85, 1983.

50. K. Barney, "Unification of work stations," Elektronika, no. 3, 5-7, 1983.

51. S. Sazegari, "Metropolitan networking: Theory and practice," Data Communications, 99-113, May 1983.

52. "Monolithic receiver enhances data rates," Elektronika, no. 6, 6-7, 1980.

53. A. Dahod, "Local network standard: no utopia," Data Communications, 173-180, March 1983.

54. DPS-25. Packet Switching System. SESA, 1-23, 1980.

55. J. Guyon, "A multi-microprocessor-based internetwork net-

work Hermes," Network 80, 119-128, London, June 1980.

56. M. Edwards, "Deregulation heralds new era for digital PBX," Communications News, 32-36, December 1982.

57. J. Jones, "Consider fiber optics for local-network designs," EDN, no. 5, 105-107, 1983.

58. J. Saltzer and D. Clark, "Why a ring?" IEEE CH 1694-9, 211-217.

59. R. Cole, P. Higginson, P. Lloyd, and R. Moulton, "International net faces problems handling mail and the transfer," Data Communications, 175-187, June 1983.

60. "Plan for combining local-area networks," Elektronika, no. 4, 127, 1983.

61. C. Smith, "Joining local-area networks via a satellite communications system," Elektronika, no. 5, 16-17, 1983.

62. E. Spratt, "Local area networks: management and quasi-political issues," ICCC-82, 143-148, London, 1982.

63. A. Ahtiainen and L. Marttinen, "International standardization of network protocols," Research Report No. 14, 1-26, University of Helsinki, 1983.

64. C. Bernick, "Drafts for ISDN standard," Elektronika, no. 15, 7, 1983.

65. Standard ECMA-72. Transport Protocol (2nd edition), 1-55, Geneva, September 1982.

66. Standard ECMA-75. Session Protocol. 1-137, Geneva, January 1982.

67. Standard ECMA-80. Local Area Networks (CSMA/CD Baseband). Coaxial Cable System, 1-16, Geneva, September 1982.

68. Standard ECMA-81. Local Area Networks (CSMA/CD Baseband). Physical Layer, 1-11, Geneva, September 1982.

69. Standard ECMA-82. Local Area Networks (CSMA/CD Baseband). Link Layer, 1-35, Geneva, September 1982.

70. Standard ECMA-84. Data Presentation Protocol, 1-62, Geneva, September 1982.

71. Standard ECMA-85. Virtual File Protocol, 1-114, Geneva, September 1982.

72. Standard ECMA-86. Generic Data Presentation. Services Description and Protocol Definition, 1-88, Geneva, March 1983.

73. Standard ECMA-87. Generic Virtual Terminal. Service and

Protocol Description. 1-64, Geneva, March 1983.

74. Standard ECMA-88. Basic Class Virtual Terminal. Service Description and Protocol Definition, 1-143, Geneva, March, 1983.

75. ECMA TR/13. Network Layer Principles, 1-33, Geneva, September 1982.

76. ECMA TR/14. Local Area Networks. Layers 1 to 4 Architecture and Protocols, 1-16, Geneva, September 1982.

77. Standard ECMA-89. Local Area Networks. Token Ring Technique. ECMA, 1-63, September 1983.

78. Standard ECMA-90. Local Area Networks. Token Bus Technique. ECMA, 1-126, September 1983.

79. P. Bucciarelli, A. Poublan, J. Schumacher, and W. Thiele, "ECMA virtual file protocol: an Overview," ICCC-82, 859-864, London, 1982.

80. ISO/TC 97/SC 16. Basic Connection-Oriented Session Service Definition, 1-39, March 1983.

81. ISO/TC 97/SC 16. Basic Connection-Oriented Session Protocol Specification, 1-119, March 1983.

82. K. Knightson, "The transport layer," ICCC-82, 787-791, London.

83. P. Studnitz, "Transport protocols: their performance and status in international standardization," (July 1982). Computer Networks, no. 7, 27-35, 1983.

84. CCITT Recommendation X.25. Document AP VII Num. 7-E, 1-129, Geneva, June 1980.

85. CCITT Yellow Book. Volume VIII-VIII.2. Data Communication Networks Services and Facilities. Terminal Equipment and Interfaces X.2-X.29, CCITT VIIth Plenary Assembly, Geneva 1980, 83-93 (September 1981).

86. Data Transmission. HDLC Procedures. Unification of Elements of HDLC Procedures. ISO/TC 97. Draft of International Standard ISO 4335, 1982.

87. M. Graube, "IEEE-802 standards committee selects multiple LAN techniques," EDN, no. 5, 90-91, 1983.

88. Computer Standards. Designer's Reference. Electronic Design, 108-111, December 1982.

89. J. Nelson, "802: a progress report," Datamation, 136-152, September 1983.

90. H. Hindin, "Minis fighting way into office market," Electronics, no. 9, 101-102, 1983.

91. N. Olster, "Transmission of intelligible speech using a digital code at 150 bps," Elektronika, no. 8, 10-11, 1983.

92. O. Mofawi and W. Kelly, "Integrated voice/data packet switching techniques for future military networks," IEEE Trans. Commun., no. 9, 1655-1662, 1980.

93. "Voice/data PBX survey," Datamation, 155-160, August 1983.

94. ISO/TC 97/SC 6 N 1784. First draft proposed communication heading format standard. 1-22, February 1979.

95. ISO/TC 97/SC 16 N 318. A session layer protocol, 1-35, April 1980.

96. W. Franta, Local Networks, 1-473, Lexington Books, Toronto, 1981.

97. "Users pick up pace to incorporate evolving datacomm technologies," 38-39, Communications News, December 1982.

98. S. Middelboe, "Local area networks," Microprocessors and Microsystems, 25-32, January/February 1982.

99. J. Murphy, "Token-passing protocol boosts throughput in local networks," Electronics, no. 18, 158-163, 1982.

100. ARC. Datapoint Attached Resource Computer, 1-12, Datapoint, 1982.

101. A. Goldberger, C. Caplinsky, and A. Moelands, "Small-area network fit jobs too small for local nets," Electronics, no. 22, 119-122, 1982.

102. E. Dane and K. Stank, "One chip carries out Ethernet protocol," Electronic Design, no. 20, 121-128, 1982.

103. J. Mason and G. Shaw, "Implementing Ethernet from soup to nuts," Data Communications, 74-80, December 1981.

104. "Using Ethernet for communication between desktop computers," Elektronika, no. 20, 107, 1982.

105. Net/One. The User's Network, 1-2, Ungermann-Bass Inc., 1982.

106. Net/One. Network Configuration Facility, 1-2, Ungermann-Bass Inc., 1982.

107. Net/One. Network Interface Unit, 1-2, Ungermann-Bass, Inc., 1982.

108. "Net/One turns the equipment you have into the network you want. Now," Datamation, 200-201, May 1983.

109. J. Davidson, "Net/One's answer to packet and circuit switching," Data Communication, 84-87, December 1981.

110. "Communications processors for Ethernet that implement X.25," Elektronika, no. 23, 1982.

111. S. Zollo, "Fiber-optic lines for Ethernet," Elektronika, no. 19, 10-11, 1982.

112. H. Frank, "On the road to Hyperbus," Datamation, 80-84, March 1981.

113. J. Malone, "The microcomputer connection to local networks," Data Communications, 101-104, December 1981.

114. "Motorola supports Ethernet," Elektronika, no. 24, 98-99, 1982.

115. R. Godin, "Deregulation sparks telecom chip surge," Electronics, no. 4, 103-106, 1983.

116. "Ethernet controllers" Elektronika, no. 18, 5-6, (no year given).

117. I. Chlamtac and W. Franta, "Message-based priority access to local networks," Computer Communications, no. 2, 77-84, 1980.

118. "Communication in a mixed environment," Network Systems Corporation, Datamation, 135, April 1982.

119. Wangnet, Wang Laboratories Inc., 1-8, 1982.

120. "Wang Laboratories' Wangnet," The Localnetter Newsletter, Architecture Technology Corporation, vol. 2, no. 3, 1-8, March, 1982.

121. K. Berney, "Patent office prepares to automate," Electronics, no. 8, 101-102, 1983.

122. S. Wilbur, "Low-level protocols in the Cambridge Ring," Data Network Conference, 265-276, London, 1980.

123. "Polynet," Network Manual, Logica VTS Limited, 1-78, 1981.

124. R. Sterry, "Ring net: passing the token in local network circles," Data Communications, 97-100, December 1981.

125. J. Favre, "CARTHAGE: a multiservice local network on a fiber optics loop. Local computer networks," IFIP, 23-37, 1982.

126. IEEE Project 802. Local Area Network Standards. Draft D. Draft Standard P802.2 Logical Link Control, 1-104, November 1982.

127. IEEE Project 802. Local Area Network Standards. Rev. E. Draft Standard 802.4. Token Bus, 1-294, 1983.

128. "Special report: NEC NEAX 2400," The Localnetter Newsletter. Architecture Technology Corporation, no. 12, SR-88.1/SR-88.8, December 1983.

129. D. Alpert, D. Carberry, M. Yamamura, C. Ying, and P. Mak, "32-Bit processor chip integrates major system functions," Electronics, no. 14, 113-119, 1983.

130. "If X.25 software is throwing you a curve, cut it out," Data Communications, November 1983.

131. "Etherway," INTERLAN, 1-4, 1983.

132. "Microsystems for network operation," Elektronika, no. 22, 100-101, 1982.

133. E. Yakubaitis, Yu. Vishnyakov, Yu. Mikheev, and P. Treis, "Architecture of the computer network of the Academy of Sciences USSR and of the allied republics (ACADNET)," in: Problems of Cybernetics: Problems of the Theory of Computer Networks [in Russian], Izd. AN SSSR, pp. 3-11, 1983.

134. N. Strole, "A local communications network based on interconnected token-access rings: a tutorial," IBM J. Res. Develop., no. 5, 481-496, 1983.

135. W. Bux, "Local-area subnetworks. A performance comparison," IEEE Trans. Commun., vol. 29, 1465-1473, 1981.

136. B. Stuck, "Calculating the maximum mean data rate in local area networks," Computer, no. 5, 72-76, 1983.

137. T. Kunihero, "Fiber-optical local network sets its sights on offices and factories," Electronics, no. 15, 125-128, 1983.

138. H. Hindin, "Unix System V sets out to make its hardware mark," Electronics, no. 18, 108-109, 1983.

139. G. Brooksby, "Two iAPX 286-based computers feature Unix System V," Electronics, no. 18, 110-111, 1983.

140. F. Harteloo, "Development systems and VAX-like chips suit Unix," Electronics, no. 18, 112-113, 1983.

141. R. Freud, "Unix fits microprocessors with high-level language," Electronics, no. 18, 114-115, 1983.

142. L. Bender, "'Superminicomputer' system is readied for latest Unix," Electronics, no. 18, 116-117, 1983.

143. J. Groff, "Modified Unix system tames network architecture," Electronics, no. 19, 159-163, 1983.

144. W. Rauch-Hindin, "Unix: An operating system that means business," Data Communications, 71-77, December 1983.
145. "Compac: The solution to compatibility problems," TRT, 1-6, Paris, 1983.
146. "Automatic network management system," TRT, 1-4, Paris, 1983.
147. L. Lou, "Carrier-sensing multiple-access with collision detection," Electronics, no. 20, 61-64, 1983.
148. "IBM ponders UNIX," Datamation, 80-82, December 1983.
149. J. Johnson, "IBM's two-LAN plan," Datamation, 120-128, February 1984.
150. K. Barney, "Competing 32-bit busses manufactured by Intel and Motorola," Elektronika, no. 20, 7-9, 1983.
151. "Information technology," Elektronika, no. 21, 27-54, 1983.
152. F. Borgonovo, L. Fratta, and F. Tobagi, "The Express Net: a Local Area Communication Network Integrating Voice and Data," Progetto finalizzato informatica C.N.R., 1-46, Pisa, 1982.
153. J. Shoch and A. Hupp, "Measured performance of an Ethernet local network," Communications of the ACM, no. 12, 711-721, December 1980.
154. "Local network communication transfer TRX 1000. Technical specifications," Olivetti, 1-2, 1983.

GLOSSARY*

ACCESS — A procedure that provides shared use of a **multipoint connection** for transmission of **data**

ACCESS METHOD — Procedure by which a **subscriber system** gains access to a **baseband system, multipoint frequency channel** of a **broadband system** or **ring subnetwork**

ACCESS UNIT — Hardware for interfacing a **station** and **physical medium**

APPLICATION CONTROL — **Application-layer** function associated with control of **application processes**

APPLICATION LAYER — **Layer** that supports various modes of interaction of **application processes**

APPLICATION PROCESS — Aggregate of procedures associated with information processing

BACKBONE (LINE) — A **data link** that connects two **communications systems**

BASEBAND — A technique for transmitting **data** in which only one signal at a time is transmitted over the **physical medium**

BASEBAND (BROADCAST) SYSTEM — A **communications subsystem** based on a monopolistically-used **physical medium,** that supports transmission from the sending **subscriber system** to all the other subscriber systems at once (to within the signal propagation time)

BASEBAND COMPUTER NETWORK — A **computer network** which effects **selection** of **data blocks,** in parallel by all **subscriber systems** of the network, to deliver information to the addressee

BASEBAND TRANSMISSION — Transmission of **data** via a **baseband system**

BASIC REFERENCE MODEL OF OPEN SYSTEMS INTERCON—NECTION — The conceptual framework that defines the characteristics and facilities of **systems;** proposed by the International Standards Organization

BROADBAND SYSTEM — A group of independent **communications subnetworks,** based on a single unified **physical medium,** in which a set of **point-to-point** or **multipoint frequency channels** is allocated through frequency-division multiplexing

---

*Words in **boldface** are defined in the Glossary.

BROADBAND TRANSMISSION — Transmission of **data** via **multipoint frequency channels** run in a **broadband system**

BROADCAST ADDRESS — See GLOBAL ADDRESS

BROADCASTING — Transmission of **data blocks** to all **subscriber systems** at once

BUS (LINE) — See BACKBONE (LINE)

CABLE SEGMENT — Portion of a cable without **repeaters**

CARRIER-SENSE MULTIPLE-ACCESS WITH COLLISION DETECTION (CSMA/CD) — An access procedure for a **baseband system** or **multipoint frequency channel** that provides detection and elimination of **frame collisions** by repeat transmission of frames

COMMUNICATIONS SUBNETWORK — An aggregate of **physical medium,** hardware, and (possibly) software that supports interaction between **subscriber systems**

COMPUTER NETWORK ARCHITECTURE — Multilayer organization of hardware and software that provides various structures of **systems** and modes of interaction of these systems

COMPUTER NETWORK WITH INFORMATION ROUTING — A **computer network** in which **routing** is employed to deliver information from the sending **application process** to the recipient application process

COMPUTER NETWORK WITH INFORMATION SELECTION — A **computer network** in which **selection** is employed to deliver information from the sending **application process** to the recipient application process

COMPUTER (OR DATA) NETWORK — An association of **subscriber systems** that interact with one another via a **communications subnetwork**

CONNECTION — Line via which **entities** on the same **layer** interact

CONTENTION — Attempt by more than one **subscriber system** to simultaneously utilize a **baseband system** or **multipoint frequency channel** of a **broadband system** to transmit **data blocks**

DATA — 1) Information received or issued by **application processes;**
2) Information for whose transmission the **layer** under consideration of the **open systems interconnection environment** is set up

DATA BLOCK (OR UNIT) — Unit of information transmitted between **entities**

DATAGRAM — A **data block** transmitted via the **communications subnetwork** without organization of a **connection** between **entities** of the **transport layer**

DATA-LINK LAYER — **Layer** that controls the operation of **physical connections**

DATA LINK (or CHANNEL) — The aggregate of **physical medium** and hardware that interconnects two systems

DATA-LINK SUBNETWORK — An association of a **baseband system, multipoint frequency channel** or **ring subnetwork** with **stations** that implement the **protocols** of the **data-link** and **physical layers**

DATA TERMINAL EQUIPMENT (DTE) — A **subscriber system** that is a source and receiver of **data**

DOCUMENT — An array of information (text, graphics, images, speech, etc.) with a name (or address) of specified form, and whose contents are of limited size

ELECTRONIC MAIL — Type of service used to transmit **documents** to "mailboxes" of **users**

ENTITY — Active element on one of the layers of a **system**

FILE — Array of **data** having a name

FLOW CONTROL — Organization of transmission of **data** that supports subscriber interaction with a high degree of reliability and without congestion of the **communications subnetwork**

FRAME — Continuous interrelated bit sequence that is delivered to the **physical layer,** or taken from this layer, as a whole

FRAME COLLISION — Result of superposition of **frames** transmitted simultaneously by several **subscriber systems** via a **baseband system** or **multipoint frequency channel** of a **broadband system**

GATEWAY SYSTEM — A **system** used to transmit data between **subscriber systems**

GLOBAL ADDRESS — Address of a **data block** that is intended for all **subscriber systems**

GLOBAL COMPUTER NETWORK — A **computer network** whose **subscriber systems** extend over a very large territory (different countries, continents, etc.)

GROUP ADDRESS — Address of a **data block** that is intended for several **subscriber systems**

HOST SYSTEM — **System** that provides basic information or computing resources

INDIVIDUAL ADDRESS — Address of a **data block** that is intended for just one **subscriber system**

INTERLINK GATEWAY — A **system** that supports interaction between **data links**

INTERNETWORK GATEWAY — A **system** that supports interaction of **computer networks**

INTERSUBNET GATEWAY — A **system** that supports interaction between **communications subnetworks**

JAM — Sequence of encoded bits used to intensify **frame collisions** so that they can be more readily detected

LAYER — Level of hierarchical logical description of **open systems interconnection environment**

LAYER CONTROL — Function involving the performance of management functions of **layers;** resides on the layer and on the **application layer** (as a subset of **systems control**)

LAYER INTERFACE — Interaction rules for **entities** on adjacent **layers** of a **system**

LOCAL-AREA NETWORK — A **computer network** whose **systems** are not widely separated from one another

MANAGEMENT — Functions associated with activation and deactivation of **systems, terminals,** and **data links,** fault diagnostics, assembly of statistics, status reports, and other operations required to support operation of a **computer network**

MANAGEMENT SYSTEM — A **system** used for **management** of all or part of a **computer network**

MANCHESTER ENCODING — A procedure for combining **data** and synchronization signals into a single self-synchronizing stream to be transmitted over a serial **data link**

MIXED SYSTEM — A system that performs functions of two (rarely three) of the following types of systems: **host, terminal, management**

MULTIPLE-NODE COMPUTER NETWORK — A **communications subnetwork** consisting of several **communications systems** and the **backbones** (or busses) that interconnect them

MULTIPLEXING — Establishment of a group of N-layer **connections** in one (N − 1)-layer connection

MULTIPOINT FREQUENCY CHANNEL — Frequency band of a **broadband system** over which more than two **subscriber systems** interact

NETWORK LAYER — Layer that supports establishment of **connections** via one or more **systems** that provide retranslation of data

OPEN SYSTEM — A **system** that meets the specifications of Standard 7498 of the International Standards Organization

OPEN SYSTEMS INTERCONNECTION ENVIRONMENT — A term

in the **Basic Reference Model of Open Systems Interconnection** that specifies the group of functions residing in the **systems** between the basic parts of **application processes** and **physical interconnection facilities**

PHYSICAL CONNECTION — **Connection** that supports interaction between **entities** of **physical layer**

PHYSICAL INTERCONNECTION FACILITIES — Aggregate of physical medium, hardware, and (possibly) software that support data transmission between **systems**

PHYSICAL LAYER — Layer that specifies the mechanical, electrical, and procedural facilities for data transmission via **physical interconnection facilities**

PHYSICAL MEDIUM — Space or material whose properties support signal propagation: twisted pair, coaxial cable, "open air," light guide, etc.

POINT-TO-POINT CONNECTION — **Connection** linking two **entities**

POINT-TO-POINT FREQUENCY CHANNEL — Frequency band (or subband) of a **broadband system** over which two **subscriber systems** interact

PRESENTATION LAYER — The **layer** which presents (represents, describes) received and transmitted **data** in the requisite form

PROTOCOL — Set of rules and formats that specify interaction between **entities** on similar **layers** of different **systems**

PROTOCOL DATA UNIT — Unit amount of data exchanged by **entities** of the same **layer**

RANDOM ACCESS — An access procedure that enables a **subscriber system** to transmit **data** via **physical interconnection facilities** without explicit advance coordination with other subscriber systems

REPEATER — Device for restoring the shape of a distorted signal; used to increase the length and expand the topology of a **communications subnetwork**

RING COMPUTER NETWORK — **Computer network** in which information is delivered to the addressee through **selection** of **data blocks**, performed successively by all **subscriber systems**

RING SUBNETWORK — **Communications subnetwork** that provides successive signal transmission from one sending **subscriber system** to all the remaining subscriber systems

ROUTING — A procedure for determining the transmission paths of **data blocks** on the basis of their destination addresses

SEGMENTATION — Procedure for dividing a **data block** into smaller data blocks

SELECTION — Procedure for selecting **data blocks** on the basis of their destination addresses

SESSION LAYER — **Layer** that controls transmission of **data** between **application processes**

SINGLE-NODE COMMUNICATIONS SUBNETWORK — **Communications subnetwork** consisting of a single **communications system**

SINGLE-NODE COMPUTER NETWORK — A **computer network** in which one **communications system** is employed for transmission

SPLITTING — Establishment of a group of N-layer connections in one (N + 1)-layer connection

STAR NETWORK — A **computer network** whose topology is that of rays that depart from a single point

STATION — Auxiliary part of a **subscriber system**, used for connecting the **subscriber** to the **communications subnetwork**

SUBLAYER — Hierarchical part of a **layer** that performs a self-contained group of interrelated functions

SUBSCRIBER — Principal part of a **subscriber system**, which executes **application processes** and implements **protocols** of upper **layers**

SUBSCRIBER LINK — **Data link** that connects **subscriber system** to **communications subnetwork**

SUBSCRIBER SYSTEM — A **system** that executes **application processes** of **users**

SUBSYSTEM — A component in the hierarchical subdivision of a **system**

SYSTEM — An aggregate comprising one or more computers, software, peripherals, terminals, data-transmission facilities, and operating personnel

SYSTEMS CONTROL — An **application-layer** function involving control of data-processing resources, all **layers** of the **open systems interconnection environment**

TERMINAL SYSTEM — A **system** that provides terminal control and service for users

TOKEN — A command that enables a **subscriber system** to transmit a specified number of **frames** via a **baseband system, multipoint frequency channel** or **ring subnetwork**

TOKEN ACCESS — An **access** procedure that enables a **station** to send data to a **baseband system, multipoint frequency channel** of a

broadband system or **ring subnetwork** after receiving an authorizing **token**

TOKEN CONTROL — Procedure involving passing of **token,** elimination of loss of token or appearance of multiple tokens

TRAFFIC — Flow of **data** in a **computer network** or between networks

TRANSPARENCY — The capability of a **protocol, data link,** or **connection** for handling commands, responses, instructions, or **data** without distorting their meaning and without altering their formats and codes

TRANSPORT LAYER — Layer that furnishes **application processes** with transmission of **data blocks** via **communications subsystem**

TRANSPORT SUBNETWORK — Part of a **computer network** that includes **physical interconnection facilities** and **stations** that implement the **protocols** of the **transport, network, data-link,** and **physical layers**

TREE COMPUTER NETWORK — **Computer network** whose topology is that of a branching tree.

USER — One who interacts with the resources of a **computer network**

VIRTUAL CIRCUIT — A **connection,** via the **communications subnetwork,** between interacting **entities** on the **transport layer**

VIRTUAL FILE — Standard form of representation of a **data** set (or array)

VIRTUAL JOB — Standard form of representation of a job

VIRTUAL TERMINAL — Logical description of a standard **terminal**

WIDE-AREA NETWORK — A **computer network** whose **subscriber systems** are separated considerably from one another (usually over a geographical region)

LIST OF ABBREVIATIONS
AND SYMBOLS

CCITT Comité Consultatif International de Téléphonie et Télégraphie (International Consultative Committee on Telephony and Telegraphy)

ECMA European Computer Manufacturers Association

ISO International Standards Organization

KAMA Remote control system for data for Soviet Unified System computers

KROS Remote job input planning system for Unified System computers

POISK Interactive information-retrieval system for Unified System computers

SM Line of Soviet minicomputers

TSS Time-sharing system for Unified System computers (Russian abbreviation: SRV)

US Computers (Unified System) Line of large Soviet mainframes (Russian abbreviation: ES)

⌐	terminal	⊞	plotter
⊖	disk drive	⊠	gateway system
◯	tape drive	△	telephone set
▢	printer	▢	subscriber system
◯	symbol display	AU	access unit
▦	graphics display	ST	station of subscriber system
M	modem		

SUBJECT INDEX*

---

*Terms in the index are given in **boldface** in the text.

Data-link subnetwork, 246, 270
Data network, 5, 6
Data network architecture, 5
Data presentation protocol, 158
Data terminal equipment, 173
Data unit (or block), 24
Destructive connection to cable, 113
Deterministic access, 257
Differential Manchester encoding, 189
Digital data processing methods, 9
DISPATCHER service, 225
Distributed internetwork gateway, 139
Document, 14
D^2B bus, 267
ECMA-72 standard, 168
ECMA-75 standard, 163
ECMA-80 standard, 185
ECMA-81 standard, 186
ECMA-82 standard, 190
ECMA-84 standard, 158
ECMA-86 standard, 158
ECMA-87 standard, 159
ECMA-88 standard, 159
ECMA-89 standard, 201
ECMA-90 standard, 206
ECMA-TR/14 standard, 183
Electronic mail, 14
Electronic-mail protocol, 32
End-to-end transit time, 93
End-to-end transmission, 37
End-to-end transmission rate, 92
Entity, 22
Ethernet data-link subnetwork, 269
Etherway data-link subnetwork, 271
Expedited data, 162
Experimental Computer Network (ECN), 222
External communications-subnetwork interface, 173
Facsimile terminal system, 70
Fiber optics, 116, 274
Fifth-generation computer, 50
File, 56, 154
File control protocol, 32